D. H. LAWRENCE

A Critical Study of the Major Novels and Other Writings

D.H. LAWRENCE

A Critical Study of the Major Novels and Other Writings

EDITED BY

A. H. GOMME

Department of English, University of Keele

THE HARVESTER PRESS · SUSSEX

BARNES & NOBLE · NEW YORK

First published in 1978 by
THE HARVESTER PRESS LIMITED
Publisher: John Spiers
2 Stanford Terrace, Hassocks, Sussex

and published in the USA by
HARPER & ROW PUBLISHERS, INC.,
BARNES & NOBLE IMPORT DIVISION
10 East 53rd Street, New York 10022

British Library Cataloguing in Publication Data

D. H. Lawrence.
   1. Lawrence, David Herbert—Criticism and
interpretation
   I. Gomme, Andor Harvey
   823'.9'12   PR6023.A93Z/

ISBN 0–85527–830–7

Library of Congress Cataloging in Publication Data

Main entry under title :

D. H. Lawrence : a critical study of the major novels
   and other writings.

   Bibliography : p.
   1. Lawrence, David Herbert, 1885–1930—Criticism
and interpretation. I. Gomme, Andor Harvey.
PR6023.A93Z62338   1978   823'.9'12   77–23636
ISBN 0–06–492480–7

Printed in Great Britain by
REDWOOD BURN LIMITED
Trowbridge & Esher

CONTENTS

In Russia the power of literature has always been taken very seriously : throughout her history, and especially in this century, the efforts of the State to prevent literature have been eloquent evidence of the fear of the word and of its capacity, by celebrating individual experience, to undermine the complacencies of power. So Osip Mandelstam was harried round Russia for ten years and finally done to death; so Pasternak was—so far as his own people are concerned—stifled; so Solzhenitsyn was eventually driven from the country which is the core and inspiration of his experience and his art and is now allowed to know almost nothing of it.

In England we have learnt, it seems, to worry less. It was not always so. In 1915 publication of *The Rainbow* was stopped, and unsold copies were destroyed, after a court action. The ostensible grounds were an alleged offence against the Obscene Publications Act; but it was widely believed at the time and has been asserted convincingly since that the real reason for the suppression of *The Rainbow* was political rather than moral. Lawrence had made no secret of his opposition to the war, and the explicitly individualist, anti-utilitarian stand of his heroine Ursula against her lover Skrebensky, the stiff-necked upholder of 'the nation' and fighting for it as 'the most serious' cause there is, was itself a challenge which a State at war could hardly ignore : Ursula asserts the primacy of the self as the only place where life exists, and life and the self are in fundamental opposition to the dictatorial or bureaucratic, but always mechanistic, State.

With *The Rainbow* banned, it was five years before Lawrence could find a publisher willing to risk *Women in Love*. He himself was forced in 1917 to leave Cornwall, where he was then living, for inland England, where the military authorities considered he was less of a danger; and soon after the war ended he left the country, never to return for more than brief visits. (Yet he insisted to the end on his Englishness; and the Erewash valley where he was born and brought up remained 'the country of his heart'.)

It may astonish readers coming new to Lawrence in the 1970s, when there seems virtually no limit to what is licensed to appear in print, that it was not until 1960, and then only after an extensive court action, that the full text of *Lady Chatterley's Lover* could be published in England. The dubious character of the Defence in this famous trial and the nature of the 'victory' it achieved in the cause of freedom and culture are now perhaps more obvious than at the time; but the contemporary witness of the chief of Lawrentian critics and the man who has done more than anyone else to explore and lead us into the nature of his greatness, should make the reader in the seventies think about what this process has done for Lawrence and for the cause which he made his own. (See F. R. Leavis, 'The Orthodoxy of Enlightenment', first printed in *The Spectator* in February 1961, and reprinted in *Anna Karenina and Other Essays*, London, 1967.) What seems to have happened since is that we have seen Lawrence's challenge (well or ill conceived as it may be) overtaken in, or by, a more 'advanced' enlightenment in which the world is made safe for the commercial pornography which he himself hated so much. During the trial, when the Defence laid much stress on the novel's purity, there appeared a cartoon showing a Charing Cross Road bookseller surrounded by girlie magazines, answering a customer's request: '*Lady Chatterley's Lover*? If that's the book that's pure enough for schoolgirls to read, we don't stock it.'

In 1977 schoolgirls doubtless read many other things as well; and whatever part the liberation of Lady Chatterley may have played in the licensing of pornography, it seems unlikely that, so long as the prevailing cultural climate in England lasts, Lawrence—or any other novelist—will be officially regarded as dangerous. Yet it is one of the marks of a great writer that his power to disturb complacency is never wholly lost: after all the horrors of the twentieth century and our habituation to them, it remains true that anyone who really exposes himself to *King Lear* will, now as always, find that the experience binds him, like Lear, on a wheel of fire; and Ursula's challenge, if we can recognize it, is as keen and important now as ever it was. Nevertheless it has been a sad character of much recent criticism of Lawrence to take him easily for granted, to assume that what makes him important is agreed and need not be seriously argued; and this is the point at which a great writer becomes, at least temporarily, neutralized.

6

All writers need to be newly interpreted, newly read through, by each new generation, not so much because their 'relevance' shifts as because how they tell on the world of each generation has to be identified through the eyes of that world. And so there is always need for fresh critical reports from the new places we have reached, new attempts to prevent reputations from becoming conventionalized and stale. The essays in this volume (which have all been written during the past few years, and only one of which—Mr. Strickland's on *Lady Chatterley's Lover* —has been published before) are a small contribution to this ongoing process. Though they range widely over Lawrence's prolific career, taking in a number of his largest and most controversial books, and are for the most part arranged chronologically, it need hardly be said that the book makes no offer at a critical survey: the essays have a common aim—to suggest new openings into what we may think is familiar territory—and so there is a readily visible concentration on work which has come to seem through the years the most demanding and the most rewarding. That may seem in itself to imply a complacency; but it would have been pointlessly eccentric to devote such a collection to the less-known merely because it is less-known. That Lawrence was a very unequal writer is one point on which all his critics are agreed, though where the inequalities lie may be more in dispute. But Lawrence himself is the best and foremost guide to his own limitations and failures. We have tried to write in the spirit of Lawrence's splendid criticism and of his constant concern for his art, for 'art-speech is the only truth'. So we hope that the fairly unadventurous selection of topics for principal discussion is not a part of the neutralizing process noted above.

To make it new is good; but it would be foolish, unjust and ungenerous to disregard the work of those who have shown us so much of the way. And it is particularly appropriate at this time to acknowledge the tireless championship of Lawrence by the greatest critic of our age. Dr. Leavis's major book on Lawrence—it is still without question the most important critical account of the centre of Lawrence's work—appeared in 1955, when Lawrence was coming to be really widely read, but it was the culmination of pioneering exploration over more than

7

thirty years, and, for all this it seems, twenty years further on, still to tell so much of the essential truth of Lawrence's art, has been in no way a stopping-place for its author. To no man, except Lawrence himself, do Lawrence's readers owe so much as to Dr. Leavis.

Lawrence is now, it may be safely assumed, a very extensively read author, at least so far as his novels are concerned, and he has become a main centre of critical industry in the world of academic English. This industry, however, has still not managed to produce a satisfactory edition of Lawrence's work. At last a really complete critical edition of the letters is under way (to be published by the Cambridge University Press), and the present situation, in which many letters are duplicated in different collections, many have never been published and those that have must be sought for in a score of assorted places, will eventually come to an end. The poems too are now in good order, and the two volumes of *Phoenix* make a tolerably comprehensive collection of the essays. Para-doxically it is the novels and stories—the obvious centre of Lawrence—which it is still next to impossible to read in reliable editions. The Penguin is the best, though some-what more selective than the Heinemann Phoenix edition, which, however, contains many inaccuracies, and the texts of two of the novels—*The Rainbow* and *The Lost Girl*— are incomplete. 1980 will be the fiftieth anniversary of Lawrence's death, 1985 the centenary of his birth. Is it too much to hope that one of these dates will be celebrated in the most fitting way possible—by the publication of a really sound edition of his work, and not at a prohibitive price (whatever that may be at the time)?

A. H. GOMME
September 1977

8

Chronological Table of Lawrence's Life

Date	Events in his life	Writing	Publication
1885	Born, Sept. 11th at Eastwood.		
1887	Family moved to the Breach ('The Bottoms' of Sons and Lovers).		
1890	Family moved to Walker St.		
1897	L won scholarship to Nottingham High School.		
1901	Met Jessie Chambers. Left school. Worked for Haywoods in Nottingham. Seriously ill with pneumonia. Death of L's brother Ernest.		
1902	Pupil teacher at British School, Eastwood.		
1903	Pupil teacher at Ilkeston.		
1905		First poems	
1906	Goes to Nottingham University College (to 1908).	The White Peacock begun (-1910)	
1907		'The White Stocking'	'A Prelude' [Nottinghamshire Guardian]
1908	Teacher at Davidson Rd. School, Croydon. Met Helen Corke.		
1909		'Odour of Chrysanthemums'	Poems [English Review]
1910	Death of Mrs Lawrence. L engaged to Louie Burrows (till 1912).	The Trespasser begun (-1912) Sons and Lovers begun (-1912)	

Date	Events in his life	Writing	Publication
1911	Meets Edward Garnett. Very ill with pneumonia. Leaves Croydon.	*Daughters of the Vicar*	*The White Peacock* 'Odour of Chrysanthemums' *The Trespasser*
1912	Meets Frieda Weekley. Goes with her to Germany and Italy.		
1913	Final break with Jessie Chambers. Meets J. M. Murry and Katherine Mansfield. In England, Germany and Italy.	*The Sisters* begun (finished as *The Rainbow* 1915) *The Lost Girl* begun (~1920)	*Love Poems and Others* *Sons and Lovers*
1914	Returns to England. Married to Frieda, July 13. Meets Catherine Carswell, Ottoline Morrell, S. S. Koteliansky. Outbreak of war. Living at Chesham.		*The Widowing of Mrs. Holroyd* *The Prussian Officer*
1915	Living at Pulborough and in London. Friendship with Bertrand Russell (to 1916). Tries to go to U.S. Condemnation and banning of *The Rainbow*.	'England, My England' 'The Crown' *Study of Thomas Hardy*	*The Rainbow* 'The Crown'
1916	Cornwall. Summoned for medical inspection for military service, declared unfit.	*Women in Love* 'The Horse-Dealer's Daughter'	*Twilight in Italy* *Amores*
1917	Ordered to leave Cornwall. Living in Berkshire.	*Aaron's Rod* begun (~1921)	*Look! We Have Come Through*
1918	Derbyshire. Second medical inspection.	'The Fox' *Education of the People*	*New Poems*
1919	To Italy (Frieda in Germany). Meets Maurice Magnus.		
1920	Sicily. With Magnus in Italy and Malta. Magnus's suicide.	*The Lost Girl*	*Touch and Go* *Women in Love* *The Lost Girl*

10

Date	Events in his life	Writing	Publication
1921	To Sardinia, Germany, Capri. Meets Earl and Achsah Brewster. Correspondence from Mabel Dodge Luhan.	'The Captain's Doll' 'The Ladybird' Introduction to Memoirs of the Foreign Legion	Movements in European History Psychoanalysis and the Unconscious Sea and Sardinia
1922	To Ceylon, Australia, U.S.A. (California, New Mexico). Settles at Del Monte Ranch.	Kangaroo (–1923)	Aaron's Rod Fantasia of the Unconscious England, My England
1923	Death of Katherine Mansfield. L visits Mexico, returns to London. Death of Lawrence's father.	The Boy in the Bush The Plumed Serpent begun (–1925)	The Ladybird Studies in Classic American Literature Kangaroo Birds, Beasts and Flowers Mastro-Don Gesualdo
1924	Returns to New Mexico. Second visit to Mexico. Very ill with tuberculosis.	St. Mawr	The Boy in the Bush Memoirs of the Foreign Legion Little Novels of Sicily
1925	New Mexico. Return to London. To Italy; settles at Florence.	The Woman Who Rode Away The Princess	St. Mawr Reflections on the Death of a Porcupine
1926	Visit to London. Return to Florence. Meets the Huxleys.	Lady Chatterley's Lover (first and second versions –1927)	The Plumed Serpent David Mornings in Mexico
1927	Florence. Travels in Etruria.	Lady Chatterley's Lover (third version –1928)	
1928	Two visits to Switzerland. Later to Port Cros (S. France).	'The Man Who Died'	Cavalleria Rusticana The Women Who Rode Away Lady Chatterley's Lover Collected Poems
1929	In France, Majorca, Germany, France again. Exhibition of L's paintings in London; some seized by police. MS. of Pansies confiscated by Customs.	'Apropos of Lady Chatterley's Lover' Apocalypse 'The Ship of Death'	The Paintings of D. H. Lawrence Pansies The Escaped Cock

II

Date	Events in his life	Writing	Publication
1930	L dies at Vence (S. France), 2nd March.		Nettles
			Assorted Articles
			The Virgin and the Gipsy
			'Apropos of Lady Chatterley's Lover'
1931			Apocalypse
1932			Etruscan Places
			The Letters of D. H. Lawrence (ed. Huxley)
			Last Poems
1933			The Ship of Death
1934			The Tales of D. H. Lawrence
1936			Phoenix (ed. McDonald)

D. H LAWRENCE AND ENGLISH PROSE *

People who do not like Lawrence's prose often say that his great fault is repetitiousness, and he comments on the charge in the Foreword to *Women in Love* :

> In point of style, fault is often found with the continual, slightly modified repetition. The only answer is that it is natural to the author : and that every natural crisis in emotion or passion or understanding comes from this pulsing, frictional to-and-fro, which works up to culmination.

Here are two other paragraphs from the same Foreword :

> The creative, spontaneous soul sends forth its promptings of desire and aspiration in us. These promptings are our true fate, which is our business to fulfil. A fate dictated from outside, from theory or from circumstance, is a false fate.

> Man struggles with his unborn needs and fulfilment. New unfoldings struggle up in torment in him, as buds struggle forth from the midst of a plant. Any man of real individuality tries to know and to understand what is happening, even in himself, as he goes along. This struggle for verbal consciousness should not be left out in art. It is a very great part of life. It is not superimposition of a theory. It is the passionate struggle into conscious being.

I want to show, by exploring the connections between these paragraphs, why and how Lawrence needed to change English prose, and what his change has to do with thought. This—a large programme for a short essay—will involve me in speculative generalizations which at greater length I

* By Ian Robinson, University College, Swansea.

might expand, defend or modify. I am not, however, essaying the last word on this subject; I only hope to show that the subject ought to exist.

Lawrence might have written his sentence about 'continual, slightly modified repetition' with this famous passage from Chapter IV of *The Rainbow* in mind:

He worked in silence. The rhythm of the work carried him away again, as she was coming near.

They worked together, coming and going, in a rhythm, which carried their feet and their bodies in tune. She stooped, she lifted the burden of sheaves, she turned her face to the dimness where he was, and went with her burden over the stubble. She hesitated, set down her sheaves, there was a swish and hiss of mingling oats, he was drawing near, and she must turn again. And there was the flaring moon laying bare her bosom again, making her drift and ebb like a wave.

He worked steadily, engrossed, threading backwards and forwards like a shuttle across the strip of cleared stubble, weaving the long line of riding shocks, nearer and nearer to the shadowy trees, threading his sheaves with hers.

And always, she was gone before he came. As he came, she drew away, as he drew away, she came. Were they never to meet? Gradually a low, deep-sounding will in him vibrated to her, tried to set her in accord, tried to bring her gradually to him, to a meeting, till they should be together, till they should meet as the sheaves that swished together.

The great difference between this and ordinary English prose is, of course, one of rhythm; but it would not do merely to say that Lawrence is rhythmic or even to point to phrases like 'drift and ebb like a wave' or 'the rhythm of the work' as characterizing the movement of the passage: for in one sense all prose is rhythmic, because all prose is a succession of phrases whose internal structure and relations to each other (their grammar and syntax) are expressed in the way we relate stresses as we read, that is, their rhythm. But in good modern prose the writing seems somehow to precede the rhythms: the rhythms of prose follow from the tidy, written progress through main and subordinate clauses. Lawrence, however, is writing strings

14

of simple clauses separated by commas or *ands* and not linked by syntactic subordination; his phrases are connected, if at all, by the tone of the speaking voice. Like the 1611 Bible or like Chaucer he relies on tone to do what Dryden would have done by complex yet easy sentence-structure. One may see this, for instance, in Lawrence's ungrammatical punctuation. Modern prose is punctuated syntactically : main clauses are separated by the correct stop, no matter how the passage is spoken, and the commas which in some passages of Henry James separate almost every word need not be rhetorical instructions to the reader to pause. But Lawrence is here using commas in exactly the same way as the mediaeval scribes used their rhetorical stops, to separate the balancing phrases of the spoken language.

If we are irritated by this prose I suggest the most likely reason is that we are reading it the wrong way and refusing to allow the tone to carry us. If we read with the alertness and expectations proper to a *Times* leader we shall certainly often object 'he's said that before'. But Lawrence is not here conducting an argument in which restatement is unnecessary repetition. A new intensity and impetus enters the passage with the 'low, deep-sounding will'. Once this is present the repeated 'together', 'near', and 'meeting' develop a new resonance and modify 'the rhythm of the work'. All these are the same words used already; there is no difference in their 'prose sense'; but the new contexts (like the new context for each repetition of a refrain in Wyatt's lyrics) make the same phrase express a further emotional development, not by describing or naming the emotion but by imaginatively creating it. Every phrase is relative to every other phrase, and the passage is a whole, though the relations and the unity are not those we expect of ordinary prose.

Lawrence is writing in this rhythmically phrasal way because it allows him to realize the feelings of the characters as he could not do in ordinary prose, which would be more analytic and descriptive. The repetitions express, in the reader's imagination, the developing impulses as they arise in the lives of these characters at these moments. We have a direct sympathy with these movements of feeling because the language has the air of following the experience, the 'pulsing, frictional to-and-fro' as it arises in the consciousness of the characters. (It is right that we should be told that they spoke but not what they say.) So, if Lawrence is here realizing the rhythm of the work and the ebb and flow towards the meeting, the prose style is functional.

And though this prose is extraordinary, it is also convincingly natural—partly because its rhythm comes from very deep roots of the language. 'Continual, slightly modified repetition' goes back to Anglo-Saxon, where it is one of the central parts of poetic style; much of the quoted passage could pass as a close translation of some Anglo-Saxon poem:

> tried to bring her gradually to him
> to a meeting till they should be together
> till they should meet as the sheaves
> that swished together.

'The rhythms' (as Mario Praz said of Donne's) 'seem to the sympathetic reader to be those of the experience itself'. This prose is, in a word, poetic, enacting an experience with a depth we do not expect from ordinary prose.

But it will not do, either, to call Lawrence a writer of poetic prose, for that would suggest the purple patches of Wilde, the more delicate preciosity of Pater, or the indefinitely trailing adjectives of that failed American Lawrence, Frank Norris, who were all, in Lawrence's early years, looking for something more poetic than ordinary prose and finding it in a turn away from tight syntax towards phrase-successions. If I call Wilde's prose 'poetic' I do so with pejorative intent, meaning that it has forsaken the collective achievement of English prose for a peculiarly restricted kind of poeticism.

Lawrence's prose is really poetic; moreover at its most poetic it is still prose. Passages like the one I quoted from *The Rainbow* stand out as remarkable, but they are not purple patches; there is no sudden break between them and the more ordinary prose that surrounds them. Frank Norris's favourite word is 'stupefied', and his prose is poetic in the worst Victorian sense, but Lawrence, with all his ambition to explore the depths of the unconscious, writes prose that is the instrument of a sharpened consciousness, the opposite of a narcotic. The poetic use of language is its centre, but it is a centre which connects all the other powers

16

of traditional prose, thus changing prose expression but leaving it as something we still have to see as prose. The difference between Lawrence and all those comparable authors classed by Professor Gordon [2] as writers of 'romantic prose' is that the others are always peripheral, related to the centre, like Sterne, as a joker, or as literary deviations. Even Dickens retains the old tightness of syntactic control most of the time.

These are the contentions I must try to substantiate, but it is worth remarking at once that the failures of Lawrence's new prose (some of the choruses in *David*, some of the descriptions in *Lady Chatterley's Lover*), where he can sound, as he says, 'willed and insistent', are not those that go with poetic vagueness or a dislike of consciousness. On the contrary, Dr. Leavis's convincing objection is to an occasional undue 'explicitness' and 'jargon'.[3] These are the faults of a writer trying unsuccessfully to be conscious in prose : jargon is a failure to develop a language for what has never been expressed before, 'explicitness' is doing so too easily.

If Lawrence's prose succeeds, he has changed expression in prose more effectively than Eliot in verse. If Lawrence's work has sunk into our consciousness and language, he has changed the idea of English prose : after him we have different ideas of what it can do.

Modern prose, developed after the Restoration, is our ordinary means of joining in the everyday world embodied in ordinary writing. With prose, our 'indispensable eighteenth century' created its own world of reason, truth and nature out of chaos; without prose the places where we use it would be again without form and void. Hence the old idea of prose : prose expresses the prosaic and 'collocates' in phrases like 'prose and reason', joining like things, and 'prose and poetry', distinguishing unlike things; and one can talk of the 'prose sense' of a poem, that is, whatever is left when the poetry is removed. Lawrence is, of course, clean contrary to this notion of prose; he needed a different prose to do what he had to do in the novels. (I have to neglect the question of how there can have been English novels *before* Lawrence's prose—imaginative works in the medium of commonsense—but I am not of course saying that there were none.) Moreover his 'change of expression' in prose is so deep down among the foundations of language that it changes at the same time the idea of thought, by putting (in our mathematical and technological age) the poetic imagination right at the centre of thought.

For the idea of ordinary prose I have so crudely sketched belongs very definitely to the same world as the search, culminating in the early years of this century, for a perfect language, guiltless of the emotion and imprecision of the languages we speak, and capable of making propositions definite enough to be demonstrably true or false. Bertrand Russell's ideal language would have been very like eighteenth-century prose *in extremis*, with everything except pure propositions analysed out of it. For this philosophical school all prose aspires to the condition of mathematics:

> If we speak for the sake of arousing emotional attitudes, then the use of emotionally toned words is good for the purpose. When, however, our purpose is to give a straightforward account of what we believe to be the case, emotionally toned language is bad language. In poetry and in oratory the use of emotionally toned language may be essential for the purpose the speaker wishes to achieve. It is, then, good language, for it is fitted to its purpose. If, however, we want to think something out, then we are hindered in our purpose by using emotionally toned language. Such language may be an insuperable obstacle to thinking effectively.[4]

If the novel is in any sense thought something like Lawrence's anti-logical, anti-analytical notion of thought in the paragraphs I began by quoting is necessary to the novelist: for what could be less like Miss Stebbing's 'thinking something out' than telling a story that exists only in the sympathy of the reader? But if Lawrence's prose is infinitely better than the comparable attempts of his contemporaries, the superiority, I would claim, can only be in some way a superiority of thought. Lawrence brought great powers of concentration to bear on language; he did not (as critics like to believe and as they used to believe of Shakespeare) arrive at the achievement of *The Rainbow* by a lucky, undisciplined outpouring of genius. No artistic development is surer, or a reward of harder work, than Lawrence's between *The White Peacock* (whose prose is adjectival and period-poetic) and *The Rainbow*, which is remarkably disciplined, for instance in the passage I quoted, in its attention to its subject.

II

Perhaps even if the foregoing were acceptable as the skeleton of an account of why Lawrence needed an extraordinary prose for the novels it could still be objected that novels have little to do with ordinary prose and that therefore assertions about Lawrence's changing the ideas of prose and of thought are extravagant. It is true that Lawrence's prose is first and foremost a novelist's prose, developed to meet a novelist's need. But there is no discontinuity between Lawrence's style in the novels and in that splendid series of works of criticism (of religion, art, history, psychology, literature and life in general) which accompanied them.

> At first the child cleaves back to the old source. It clings and adheres. The sympathetic centre of unification, or at least unison, alone seems awake. The child wails with the strange desolation of severance, wails for the old connection. With joy and peace it returns to the breast, almost as to the womb.
>
> But not quite. Even in sucking it discovers its new identity and *power*. Its own new, separate *power*. It draws itself back suddenly; it waits. It has heard something? No. But another centre has flashed awake. The child stiffens itself and holds back. What is it, wind? Stomach-ache? Not at all. Listen to some of the screams. The ears can hear deeper than eyes can see. The first scream of the ego. The scream of asserted isolation.[5]

'The child' is generalized; this is prose of exposition, but it nevertheless works in the same way as the prose of *The Rainbow*. The phrasal repetitiveness is the same; and Lawrence is making his point, as usual, by telling a story. By the second paragraph we are being invited to listen to the screams of this generalized child; the proper understanding of the passage, as of any novel, depends on the response of the reader's imagination. Yet Lawrence is thinking here, and thinking hard, about the development of the ego in a child.

19

But if 'continually slightly modified repetition' expressing a 'pulsing, frictional to-and-fro which works up to culmination' is the centre of Lawrence's prose, it is a centre
that links many other things. For instance 'The Novel',[6]
however unfair it may be to Tolstoy, is a wonderful display of intellectual versatility. There is simple seriousness
of a kind few people now dare attempt:

> And the honour, which the novel demands of you,
> is only that you shall be true to the flame that leaps in
> you. When that Prince in *Resurrection* so cruelly be-
> trayed and abandoned the girl, at the beginning of her
> life, he betrayed . . .

but this immediately continues with an effectively in-
decorous image, '. . . and wetted on the flame of his
own manhood.'
Lawrence also has a kind of spontaneous mythology, a development of the novelist's powers that can be convincing
as argument and marvellously funny at the same time:
his prose is packed with the traditional images of Christian
and other mythologies, which he brings startlingly to life:

> When the lion swallows the lamb, fluff and all, he
> usually gets a pain, and there's a rumpus. But when the
> lion tries to force himself down the throat of the huge
> and popular lamb—a nasty old sheep, really—then it's
> a phenomenon. Old Leo did it: wedged himself bit by
> bit down the throat of woolly Russia. And now out of
> the mouth of the bolshevist lambkin still waves an
> angry, mistaken, tufted leonine tail, like an agitated ex-
> clamation mark.

All this from the notion of the lion lying down with the
lamb and Tolstoy's Christian name! Similarly, from the
fable of the frog and the ox (mixed with Cadmus and the
dragon's teeth?)

> Leo was too tight for Tolstoi. He wanted to puff, and
> puff, and puff, till he became Universal Brotherhood it-
> self, the great gooseberry of our globe.
> Then pop went Leo! And from the bits sprang up
> bolshevists.

The opposite extreme in Lawrence from the biblical earnestness is the frequent slang. The next sentence to the above

20

passage is, 'It's all bunk'. Frequently Lawrence's simplicity of style enables him to make a point sharply : this is wit as usually understood, an inheritance from the eighteenth century. Still from 'The Novel' :

> The novel is a great discovery : far greater than Galileo's telescope or somebody else's wireless. The novel is the highest form of human expression so far attained. Why? Because it is so incapable of the absolute.

This prose is marvellously alert, alive with a depth of emotion as well as of intellect, but a depth of mind nevertheless.[7]

Lawrence is engaged on the perennial struggle of the artist 'into conscious being', in English prose. And because he is offering the artist's way of thinking in prose that remains prose, that is, central, and not merely on the periphery of a real world of mathematics or science, Lawrence's brush with Bertrand Russell is of more than anecdotal significance; their quarrel was the fight to the death between two incompatible modes of thought.

It is hardly an exaggeration to say that Russell is wholly unable to understand anything Lawrence wrote,[8] because of the way in which Russell's mind works, which shows itself in the way he writes—or, rather, the ways, for Russell has two (and only two) quite opposed styles. In one mood he is the survivor of the age of 'prose and reason' maintained by so many of his Whig ancestors, and has that air of neat finality that a mathematician's prose ought to have.

> Exactly a year after I had fallen in love with her, she fell in love with somebody else, though she did not wish it to make any difference in her relations with me. I, however, was bitterly jealous. We had violent quarrels, and things were never again quite the same between us. While I was in prison, I was tormented by jealousy the whole time, and driven wild by the sense of impotence. I did not think myself justified in feeling jealousy, which I regarded as an abominable emotion, but none the less it consumed me.
>
> I recognize now that the emotion was wholly foolish, and that Colette's feeling for me was sufficiently serious to persist through any number of minor affairs.[9]

Russell is here following his own beliefs about language

21

and using 'fell in love', 'jealous' etc. as if they are words with a referential meaning of the utmost clarity. He writes as if jealousy were as unmistakable as the sun. (So it is, but not in the same way.) He writes with confident finality, characteristically beginning the passage with 'exactly'. But really this is an obscure passage: we have no idea what really happened, because this is a prose incapable of expressing the feeling which is an essential part of the experiences referred to. The experiences are referred to, not expressed: to have expressed them would have been to show some power over language comparable to a novelist's. Even at his own level Russell cannot keep up his air of precision. Applied to himself, 'falling in love' is evidently meant to be something serious, and if this prose is to work at all, the same phrase must always mean the same thing: but Colette's falling in love is later glossed as a 'minor affair'.

This is a prose incapable of exploring the way life really goes. And underneath its definite certainties rage the untameable, *unprosable* feelings which can only emerge as Russell's other style, the Victorianate purple patch of, for instance, 'A Free Man's Worship', on which the best comment would be a remark in Lawrence's essay 'The Novel and Feelings':

> Yet unless we proceed to connect ourselves up with our own primeval sources, we shall degenerate. And degenerating, we shall break up into a strange orgy of feelings.[10]

Russell always suggests either mathematics or intoxication, and never the twain shall meet. Here one may see the force of Lawrence's insistence on 'interrelatedness' and of his dictum in the Galsworthy essay that 'an emotionally educated man is as rare as a phoenix'. Russell's proses are the evidence of a failure of emotional education, which is bound to be, where human affairs are in question, a failure of thought. Lawrence is the better thinker.

I would go further and say that even in comparison with the best that the traditional prose can offer, Lawrence can show a greater power of thought. In a recent essay [11] Mr. John Remsbury convincingly shows that Lawrence's criticism of Cézanne is superior to Roger Fry's. A very distinguished philosopher offers a third term of com-

22

parison. R. G. Collingwood is, it seems to me, one of the most brilliant minds of our century and—it follows here—a great master of English prose. It is a great triumph of mind to write with the consistent clarity and illumination of difficult problems that Collingwood achieves, for instance, in his *Principles of Art*. Collingwood is a practitioner of wholly traditional prose, always giving the impression of the best and shortest argument or the most succinct information, and having the clarity of wit in the very form of his sentences. And Collingwood makes about Cézanne remarks which, as far as prose sense goes, are almost the same as the ones ten years earlier in Lawrence's *Introduction to these Paintings*.

Both writers, in passages unfortunately too long to quote, have set themselves the difficult task of explaining how Cézanne seems to appeal to the sense of touch rather than of sight. Collingwood does it, as I have said, brilliantly: but he is not quite above the primal philosophical sin of displaying his brilliance, by a proud brandishing of paradox which may perhaps make us admire Collingwood rather than understand his idea. Collingwood says things like 'His landscapes have lost almost every trace of visuality. Trees never looked like that; that is how they feel to a man who encounters them with his eyes shut, blundering against them blindly', and talks of Cézanne's colour as ' a kind of algebraic notation [for] what in his groping he has felt'.[12] But these ways of putting it are bound to suggest the superiority of sight: why not open one's eyes rather than blundering blindly? And can 'algebraic notation' really tell how seeing can suggest touch? Lawrence manages to show Cézanne's vision of what things are like to touch to be superior to what he elsewhere[13] calls 'the kodak sort' of vision, to be the opposite of blundering. Lawrence's great advantage is that he can take us imaginatively through Cézanne's struggle in a kind of biography: his essay could only have been written by a novelist and the result is here a depth of understanding greater than the philosopher can achieve.

At this point, having worked frictionally to-and-fro as best I can, I have a sensation more commonly felt than stated by critics, namely, that the hoped-for culmination has already been finely stated by Dr. Leavis. Discussing Lawrence's claim for the novel as the 'highest form of

23

human expression', after pointing out that 'by highest form of human expression he meant the highest form of thought, the thought in question necessarily being, for him, thought about the nature, meaning and essential problems of human life', Dr. Leavis says:

> Thought, to come at all near truth and adequacy, must engage the whole man, and relate in a valid way—such a way, that is, as precludes and defeats the distorting effects of abstraction and selection (both inevitable)— all the diverse elements of experience.[14]

Put beside that this passage of Lawrence's:

> Now I absolutely flatly deny that I am a soul, or a body, or a mind, or an intelligence, or a brain, or a nervous system, or a bunch of glands, or any of the rest of these bits of me. The whole is greater than the part. And therefore, I, who am man alive, am greater than my soul, or spirit, or body, or mind, or consciousness, or anything else that is merely a part of me. I am a man, and alive. I am man alive, and as long as I can, I intend to go on being man alive.
>
> For this reason I am a novelist. And being a novelist, I consider myself superior to the saint, the scientist, the philosopher, and the poet, who are all great masters of the different bits of man alive, but never get the whole hog.[15]

The novelist—and Lawrence as thinker outside the novels —connects the different parts of 'man alive' to concentrate him in thought. For Lawrence, the medium of that connection had to be that prose.

III

I suggest that in common experience 'thinking something out' is quite unlike what Miss Stebbing describes and much more like Lawrence's 'passionate struggle into conscious being'. We are not likely to think anything out unless we have a strong enough passional urge to make us want or need to, and the thought is then manoeuvring ourselves into the position where a voice can come from

> the individual in his pure singleness, in his totality of consciousness, in his oneness of being . . . This voice of

24

my being I may *never* deny . . . Conscience is the being's consciousness, when the individual is conscious *in toto*, when he knows in full.[16]

All the same there is something wrong here. 'Thinking something out' *is* like this, but there is something missing from Lawrence's statement, some necessary safeguard which goes with the oversimplicity of the belief that any individual can live in 'pure singleness'. For if one must *never* deny one's 'whole being speaking in one voice' [*Ibid.*] then, for instance, Macbeth's career is virtuous : it belongs to Lawrence's case if not to his feeling that the voice which whispers to Macbeth to murder Duncan is from the Holy Ghost.

The missing safeguard is : ordinary language. Lawrence falls into this position—and into his hatred of words like 'thought' and 'understanding' because of an unduly simple notion of 'outside fate', which is closely connected with his strange distrust of language and with his sense of the hostility of the world.

For Lawrence, language is part of the social world, an 'outside fate' that must not be allowed to dictate to the individual.[17] Lawrence even comes close to denying the possibility of an intelligible language :

There is no straight path between you and me, dear reader, so don't blame me if my words fly like dust into your eyes and grit between your teeth, instead of like music into your ears . . . As for the profanation of your sacred ears, just apply a little theory of relativity, and realize that what I say is not what you hear, but something uttered in the midst of my isolation, and arriving strangely changed and travel-worn down the long curve of your own individual circumambient atmosphere. I may say Boh, but heaven alone knows what the goose hears.[18]

If Lawrence were right here he couldn't possibly say so. It is true that as individuals we are quite different; it is also true that we talk to each other and by so doing keep going a world we have in common. The fact that language works is the proof that our individual visions of the world are at least not incomparable. This is the relevant different between us and geese. Yes, heaven knows what any goose hears if you say 'Boh!'—but whatever the goose hears it is certainly not the *word* 'boh' which, equally certainly, is what I hear if you say it to me. So there is an important sense in which 'what I say' is certainly 'what you hear'. You prove that there *is* a straight path between us if you make an intelligible reply.

Lawrence also said, 'It is grass that renews its youth like the Eagle, not any Word.' [19] This too is his failure to realize that he needed to co-operate with language, for, on the contrary, any word has the chance of renewing its youth every time anybody uses it. Any use of language is the chance to say something of our own—which is the same as the chance to achieve sincerity, with which Lawrence as literary artist is necessarily concerned.

Lawrence's way of talking about 'fate dictated from outside' confuses this issue. Neglecting the question of why it is worse to be dictated to by outside fate than by one's innards, one may ask whether it was not an 'outside fate' that Lawrence was an Englishman. He did not choose his language: he was fated to be born in an English-speaking land. But seeing language as 'outside fate' is unhelpful because a language only dictates to an individual insofar as that individual voluntarily accepts it. By using language we simultaneously express our individuality and our connection with humanity: we imitate and use the language of others because that allows us to be ourselves.

I think this is worth saying, because if Lawrence had arrived at an explicit awareness [20] of the necessity of other individuals for the existence of an individual—of the nature of language—he might have achieved more respect for the proper authority of language in its judgment, and restraint, of such characters as Macbeth. Macbeth struggles into conscious being, but against the grain of the language: foul has to be fair before he can be himself; and for ordinary mortals the sense of words like 'foul and fair' (which only exist insofar as they are co-operatively re-created in each use) is a great safeguard. A language may be wrong, and it may be necessary to amend it, as Lawrence courageously set out to do in the case of the common English language of sex. But a man who finds his language against him to the extent of being in basic opposition to it simply cannot speak. I have been trying to show the magnitude of Lawrence's change of English prose, which shows

26

how far he felt English prose as he found it insufficient; and the feeling of desperation was certainly one of the necessary goads to his heroic career: he *had* to see himself as opposing the whole trend of life expressed in the language he spoke. But really Lawrence was co-operating with English and helping it to be itself, just as without it he could not have been *him*self. For all his distaste of 'humanity', Lawrence's work had to belong to the human world, and for all his distrust of 'mental consciousness' his achievement is to extend consciousness in a medium that can only work through the mind. He is concerned with bringing thought to mind and making it available to other minds. It may be true that reading Lawrence involves a more physical response than reading Bertrand Russell—that the perception of the meaning of that *Rainbow* passage may involve the mind in sending and receiving messages from various parts of the body not active in mathematics; it may be true that as Lawrence sometimes asserts, we think with the blood (or other parts) as well as the brain: yet if the thought is to be transmitted on paper it has to go through the brain. All Lawrence writes is under the control of the imagination working in prose, which can only operate through the conscious mind. Lawrence perhaps extends consciousness downwards, but it is consciousness that he extends. All this is only a gloss on the assertion that Lawrence is a great imaginative genius at work on the English language and that without either term, the genius or the language, his achievement would have been impossible—an obvious gloss, perhaps, to everybody except Lawrence.

But, finally, it is possible to see the achievement of Lawrence's prose as an extension of the powers English permits to the human mind. Lawrence vindicates for our age the centrality of the creative imagination in thought and, since that vindication could not be merely static, the claim implies that he took English a step further than it had ever gone before—this, too, in the century when in common belief all the best thought has gone into science. This is only to say that Lawrence is our most recent great author.

But subsequent history has shown that Lawrence's alteration of expression has been only partly effective: he has had little influence, and what there is is almost always regrettable; so his achievement is very unlike Dryden's which

27

at once altered prose for everybody. Perhaps I could say merely that he has changed the idea of prose without changing our practice: English prose now includes Lawrence. But I think the real explanation of his apparent lack of effect is teleological. The change Lawrence has made is so profound that (like Shakespeare's) it may not be fully discovered for hundreds of years. In the unlikely event of the survival of English civilization, Lawrence and his prose may be known in the future in ways impossible to us. It may well be that the impact of D. H. Lawrence on English prose will not be fully felt before the next millennium.

NOTES

1. Included in *Phoenix II* (edited by Warren Roberts and Harry T. Moore, London, 1968), pp. 275–6.
2. I. A. Gordon, *The Movement of English Prose.*
3. F. R. Leavis, *D. H. Lawrence, Novelist* (London, 1955), p. 148.
4. L. S. Stebbing, *Thinking to Some Purpose* (London, 1939), chap. V. For a brilliant demonstration that *all* language is 'emotionally toned', v. R. G. Collingwood, *The Principles of Art* (Oxford, 1938), chap. X, section 4. Miss Stebbing's tone is that of a nice, fussy, conscientious public lecturer.
5. *Psychoanalysis and the Unconscious*, chap. III.
6. First collected in *Reflections on the Death of a Porcupine* (Philadelphia, 1925), reprinted in *Phoenix II*.
7. For all Lawrence's dependence on the speaking voice one can sometimes say that his prose is written as opposed to spoken:

The universe, in short, adds up to ONE.
ONE.
1.
Which is Walt.

('Whitman' in *Studies in Classic American Literature*) The cheeky finality of the repetition of 'ONE' as '1' is effective, but not an effect that could be expressed orally.
8. Cf. Russell's most recent anti-Lawrence outburst in *Autobiography*, vol. II, where he confounds Lawrence with

Hitler apparently on the grounds that both were emotional men.

9. Russell, op cit.

10. *Phoenix* (edited by Edward McDonald, London, 1936), p. 758.

11. " 'Real Thinking': Lawrence and Cézanne' (*Cambridge Quarterly*, Vol. II, no. 2, Spring 1967).

12. Collingwood, op. cit., chap. VII, sec. 6.

13. 'Accumulated Mail' (*Phoenix*, p. 802).

14. F. R. Leavis, '*Anna Karenina*: Thought and Significance in a Great Creative Work (*Cambridge Quarterly*, vol. I, no. 1, Winter 1965, reprinted in '*Anna Karenina*' *and other essays* (London, 1967): see p. 11).

15. 'Why the Novel Matters' (*Phoenix*, p. 535).

16. *Fantasia of the Unconscious*, chap. XI.

17. Cf. for instance the remarks about 'bread' in 'Pornography and Obscenity' (*Phoenix*, p. 171).

18. *Fantasia of the Unconscious*, chap. II.

19. 'Why the Novel Matters' (*Phoenix*, p. 536).

20. Such an awareness is wonderfully worked out in *Women in Love*, one of the ways in which the novels are better than Lawrence's own pronouncements.

JESSIE CHAMBERS AND MIRIAM LEIVERS

An Essay on *Sons and Lovers* *

Late in 1912 Lawrence finished his last revision of *Sons and Lovers*, and, having sent the manuscript to the publishers, wrote to Edward Garnett that he wanted 'to defend it quick'. He did so in the following schematic synopsis:

A woman of character and refinement goes into the lower class, and has no satisfaction in her own life. She has had a passion for her husband, so the children are born of passion, and have heaps of vitality. But as her sons grow up she selects them as lovers—first the eldest, then the second. These sons are *urged* into life by their reciprocal love of their mother—urged on and on. But when they come to manhood, they can't love, because their mother is the strongest power in their lives, and holds them. . . . As soon as the young men come into contact with women, there's a split. William gives his sex to a fribble, and his mother holds his soul. But the split kills him, because he doesn't know where he is. The next son gets a woman who fights for his soul—fights his mother. The son loves the mother—all the sons hate and are jealous of the father. The battle goes on between the mother and the girl, with the son as object. The mother gradually proves stronger, because of the tie of blood. The son decides to leave his soul in his mother's hands, and, like his elder brother go for passion. He gets passion. Then the split begins to tell again. But, almost unconsciously, the mother realizes what is the matter, and begins to die. The son casts off his mistress, attends to

* By A. H. Gomme (University of Keele).

his mother dying. He is left in the end naked of everything, with the drift towards death.[1]

And then he went on to insist:

It is a great tragedy, and I tell you I have written a great book. It's the tragedy of thousands of young men in England.

What I want to ask in this essay turns on both these quotations, and may be put preliminarily in the form, 'Whose tragedy?' The first and simplest answer, likely to occur in some form to anyone at all familiar with the story of Lawrence's early life is: 'Lawrence's own'. Obviously this cannot be the whole truth. Though every novelist must in some way draw deep on his own experience (and Lawrence later became almost notorious in some people's eyes for helping himself fictionally to the characters and fortunes of others), *Sons and Lovers* does this in a peculiarly detailed and intimate way: how much so we know from the memoirs that his friends and acquaintances have given us, and especially from that of Jessie Chambers, originally published in 1935 as *D. H. Lawrence: a Personal Record*, by 'E.T.'.[2] Telling us of Lawrence's early interest in George Borrow, she reports him as saying that

Borrow had mingled autobiography and fiction so inextricably in *Lavengro* that the most astute critics could not be sure where the one ended and the other began. From his subtle smile I felt he was wondering whether he might not do something in the same fashion himself.[3]

This suggests that at one stage Lawrence was perhaps looking forward to writing a kind of semi-fictional autobiography. And to many people—to Jessie herself—this is what, despite obvious departures from the factual record, *Sons and Lovers* became. Yet surely *Sons and Lovers* is a novel: what I am concerned with is how far such a statement defines and justifies itself. 'I tried hard', Jessie reports, when Lawrence sent her the manuscript which hurt her so much, 'to remind myself that after all *Sons and Lovers* was only a novel.'[4] Now obviously, for her it could not be: the narrative was so intimately linked to the story of her own life and her relationship with Lawrence that such detachment would be inconceivable. Moreover there is a difference

31

between saying that it is a novel and saying that it is *only* a novel. She was perhaps using the word in a depreciatory sense, as a help in keeping up her own strength in the face of what was to her a terrible betrayal; but for the most disinterested and uninvolved of readers, *Sons and Lovers* must always be more and less than 'only a novel', so poignantly does it expose the personal tragedy and contradictions which brought it into being and remain at its heart.

The questions that we can properly ask about *Sons and Lovers* have to be very delicately poised. Jessie tells us of her disappointment with the first draft of the book, which Lawrence sent to her when he was two thirds of the way through 'and seemed to have come to a standstill':

> As I read through the manuscript I had before me all the time the vivid picture of the reality. I felt again the tenseness of the conflict, and the impending spiritual clash. So in my reply I told him I was very surprised that he had kept so far from reality in his story; that I thought what had really happened was much more poignant and interesting than the situations he had invented. In particular I was surprised that he had omitted the story of Ernest [Lawrence's elder brother], which seemed to me vital enough to be worth telling as it actually happened. Finally I suggested that he should write the whole story again, and keep it true to life.[5]

That certainly sounds, with its reference to a particular episode in the family's life, as if she was urging him to write an autobiography, to keep 'true to life' in the sense of keeping to the 'facts' as they were and had happened. But whether or not that is so, her main criterion here is a truly critical one: 'I thought that what had really happened was much more poignant and interesting than the situations he had invented'—that is, that the human value and significance were what really counted, and the virtue of keeping 'true to life' was that, to her, the factual story was more profoundly representative than the fictitious one. (To judge from the brief summary she gives of the first draft she was certainly right.) But much later, when she read the final version, the issue for her had shifted, and the basis for judgement had subtly changed:

32

Neither could I feel that he had represented in any degree faithfully the nature and quality of our desperate search for a right relationship.[6]

Here the issue is not one of broad human values but of fidelity to what specifically had been the case between them, and her charge is that Lawrence has falsified the record. Immediately, however, this appears too crude an analysis: for her human values could in the nature of the case only be served by such fidelity: how could it have been otherwise for Jessie Chambers at such a time? Moreover for Lawrence himself it seems to have been at one time a matter of real moment that he should get the record straight, for he 'fell in absolutely' with Jessie's suggestion that he should rewrite the story, keeping it true to life, and asked her 'to write what I could remember of our early days, because, as he truthfully said, my recollection of those days was so much clearer than his'.[7]

Exactly what she wrote, and in consequence the precise use that Lawrence made of her reminiscences, are now beyond recovery; but certain comparisons remain open to us. Consider the following two passages relating an apparently trivial incident on one of the communal walks that they went on with various friends:

It was on one of these walks . . . that I had a sudden flash of insight which made me see Lawrence in a totally new light. We were walking along anyhow, singly, or in twos and threes. I happened to be alone, admiring the bronze tips of the maple in the hedge. Suddenly I turned and saw Lawrence in the middle of the road, bending over an umbrella. There was something in his attitude that arrested me. His stooping figure had a look of intensity, almost of anguish. For a moment I saw him as a symbolic figure. I was deeply moved and walked back to him.

'What is the matter?' I asked.

'It was Ern's umbrella, and mother will be wild if I take it home broken', he replied.

We walked on together, but I did not tell him what I had seen. This was perhaps the beginning of our awareness of sympathy for one another.[8]

That is Jessie's report, from which, though she does not

33

make it easy for us to understand just what Lawrence symbolized for her, we become aware of her being drawn to him *through* a vision of his aloneness, of something which separated him from the rest of those she knew. When Lawrence wrote up the incident in *Sons and Lovers* (chap. 7), the scene is virtually unchanged, but the outcome is very different:

> . . . Turning a corner in the lane, she came upon Paul, who stood bent over something, his mind fixed on it, working away steadily, patiently, a little hopelessly. She hesitated in her approach, to watch.
>
> He remained concentrated in the middle of the road. Beyond, one rift of rich gold in that colourless grey evening seemed to make him stand out in dark relief. She saw him, slender and firm, as if the setting sun had given him to her. A deep pain took hold of her, and she knew she must love him. And she had discovered him, discovered in him a rare potentiality, discovered his loneliness. Quivering as at some 'annunciation', she went slowly forward.
>
> At last he looked up.
>
> 'Why', he exclaimed gratefully, 'have you waited for me!'
>
> She saw a deep shadow in his eyes.
>
> 'What is it?' she asked.
>
> 'The spring is broken here'; and he showed her where his umbrella was injured.
>
> Instantly, with some shame, she knew he had not done the damage himself, but that Geoffrey [her brother] was responsible.
>
> 'It is only an old umbrella, isn't it?' she asked.
>
> She wondered why he, who did not usually trouble over trifles, made such a mountain out of this molehill.
>
> 'But it was William's, an' my mother can't help but know', he said quietly, still patiently working at the umbrella.
>
> The words went through Miriam like a blade. This, then, was the confirmation of her vision of him! She looked at him. But there was about him a certain reserve, and she dared not comfort him, not even speak softly to him.

No-one will dispute that Lawrence's version is incomparably the more vivid : that, we may say, is why Jessie wrote out her memories for him 'to translate the raw material of life into significant form', as she herself said. But now, though it is evident that Lawrence has used material (including her 'vision') that she has given him, the episode becomes the occasion of division rather than of unspoken sympathy, or at least a sign to Miriam of the divisive force of his mother standing between them. Moreover Lawrence makes Miriam draw back from Paul (sensing that what she has seen has been a deception which has now been punctured), just when, if we accept Jessie's account, the real Jessie felt for the first time deeply linked to him. After she and Lawrence had parted for good, Jessie wrote to their common friend Helen Corke [9] that 'the "Miriam" part of the novel is a slander—a fearful treachery. David has interpreted her every word, action and thought in the light of "Mrs. Morel's" hatred of her.' This episode, then, is a small but specific instance where, thanks to Jessie's having included it in her book, we can see the 'treacherous' transformation taking place. But of course it is a betrayal in a straightforwardly literal sense only if we take Miriam Leivers as being meant by Lawrence as a faithful and literal portrait of Jessie Chambers, and the story of Paul and Miriam as her and Lawrence's own story.

A novel can, however, betray the truth in a subtler, more profound and more humanly significant way than this; and I believe that it is a betrayal of this deeper and less tangible kind that we have to enquire into in *Sons and Lovers* —from, as it were, a critical position within the novel itself. Jessie's crucial charge against Lawrence is that he interpreted Miriam through Mrs. Morel, or in other words and from another point of view, Jessie herself through his own mother. This attitude is endorsed, at least implicitly, by, among others, Helen Corke, who had no reason to be biased :

> The least thing—the only thing the son felt he could do in the presence of her [his mother's] suffering—was to defer to her judgment, to endorse her standard of values, to deny Jessie Chambers. He began to write the story of Paul Morel; it was to be his mother's justification and apotheosis.[10]

Certainly, so far as outward events are concerned, the end

35

of *Sons and Lovers*—Paul's final rejection of Miriam—is a victory for the spirit of Mrs. Morel, whose constant and explicit hostility to Miriam Lawrence does nothing to conceal. To judge from his own summary of the novel, Lawrence is keen to emphasize how far Mrs. Morel's possessive love thwarts the possibility of a full relationship between her son and any other woman. But the novel itself makes the hostility specific and particular:

> Mrs. Morel hated her for making her son like this. She watched Paul growing irritable, priggish, and melancholic. For this she put the blame on Miriam. (Ch. 7)

She singled out Miriam personally as the object of her resentment and cause of her misery:

> 'She exults—she exults as she carries him off from me . . . She's not like an ordinary woman, who can leave me my share in him. She wants to absorb him. She wants to draw him out and absorb him till there is nothing left of him, even for himself. He will never be a man on his own feet—she will suck him up.' (Ch. 8)

This of course is in Mrs. Morel's own voice, and it makes her attitude unequivocal (it will be important later to try to distinguish whether her dislike stems from her view of Miriam's nature, or whether she would take against *any* rival to herself and in doing so find the justification in a particular 'interpretation' of what the rival was really like). Lawrence, then, acknowledges the fact of the hostility without reserve, acknowledges, that is, that Mrs. Morel sees Miriam in just this light. But somewhat later there is a subtle shift, of which I feel sure he was not altogether conscious, but whose effects may be really damaging to the credit which the narrative technique implicitly claims for a disinterested presentation of facts working themselves out:

> . . . he came back to her [Mrs. Morel]. And in his soul was a feeling of the satisfaction of self-sacrifice because he was faithful to her. She loved him first; he loved her first. And yet it was not enough. His new young life, so strong and imperious, was urged towards something else. It made him mad with restlessness. She saw this, and wished bitterly that Miriam had been a woman who

36

could take this new life of his, and leave her the roots.
(Ch. 9)

Here, what seem still to be Mrs. Morel's reflexions have the
only partly veiled endorsement of Lawrence the narrator
(at such a moment one hardly knows whether to say 'Lawrence' or 'Paul'). And it is precisely *this* Miriam, worked
out at length in the novel, that Jessie saw as herself 'reflected in the distorting mirror of Mrs. Lawrence's mind';[11]
what is at issue is not the fact of Mrs. Morel's or Mrs.
Lawrence's hostility, but Lawrence/Paul's endorsement of
it, his identification of himself with her point of view.
And the question for the critical reader is not whether
Lawrence is being fair to Jessie Chambers, but whether he
is honest about Miriam Leivers. What is the evidence here?

In trying to make a critical assessment of this issue so
much at the heart of the novel, we are faced immediately
with a very special difficulty and a special need for delicate
discrimination. I have just now hinted at how hard it is
at times to distinguish Lawrence from Paul; but that is
only one aspect of the striking—if somewhat perplexing—
narrative technique of the novel, in which the convention
of the omniscient narrator has gone through a process of
being, as it were, absorbed into the internal consciousness
of several characters in turn. Raymond Williams has observed recently of Lawrence[12] that in him as never before
in the English novel, 'the language of the writer is at one
with the language of his characters'. And while this instinctive atoneness with his people has undoubtedly given
Lawrence the ability to open up to us great new areas of
experience, it can put a very real strain on the careful
reader. Consider the following passage from the chapter
(number 11)[13] rather grimly called 'The Test on Miriam'
(who sees it as a test? and who—is it within the novel or
an outside narrator?—is putting her to it?):

> Frequently he hated Miriam. He hated her as she bent
> forward and pored over his things. He hated her way of
> patiently casting him up, as if he were an endless
> psychological account. When he was with her, he hated
> her for having got him, and yet not got him, and he
> tortured her. She took all and gave nothing, he said. At
> least, she gave no living warmth. She was never alive,

37

and giving off life. Looking for her was like looking for something which did not exist.

It may seem, on a first and casual glance, to be in the voice of an attentive but neutral (though privileged) descriptive narrator—until one comes to the fifth sentence, with its revealing 'he said', coming at the end almost as an after-thought. Once it has come we can hardly help feeling that the following sentences also give us what 'he said' or thought, even though there is nothing to make this explicit. But then, if we look back, it seems that the preceding sentences equally represent 'Paul's thought': 'her way of patiently casting him up, as if he were an endless psycho-logical account'—is this not *his* view of her? Yet it merges imperceptibly into what passes as neutral description. In fact all the generalized descriptions of Miriam, from the first important one at the beginning of chapter 7, come to sound as if they were spoken by Paul, even when they relate things that he could not know at first hand. Hence, if such a passage does represent some kind of betrayal of 'the true Miriam', it is not Paul's alone: Lawrence too is insidiously implicated.[14]

But because of the constant shifting of narrative insight through the book, as Lawrence strives to present as directly and as naturally as possible the immediate feelings of his characters, he must also involve Miriam herself in the betrayal. When she first gives herself to him sexually, we read (chap. 11):

> He stood against a pine-tree trunk and took her in his arms. She relinquished herself to him, but it was a sacri-fice in which she felt something of horror.

Whose voice is that? the narrator's or Miriam's? A little later the notion of sacrifice, on which Lawrence is so insistent, gets repeated stress in a passage in which the language undergoes a further subtle corruption:

> Her big brown eyes were watching him, still and re-signed and loving; she lay as if she had given herself up to sacrifice: there was her body for him; but the look at the back of her eyes, like a creature awaiting immolation, arrested him, and all his blood fell back.
>
> 'You are sure you want me?' he asked, as if a cold shadow had come over him.

38

'Yes, quite sure.'

She was very quiet, very calm. She only realized that she was doing something for him. He could hardly bear it. She lay to be sacrificed for him because she loved him so much.

Whose voice have we here? Except for the two short sentences of direct speech, there is no change of tone anywhere. We begin in some unspecified consciousness ('she lay *as if* she had given herself up to sacrifice'), and then move from what Paul sees ('the look at the back of her eyes . . . arrested him') to what she feels ('She only realized . . .'), and then back to him or to some detached mind outside them both. Moreover *what* she feels—what, that is, we are told she feels—confirms completely *his* view of her, contradicting her speech. It is as if Lawrence has established an unholy alliance between Paul and Miriam's unspoken feelings against her conscious and deliberate self: there can be no appeal from Paul's interpretation of her, because, through a subtle, though surely unconscious, linguistic device, Lawrence has ensured that Miriam's own deepest promptings are already leagued against her. It is the identity of tone which obliges the reader to take it all as carrying the guarantee of omniscience: so poor Miriam has no chance against the alliance of Lawrence and Paul. Passage after passage could be quoted to confirm the way in which the very technique of the novel is enlisted in the service of one particular interpretation of the events of the story. I give one more, which also illustrates how the overall tone embraces both protagonists and implicates them together in a conspiracy, because it points more specifically to the explanation of why the real Miriam who struggles to emerge in the book becomes falsified through being seen through Paul's eyes:

She felt she could bear anything for him; she would suffer for him. She put her hand on his knee as he leaned forward in his chair. He took it and kissed it; but it hurt to do so. He felt he was putting himself aside. He sat there sacrificed to her purity, which felt more like nullity. How could he kiss her hand passionately, when it would drive her away, and leave nothing but pain? (Ch. 11)

Here it is Paul who is sacrificed, but it seems to make

39

curiously little difference: the point is that it is the Lawrence–Paul voice which is regulative throughout, and which is determined to interpret the relationship in terms of sacrifice, and to see this as the true cause of their failure to bring it to a whole-hearted consummation. For what do we see on the next page? Surely an eager, passionate girl struggling to understand, to accept and come to live with strong new urges within herself, and in the process inevitably scared. It is in fact Paul who repulses and stigmatizes these promptings in her. Long before this (chapter 8), in answer to his weary complaint, 'If only you could want *me*, and not what I can reel off for you!' she comes out with the true voice of passion:

'I!' she cried bitterly—'I! Why, when would you let me take you?'

The rhythm of her words here compels acceptance, as do all her spontaneous actions and speech: it is the reflective prose which interprets her according to Paul's image of her, as he is determined she should be seen. And this seems to be very close to what Lawrence did to Jessie when, as she puts it, he stuck labels on her:

Lawrence had found a new name for me. I was no longer Emily Brontë; I was a pre-Raphaelite woman. I disliked the new label even more than the old one. It made me feel that for him I was becoming less and less of a suffering, struggling human being, and more and more of a mental concept, a pure abstraction.[15]

How nearly this describes the method of *Sons and Lovers* hardly needs stressing.

Curiously, therefore, the living Miriam who is directly revealed to us tells against and even undermines the Miriam who is described and interpreted. Occasionally this contradiction appears to come to the conscious surface of the novel. At the end of chapter 10, Paul complains to Clara that Miriam wants 'a sort of soul union'. Clara retorts:

'But how do you know what she wants?'
'I've been with her for seven years.'
'And you haven't found out the very first thing about her.'
'What's that?'

'That she doesn't want any of your soul communion. That's your own imagination. She wants you.'

He pondered over this. Perhaps he was wrong.

'But she seems—' he began.

'You've never tried,' she answered.

It is almost directly after this in the narrative that (as the novel asks us to believe) Paul forces Miriam to surrender herself to a sexual relationship. But it is instructive to remark how chapter 11 begins, immediately on the close of the conversation just quoted. 'You've never tried,' Clara insists. And then :

With the spring came again the old madness and battle. Now he knew he would have to go to Miriam. But what was his reluctance? He told himself it was only a sort of overstrong virginity in her and him which neither could break through.

So he goes to her as under some strong impulse, but already withdrawn into abstraction, wrestling with his own mental interpretation of them both, and particularly of her. It is this of course—in Paul's voice—and not the Miriam that, I suggest, we can see struggling against its dominance that determines the course of the story (as perhaps it was Lawrence's interpretation of Jessie that determined *theirs*). And so much is indeed 'his own imagination', his casting Miriam in the image he has made for her. When Paul has made up his mind to break with her,

Miriam met him at the lane-end. She was wearing a new dress of figured muslin that had short sleeves. Those short sleeves, and Miriam's brown-skinned arms beneath them—such pitiful, resigned arms—gave him so much pain that they helped to make him cruel. She had made herself look so beautiful and fresh for him. She seemed to blossom for him alone. Every time he looked at her— a mature young woman now, and beautiful in her new dress—it hurt so much that his heart seemed almost to be bursting with the restraint he put on it. But he had decided, and it was irrevocable. (Ch. 11)

Yes, he had decided. It is astonishing that Lawrence appears not to see what he has done here : he has given us a Paul who cannot see the real Miriam because he has already decided what will be there to see, and because she does not—what living being could?—fit the abstraction, the categories which determine the lines of what he can see. Once again the focus of the language shifts from sentence to sentence : the first two are quite neutral, the fourth and fifth ambiguous, though seeming to point towards Paul's view of her: and in between one that starts innocuously enough and then traps her and the reader with a phrase that corrupts all attempts at honest dealing—'such pitiful, resigned arms'. What justification can there be for such adjectives? What indeed do they mean, in this context? Only that Paul wills himself to see *her* as pitiful and resigned to the fate he is about to deal her. In the light of so betraying a trick, we can look back to the quotation on p. 6 and realize that the constant shifting of focus which I noted there is an expression not only of a not fully conscious wish on Lawrence's part to equate Miriam with Paul's view of her, but worse, of his recurrent inclination to credit Miriam with Paul's own weakness (and—though this departs from strict critical relevance into the psychology of literary creation—probably therefore with his own). This is nowhere more tellingly visible than in a passage at the very end of the book which, in its naked self-exposure, makes one wonder how much of the truth of what he had done Lawrence now at last consciously saw : last consciously saw :

The despairing doggedness in his tone made her go on her knees on the rug before the fire, very near to him. There she crouched as if she were crushed by something, and could not raise her head. His hands lay quite inert on the arms of his chair. She was aware of them. She felt that now he lay at her mercy. If she could rise, take him, put her arms round him, and say, 'You are mine', then he would leave himself to her. But dare she? She could easily sacrifice herself. But dare she assert herself? She was aware of his dark-clothed, slender body, that seemed one stroke of life, sprawled in the chair close to her. But no; she dared not put her arms round it, take it up, and say, 'It is mine, this body. Leave it to me.' And she wanted to. It called to all her woman's instinct. But she crouched, and dared not. She was afraid he would not let her . . . Her eyes, shuddering, appealing, gone almost distracted, pleaded to him suddenly. His heart caught with pity. He took her hands, drew her to him, and comforted her.

'Will you have me, to marry me?' he said very low.

Oh, why did not he take her? Her very soul belonged to him. Why would he not take what was his? She had borne so long the cruelty of belonging to him and not being claimed by him. Now he was straining her again. It was too much for her . . . She pleaded to him with all her love not to make it *her* choice . . .

It was the end then between them. She could not take him and relieve him of the responsibility of himself. She could only sacrifice herself to him—sacrifice herself every day, gladly. And that he did not want. He wanted her to hold him and say, with joy and authority: 'Stop all this restlessness and beating against death. You are mine for a mate.' She had not the strength. Or was it a mate she wanted? or did she want a Christ in him? (Ch. 15)

The flickering alertness of Miriam's mind, as it moves among her own thoughts and desires and the signs immediately presented to her senses, is marvellously caught. Yet once again we find the shifting, ambiguous focus of consciousness. But for a moment the real Miriam and the predicament she is forced into are recognized in the novel's own voice: 'She was afraid he would not let her . . . Why would he not take what was his? She had borne so long the cruelty of belonging to him and not being claimed by him . . . She pleaded to him with all her love not to make it *her* choice.' What this seems to me to amount to is that Paul has all along tried to make her not just take him on his terms, but *choose* him on his terms, including the abstraction of herself: the crucial weakness, the refusal of responsibility, is Paul's; and this is here at last explicit. Hence the extraordinary and impossible choice which she is made to face of 'self-sacrifice' or taking all responsibility from him. It has throughout been Paul who has insisted that she wants only his soul ('a Christ in him') and has tried in his alter ego as Lawrence to prevent our seeing the Miriam whose instinct for life would contradict this self-defensive view of what would otherwise be a threat to his conception of himself.

43

What Lawrence calls in his synopsis 'the drift towards death' is very powerful at the end (so much so that Paul's new resoluteness in the final paragraph does not carry much conviction). Death is now almost equated with his mother : 'she was the only thing that held him up . . . his soul could not leave her, wherever she was' (ch. 15). So Paul's will, atrophied before, has become paralyzed in her death. It is interesting to see how inert is the image of Paul in the summary : 'the battle goes on between the mother and the girl, with the son as object'. The battle is one-sided, and the synopsis is manifestly untrue to Miriam at this point; but the sentence suggests forcefully Mrs. Morel's power over her son. She is above all the dominant *will* of the book, working out a vicarious substitute for the failure of her own married life in her relations with her sons. When Paul first goes to work she exults in having two sons 'in the world' (William is now in London) :

> She could think of two places, great centres of industry, and feel that she had put a man into each of them, that these men would work out what *she* wanted; they were derived from her, and their works also would be hers. (Ch. 5)

In such phrases the possessiveness of the will ceases to be metaphorical; the italics are Lawrence's and for a moment there is something almost vindictive in his tone. Paul's life quickly becomes a surrogate for hers :

> His life-story, like an Arabian Nights, was told night after night to his mother. It was almost as if it were her own life. (Ch. 5)

So by the time he tried to assert his right to 'please himself' —'I shall do as I like' (ch. 7)—we know all too well how powerless he is to do any such thing : ' "Very well," said his mother cuttingly, "then do as you like." '

There seems no doubt that Lawrence knows that Paul is trapped by the peculiarity and intensity of his relationship with his mother. 'You can't come out of yourself, you can't', Clara tells him (ch. 13); and it is only what Paul, in a curious passage, is made to reflect about his contemporaries :

> He looked round. A good many of the nicest men he knew were like himself, bound in by their own virginity,

which they could not break out of . . . Being the sons of mothers whose husbands had blundered rather brutally through their feminine sanctities, they were themselves too diffident and shy. They could easier deny themselves than incur any reproach from a woman; for a woman was like their mother, and they were full of the sense of their mother. (Ch. 11)

It is not only, therefore, that the mother 'selects her sons as lovers', but that the relationship becomes their deliberate choice too, so far as choice is possible. Jessie tells us that Mrs. Lawrence 'had claimed his love, all the spontaneous tenderness without which "love" is a mockery'.[16] But also, in a letter to Helen Corke,[17] she quoted Lawrence himself as having said of his mother, 'I've loved her—like a lover— that's why I could never love you.' There is nothing quite so frank as this in *Sons and Lovers*, but many episodes in which their unhealthy possessive relationship is displayed. Paul treats his mother—as (not always unconsciously) she asks to be treated—as his contemporary : on their trip to Lincoln, he is a young man out with his girl. The likeness of it all to the classic Freudian Oedipal situation has often been noted; but one does not need the apparatus of psycho-analysis to see how inevitably it leads to the bitter hostility of the son to his father, of the mother to the girl who is truly her rival. Paul's young ambition 'was quietly to earn his thirty or thirty-five shillings a week somewhere near home, and then, when his father died, have a cottage with his mother, paint and go out as he liked, and live happy ever after' (ch. 5). That is a child's eye view of course, but the casual dismissal of the father—'the poor disinherited father', as Jessie calls Mr. Lawrence—hardens later into a hatred which gets almost to the point of physical violence. In after life Lawrence admitted that his treatment of his father was unjust ('I was born hating my father', he said in 1910[18]) : this is undoubtedly true to the extent that Walter Morel is thought of as a literal portrait—the interest for us lies in the confirmation it gives of Lawrence's continuing to see the novel as autobiographical. But for the critical reader of the novel, the important issue is how far there is internal falsification. The scenes between the elder Morels are observed with a hard, unflinching brilliance which keeps them astonishingly vivid; but that is not the same thing as saying that Lawrence really understands what is going on. Walter Morel of course repeatedly puts himself terribly in the wrong, as much by his whining self-pity as by the coarse drunken violence to which the mother and child react so bitterly. After he has flung the table drawer at Mrs. Morel (ch. 2), cutting her forehead, we know how frightened and miserable he has made himself :

> He lay and suffered like a sulking dog. He had hurt himself most; and he was the more damaged because he would never say a word to her, or express his sorrow. He tried to wriggle out of it. 'It was her own fault', he said to himself. Nothing, however, could prevent his inner consciousness inflicting on him the punishment which ate into his spirit like rust . . .
> . . . He always ran away from the battle with himself. Even in his own heart's privacy, he excused himself, saying, 'If she hadn't said so-and-so, it would never have happened. She asked for what she's got.'

This is all most brilliantly observed; yet we may ask how far Lawrence understands the impulses that drove Walter Morel out of his family, and not find a satisfactory answer. 'He was an outsider. He had denied the God in him' (ch. 4). But had he? This is mere assertion : it is remarkable that Lawrence the artist seems unconscious of the effect of the cutting edge of Mrs Morel's scornful pride. When Walter Morel is really and visibly shocked at the outcome of his violence, she was 'cold and impassive as stone, with mouth tight shut', so that he 'sickened with feebleness and hopelessness of spirit' and 'turned drearily away' (chap. 2). But even more remarkable is the power of the story to counteract the conscious contempt and condemnation of Morel, and to make us feel the terrible effect on him of Mrs Morel's pride and sense of a superiority which she has degraded by associating herself with him. This is not the whole story : there is a profound and inborn weakness in Morel, on which she rests all the moral weight of her self-justifying rejection of him (of which his childish spite in the passage quoted above is a helpless reflexion); and this is something which it does not seem to have occurred to Lawrence that he must, to preserve the full integrity of this part of the novel, come to grips with.[19]

I think that few people can read *Sons and Lovers* without

feeling a good deal of pathos in the portrait of Walter Morel: he is as much victim as villain; and this seems to be against Lawrence's conscious intention. With Mrs. Morel the situation is at once plainer and more obscure. For who comes away from the book without feelings of deep disquiet about her and her relation to Paul (and Lawrence)? To judge from the synopsis, Lawrence was well aware of the devastating effect of her possessive love on her sons. And there is much in the novel to confirm this: 'She could not bear it when he was with Miriam. William was dead. She would fight to keep Paul.' (chap. 9). So 'the deepest of his love belonged to his mother' (ib.) and would always do so. But it is hard to feel that Lawrence is aware of how damaging to his overt idea of his mother the direct revelation is. Even more puzzlingly Jessie Chambers was not aware of it either: for her the book not only displayed Paul's bondage to his mother but glorified it: 'His mother had to be supreme, and for the sake of that supremacy every disloyalty was permissible'.[20] But just as she realized that she 'had naïvely credited Lawrence with superhuman powers of detachment',[21] so perhaps it is asking too much of her, even twenty years afterwards, to detach herself enough from her involvement in the book to find the truly critical response. For how does the critical reader react to this?

He had taken off his collar and tie, and rose, barethroated, to go to bed. As he stooped to kiss his mother, she threw her arms round his neck, hid her face on his shoulder, and cried, in a whimpering voice, so unlike her own that he writhed in agony:

'I can't bear it. I could let another woman—but not her. She'd leave me no room, not a bit of room—'

And immediately he hated Miriam bitterly.

'And I've never—you know, Paul—I've never had a a husband—not really—'

He stroked his mother's hair, and his mouth was on her throat.

'And she exults so in taking you from me—she's not like ordinary girls.'

'Well, I don't love her, mother', he murmured, bowing his head and hiding his eyes on her shoulder in misery. His mother kissed him in a long, fervent kiss.

47

'My boy!' she said, in a voice trembling with passionate love. (Ch. 8)

It is a very painful scene, and especially so in the way that Mrs Morel's pain gives way to triumph as Paul pushes the thought of Miriam away from him. Here surely one can see that it is not just Miriam in particular who is the object of her bitterness, but anyone who would claim Paul's new life. Openly—to the reader if not to Paul or Lawrence —*she* claims Paul as the replacement for the husband who has failed her; he responds, and from that point the distortion of the picture of Miriam becomes patent. For there is no evidence anywhere of Miriam's 'exulting' in 'taking Paul from her' (if there were Paul might indeed yield to it). It is a manifest untruth which Paul will not or cannot contradict: Mrs Morel falsifies the truth about Miriam to find a justification for claiming unnatural possession of him. One says, 'Mrs Morel', but both Paul and Lawrence implicitly but unhesitatingly accept that the lie does justify her—so close is the identification here. Indeed for Lawrence it is not a lie: this then is the treacherous reinterpretation, but now seen from the inside. (It is significant of the double disloyalty that Walter Morel is made to come in immediately after in a particularly brutal mood.)

The damage, to the picture of Mrs Morel that I believe the conscious artist in Lawrence wanted to present, seems to me fatal. Now when Lawrence asked Jessie for her opinion on the development of this crucial theme in the book, she felt comment was useless:

> Either he was aware of what he was doing and persisted, or he did not know, and in that case no amount of telling would enlighten him. It was one of the things he had to find out for himself. The baffling truth, of course, lay between the two. He was aware, but he was under the spell of the domination that had ruled his life hitherto, and he refused to know. So instead of a release and a deliverance from bondage, the bondage was glorified and made absolute. His mother conquered indeed, but the vanquished one was her son. In *Sons and Lovers* Lawrence handed his mother the laurels of victory.[22]

That was written in the 1930s, but it must reflect very closely Jessie's nearly immediate reaction. It seems to me only a partial truth (though one can well understand why to her it was all of it). If Lawrence handed his mother the laurels of victory, they have now turned to ashes. That he consciously meant her to have the victory, I see no reason to doubt. But the overwhelming impression I retain is that, so far as posterity is concerned, the victory, if there is one, is Miriam's. The integrity that Jessie had counted on in Lawrence and which she believed had failed him is there in the truth that comes out against the conscious intention, when Lawrence writes with all his brilliant perception of spontaneous life. That the tension between conscious aim and concrete truth obstinately refusing to be turned into abstraction results in a flawed novel is certain: *Sons and Lovers* seems to me to illustrate with touching piquancy the truth in Lawrence's own maxim, 'Never trust the artist. Trust the tale.'[23] I think the tale of *Sons and Lovers* reveals the truth steadily, plainly, even inexorably, but it is not what 'Lawrence the artist' wanted us to see. Lawrence said later, in 'Morality and the Novel',[24] 'If you try to nail anything down in the novel, either it kills the novel, or the novel gets up and walks away with the nail.' That Jessie should feel the first had happened was inevitable in the devastation done to her life; and no 'literary victory' could make up for her personal unhappiness. Yet *Sons and Lovers* is after all a remarkable work of genius, a tragedy whose heart is in the very tension between aim and achievement, what is said and what is shown. That may sound like a sophistical defence of failure: it is only not this, para-doxically because Lawrence is so closely identified with Paul that the tension in the writing becomes the natural expression of the partial paralysis and blindness of the hero. Paul's tragedy is the corruption of spontaneous life in the service of an inflexible ideal, Lawrence's and Jessie's in the impossibility of self-detachment from the forces which make the idea all-powerful. Years later Lawrence saw half of this: 'I would write a different *Sons and Lovers* now: my mother was wrong and I thought she was ab-solutely right.'[25] But the novel knew all along that she was wrong; and 'the proper function of a critic is to save the tale from the artist who created it'.[26]

NOTES

1. Letter to Edward Garnett, 14th November, 1912. Cf. *Collected Letters of D. H. Lawrence*, edited by Harry T. Moore (London, 1962), p. 160.

2. Reprinted photographically with extra material (London, 1965). E. T. were the initials of Eunice Temple, the eponymous heroine of a novel, originally called *The Rathe Primrose*, which Jessie Chambers wrote while Lawrence was finishing *Sons and Lovers*, and which she later destroyed.

3. Jessie Chambers, op. cit., p. 110.

4. *Ibid.*, p. 204.

5. *Ibid.*, pp. 191–2.

6. *Ibid.*, p. 203.

7. *Ibid.*, p. 193.

8. *Ibid.*, pp. 41–2. For a different treatment of this episode, with evidence from an earlier draft, see Harry T. Moore, *The Intelligent Heart* (London, 1955), pp. 35ff.

9. See 'D. H. Lawrence's Princess' in Helene Corke, *The Croydon Years* (Austin, Texas, 1965), p. 36.

10. Corke, op. cit., p. 22.

11. *Ibid.*, p. 33.

12. Raymond Williams, *The English Novel from Dickens to Lawrence* (London, 1970), p. 173.

13. The chapters in *Sons and Lovers* are all long, and each contains many episodes and incidents linked to one another as on a necklace, each merging almost unnoticed into the next. The technique gives a vivid impression of the inextricable detail and the continuity of life, to which the particular characteristics I am at present discussing are closely tied.

14. Cf. chap. 11 : 'As Miriam sang her mouth seemed hopeless. She sang like a nun singing to heaven. It reminded him so much of the mouth and eyes of one who sings beside a Botticelli Madonna, so spiritual . . . It was not fair to hurt her. There seemed an eternal maidenhood about her . . .' This is fairly presented as Paul's personal and hence partial view; but it too merges without any let into the inclusive attitude of the novelist.

15. Jessie Chambers, op. cit., p. 145.

16. *Ibid.*, p. 185.

17. Corke, op. cit., p. 41. Cf. Lawrence's letter to Rachel Annand Taylor, 3rd December, 1910 (Moore, *Collected Letters*, p. 69): 'We have loved each other, almost with a husband and wife love, as well as filial and maternal. We knew each other by instinct.'

18. *Collected Letters*, p. 69.

19. So much is Walter Morel rejected and denied by the mother-dominated family that it comes as a shock, in one of those rare and touching scenes of jolly purposeful family activity in which they are all engaged together, to find Paul calling him 'Dad' and realize that he is after all Paul's father. Yet when Paul treats Miriam brutally he tried to justify himself in terms that keenly recall his father: 'He felt himself cruel towards Miriam . . . "But it serves her right", he said inside himself.' (chap. 12).

20. Chambers, op. cit., p. 201. And cf. Helen Corke's opinion quoted on p. 4 above.

21. Chambers, op. cit., p. 202.

22. *Ibid.*

23. 'The Spirit of Place' in *Studies in Classic American Literature*.

24. 'Morality and the Novel': V. *Phoenix* (London, 1936 etc.), p. 528.

25. V. Frieda Lawrence, *Not I But The Wind* (London, 1935), p. 52.

26. After completing this essay, I read the following extract from an unsigned review of *Sons and Lovers* in the *Athenaeum* of 21st June, 1913 (quoted by John Worthen in his review of Draper, *D. H. Lawrence: the Critical Heritage* in the *Cambridge Quarterly*, Vol. 5, no. 1, Spring 1970, pp. 107–8): 'A certain distortion arises from the fact that, while all the other characters are drawn, as it were, in the third person, the hero is drawn from the first . . . We are not, at the end of the story, left understanding the nature of the man about whom it is told. No doubt he himself would not, in real life, have understood it: but we cannot help thinking that to complete his achievement the novelist should have made the reader do so . . . We suspect—and it is a tribute to the strength of the illusion created—that, if the girl's story had been written, we should have found her by no means so abnormal a person as represented, and her wayward lover considerably more comprehensible.' This is notably shrewd

criticism, especially when written, as Mr. Worthen observes, in ignorance of Lawrence's biography : the problem that it wrestles with is close to that with which I have been concerned, and though in a slightly obscure way, the writer has identified the tricky technique of the narrative, which I have tried to explore in more detail. The problem, then, was spotted by an intelligent reader, without inside information, at a very early date.

I must also draw the reader's attention to an extremely interesting paper by Mr. J. C. F. Littlewood ('Son and Lover' : *Cambridge Quarterly*, vol. 4, no. 4, Autumn & Winter 1969/70, pp. 323–361) which approaches the same problem from a somewhat different angle and takes a somewhat more critical standpoint.

'THE RAINBOW' AS EXPERIMENTAL NOVEL *

I

In the course of the last twenty-five years, *The Rainbow* has lost its notoriety and acquired the status of a major classic. It can now be found on every book-stall and in every public library; no course in modern literature can afford to disregard it; no cultivated man will be content to leave it unread. Above all, it has received almost uninterrupted critical attention, some of which has attained an impressive standard. Dr. Leavis, for example, has shown that it takes its place in and enlarges the tradition of the English novel; Marvin Muldrick has claimed that it confronts some of the central problems of modern life; and, more recently, H. M. Daleski and Mark Kinkead-Weekes have argued that it exhibits a bold and original system of thought.[1] These conclusions I have no wish to deny; yet for me the novel remains, despite its deserved standing, a curiously difficult and disturbing work. A great classic, of course, will always challenge those of its readers prepared to take it seriously, but the problem I encounter with *The Rainbow* is not wholly of this order. There enters into my response an element of ambiguity, of attraction and reserve, of discovery and disorientation, which I usually associate with works of a strongly experimental inclination.

That Lawrence was aware that he was engaging in something of a deliberate experiment is revealed in his well-known correspondence with Edward Garnett during the two years preceding the First World War. I refer not so much to his qualified invocation of Marinetti and the Futurists, or to his dissatisfaction with the 'certain moral

* By Jacques Berthoud (University of Southampton).

53

scheme' within which he claimed the nineteenth-century novelists conceived their characters, or even to the new impersonal 'ego', the so-called 'carbon of character', which he affirms he has discovered,[2] but to something at once more intimate and more fundamental. 'I no longer have the joy', he writes, 'of creating vivid scenes that I had in *Sons and Lovers*. I don't care much more in accumulating objects in the powerful light of emotion, and making a scene of them'. He is now concerned, he implies, in evolving a new style, which he somewhat elliptically calls 'the exhaustive method'.[3] How much weight should be given to an author's professions of intention is of course debatable. Nevertheless, an examination of the texture of the novel will reveal, I think, in the midst of less unconventional writing, the presence of a new style, or, more accurately, of a new mode of expressing feeling. This may be brought out by contrasting two representative passages.

The first describes how Ursula Brangwen, the heroine of the novel's third generation, finds relief from the torments of adolescent sensitivity.

Even at its stormiest, Sunday was a blessed day. Ursula woke to it with a feeling of immense relief. She wondered why her heart was so light. Then she remembered it was Sunday. A gladness seemed to burst out around her. a feeling of great freedom. The whole world was for twenty-four hours revoked, put back. Only the Sunday world existed.

She loved the very confusion of the household. It was lucky if the children slept till seven o'clock. Usually, soon after six, a chirp was heard, a voice, an excited chirrup began, announcing the creation of a new day, there was a thudding of quick little feet, and the children were up and about, scampering in their shirts, with pink legs and glistening, flossy hair all clean from the Saturday's night bathing, their souls excited by their bodies' cleanliness.

As the house began to teem with rushing, half-naked clean children, one of the parents rose, either the mother, easy and slatternly, with her thick, dark hair loosely coiled and slipping over one ear, or the father, warm and comfortable, with ruffled hair and shirt unbuttoned at the neck.

Then the girls upstairs heard the continual:

'Now then Billy, what are you up to?' in the father's strong, vibrating voice: or the mother's dignified:

'I have said, Cassie, I will not have it.'

It was amazing how the father's voice could ring out like a gong, without his being in the least moved, and how the mother could speak like a queen holding an audience, though her blouse was sticking out all round and her hair was not fastened up and the children were yelling a pandemonium.[4]

Now it is true that the writing here is perhaps more fluid and relaxed than that of *Sons and Lovers*, and that the scene is offered as typical rather than unique. But a 'scene' it emphatically remains, and one unquestionably created 'in the powerful light of emotion'. The entire passage can be considered an expression of Ursula's sense of freedom and gladness. For all its domestic confusion, the family awakening is transfigured by her feeling of 'immense relief'. The children, for example, who 'chirp' and 'chirrup' and scamper about on 'quick little feet', become a kind of dawn chorus. But the expression is also an explanation. We have learnt that Ursula, with an intensity characteristic of her age, believes that the 'brutal' and 'commonplace' world of school and town is a threat to her special self, and fears that her family is becoming alien and restrictive. On Sundays, both these anxieties are banished. She feels all the delight of being able at once to belong and to be herself, and the scene conjured up by Lawrence subtly suggests why this should be so. For instance, her parents remain part of the ordinary world: they are untidy and dishevelled, they scold or reprove the children, they are involved in the general indiscipline. Yet they unobtrusively assume their fundamental roles. Will is 'the father', whose male voice sounds effortlessly through the house; Anna is 'the mother', whose bearing retains a casual dignity. Spontaneity and authority are reconciled, the commonplace blends into distinction, and for a while the household gods are placated.

Whatever he may have said to Edward Garnett, Lawrence knows perfectly well that feelings do not exist in a vacuum, but that they have a history, and are directed towards an object. The passage does not offer us the feeling

55

itself, abstracted as it were into a disembodied force; it gives us what the feeling is about. And because we are provided with object and scene, we are able not only to understand but also to share the feeling evoked. Lawrence has not denied traditional modes of expression; he has merely accommodated them to the demands of his own vision and sensibility.

The second passage, taken from the celebrated description of Will and Anna's visit to Lincoln Cathedral, seems to me to operate on different principles. Here, in part, is how Will's response to the gothic nave is rendered:

> Here the stone leapt up from the plain of earth, leapt up in a manifold, clustered desire each time, up, away from the horizontal earth, through twilight and dusk and the whole range of desire, through the swerving, the declination, ah, to the ecstasy, the touch, to the meeting and consummation, the meeting, the clasp, the close embrace, the neutrality, the perfect, swooning consummation, the timeless ecstasy. There his soul remained, at the apex of the arch, clinched in the timeless ecstasy, consummated.
>
> And there was no time nor life nor death, but only this, this timeless consummation, where the thrust from earth met the thrust from earth and the arch was locked on the keystone of ecstasy. This was all, this was everything. Till he came to himself in the world below. Then again he gathered himself together, in transit, every jet of him strained and leaped, leaped clear into the darkness above, to the fecundity and the unique mystery, to the touch, the clasp, the consummation, the climax of eternity, the apex of the arch.[5]

Given the intensity of Will's response to the cathedral, it is a little surprising to find how indistinct it remains to us. In Ursula's reaction to the family Sunday, we discover a great deal about her particular family, and about families in general. We may also recall how, elsewhere in the novel, Lawrence evokes the joy and wonder of seasonal life and landscape. For example, Ursula's ecstatic experience of a sunrise on the Sussex downs, where she has spent the night with her lover, calls up no less than five incomparably observed paragraphs; and it is hardly necessary to refer to such famous set pieces as Tom Brangwen's protection of the child Anna during her mother's confinement, or of Tom's death by drowning, or of the wedding at the Marsh, or of Anna's hay-gathering with Will under the moonlight, to realize that in his treatment of the visit to the cathedral, Lawrence's essential purpose is not the creating of 'vivid scenes'. Although in what precedes we have approached 'the great west front . . . with all its breadth and ornament' and entered into the 'pillared gloom' of the church, at the climactic moment our awareness of the object of feeling becomes vague and blurred. At most, we sense the pillars rising, bending, and meeting, but they are quite overwhelmed by the insistence on such transcendent abstractions as 'ecstasy', 'consummation', 'timeless', 'mystery', and 'eternity'. I have no positivist quarrel with religious or metaphysical language as such. All I wish to suggest is that Lawrence, having gone quite far in fulfilling his promise to Garnett to forgo object and scene, cannot avoid the stylistic consequences. To the extent to which the object of feeling dissolves, so is he forced, in order to sustain the emotional excitement, to rely on metaphor and analogy. In previous paragraphs he wove an image-pattern of flight and blossoming. Here he renders the feeling in sexual terms. Such words as 'desire', 'touch', 'clasp', 'embrace', 'consummation', and such phrases as '. . . where the thrust from earth met the thrust from earth and the arch was locked on the keystone of ecstasy' generate a rhythm so explicitly sexual that certain critics have claimed to detect parallels between Will's feeling for architecture at Lincoln and his feeling for his wife on his wedding night.[6]

But there is more to the experimental style than the exploitation of organic or sexual metaphors. Lawrence called it 'the exhaustive method', and this phrase provides a further clue. In the present context, it suggests an 'exhaustive' treatment of a character's feelings—that is to say, a complete expression not only of what a character feels consciously, but also of the whole mass of inarticulate instincts, pressures, and currents that precedes and underlines conscious feelings. To express this indistinct area, which is scarcely accessible to the character himself, the author must intervene, as it were, speak directly in his own voice, and reveal to us what is going on in the secret recesses of being. It will be seen at a glance, however, that

57

in this passage Lawrence's stance is not that of the omniscient narrator. He is not, like the Victorian novelist, communicating information to the reader over the head of his character. The incantatory intensity of the tone, the leap and pulse of the rhythm, the psalmodic, almost obsessive repetitions—all these qualities are scarcely characteristic of narrative detachment. Lawrence does indeed tell us about Will's ecstasy, but in such a way that the telling becomes a kind of enactment of this ecstasy. He deliberately reduces the distance between himself and Will; correspondingly, the reader is forced to relinquish his aloofness and involve himself in Will's experience. Essentially, the exhaustive method transforms authorial comment into lyrical representation, and the authorial voice, from a mode of description, into a mode of expression.

Whatever we may think of the exhaustive method and the kind of writing it promotes, we must accept, I think, that Lawrence does not arbitrarily turn away from the object of feeling. It becomes necessary to ask, therefore, why he found it necessary to do so.

II

There are two notable episodes, one towards the beginning of *The Rainbow*, the other right at the end, which show how someone who has lost the capacity to feel is able to regain it.[7] Lydia Lensky and Ursula Brangwen, respectively, have suffered the effects of a profoundly destructive relationship with a man, and both are shown undergoing the process of emotional renewal. For Lydia, this takes a relatively simple form. After the death of her Polish husband, a fanatical revolutionary exiled to London, she goes to a rectory in Yorkshire. Her condition is obviously serious. Lawrence tells us that she is 'blank' and 'abstracted', and that time passes by 'grey, uncoloured, like a long journey where she sat unconscious as the landscape unrolled beside her'. Gradually, however, her exposure to the solitude of the moors and the sea disturbs her 'automatic consciousness'. Tentatively and painfully, her memories and feelings begin to return. With the coming of winter, she 'shrinks back again into her darkness', but when the spring comes round again, she at last allows herself to respond. 'One morning there was a light from the

58

yellow jasmine which caught her, and after that, morning and evening, the persistent singing of thrushes from the shrubbery, till her heart, beaten upon, was forced to lift up its voice in rivalry and answer.' This process of awakening in an alien land is bewildering and difficult. She feels 'as if crushed between the past and the future, like a flower that comes above ground to find a great stone lying above it'; but the restoration, which Tom is to complete, is now well under way.

The situation in which Ursula finds herself is a far more complex one, but a similar pattern emerges. Her affair with her lover, a conventional officer in the colonial service, has ended in utter failure. When he leaves for India, she returns home, like Lydia, stunned and abstracted. Lawrence describes her as 'faint, dim, closed up', and adds, 'It was as if her energy were frozen.' She discovers that she is with child, and considers submitting herself to the role of a docile wife. But in a remarkable symbolic incident when, alone in the rain, she struggles to escape the pursuit of a menacing group of horses, she understands the danger of playing a part that will repress, and hence destructively unharness, her instinctual energies. Afterwards, she is left 'shaken and racked', and falls seriously ill, but in the midst of 'the ache of delirium' she retains 'a dull firmness of being'. She loses her child, but she continues to fight to liberate herself from the grip of the past. And as she gradually begins to recover, the process, here too, is offered in terms of organic growth. She thinks, for example, of the 'vivid reality of acorns in February lying on the floor of a wood with their shells burst and discarded and the kernel naked to put itself forth'. She feels herself to be 'the naked clear kernel thrusting forth the clear powerful shoot, and the world . . . a bygone winter, discarded'. When she finally falls into the restoring sleep of convalescence, Lawrence writes: 'She had her root in the new ground, and she was gradually absorbed into growth.'

What these two cases show is that the process of renewal is analogous to the seasonal cycle of decay and growth. As in nature, the rebirth of the emotions must be preceded by a form of death—the readiness to discard the former self. As Lydia sinks into her state of insensibility she relinquishes, almost with relief, her over-strung life with her husband. Ursula's struggle is more difficult, but she too has to rid herself of the husk of her relationship with her lover. Consideration of a further point will make clear that more is involved, however, than mere analogy. For both women, recovery implies a capacity to respond to nature. Lydia's delight in the unfolding spring is described with the greatest tact and delicacy. Ursula, who awakens not in rural Yorkshire but in industrial Nottinghamshire, feels the impulse to be part of the organic world. 'In everything she saw', we are told, 'she grasped and groped to find the creation of the living God.' It is not too much to suggest that the rhythms of feeling are not merely like the rhythms of nature, but that they are essentially the same; or, more accurately, that the human pattern is a variant of the basic and inclusive natural pattern.

This fundamental position—if it can be so called—has momentous implications. If 'nature' is understood in its ancient and full sense of 'mother nature', whose laws are the most radical laws of our being, then it follows that a corresponding claim must be made for what connects us with nature: the body and its instincts. It is there—to use one of Lawrence's favourite metaphors—that we are rooted in earth; it is thence that we derive our vital energies. Furthermore, if an emphasis on nature leads to a reappraisal of the body, it must also lead to reappraisal of the mind. Demoted to a secondary role, the mind cannot be permitted to assert itself over the body and to contradict the ebb and flow of its life. On the contrary, it must seek a collaboration with it, and allow it to direct and inform its own further functions and purposes. If the mind fails to do this and performs, as it were, a *coup d'état*, in order to become the 'author and director of life',[8] it inevitably perverts itself. Some aspects of this are illustrated by Ursula's visit to her uncle Tom, who is in charge of a new colliery in Yorkshire. The whole episode is in deliberate contrast to the one devoted to Lydia's renewal in the same county.[9] Tom too is emotionally exhausted, but his is not the death that leads to life. It is, rather, a kind of extinction, the 'stability of nullification', a settled indifference hid under 'an utterly tolerant good humour'. Here also the setting—a complete contrast to the rural order in which Lydia rediscovered herself—is related to the emotional condition. In the new township of Wiggiston, 'everything was amorphous, everything repeated itself endlessly . . . There it lay, like the new foundations of a red-brick confusion rapidly spreading, like a skin disease.' The reading room in his new house 'gave the same sense of hard, mechanical activity, activity mechanical yet inchoate, and looking out on the hideous abstraction of the town . . . and at the great mathematical colliery on the other side'. And what does this lead to? 'Tom's . . . only happy moments, his only moments of pure freedom were when he was serving the machine. Then, and then only, when the machine caught him up, was he free from hatred of himself, could he act wholly, without cynicism or neutrality.' Left to itself, it would seem that the mind can only pervert the organic energy of the body in order to transform it into its own mechanical energy. Cut off from its normative foundations, it can only destroy the given order of nature in order to reconstruct it into a landscape in its own image. This is not to say that the mind is pernicious in principle, or that Lawrence invokes an irresponsible anti-rationalism. The confident progress of the scientific West has always been accompanied by anxieties about the idea of mind it tends to promote. From Blake's 'mind-forged manacles' to Yeats' 'God save me from the thoughts men think in the mind alone', poets and philosophers have repeatedly sounded the dangers of mental self-sufficiency and its mechanical models. Lawrence's view that the mind is capable of a nihilistic destructiveness does not necessarily entail the further view that intelligence is a vice.

What we have, of course, is a modified system of good and evil based upon a modified conception of the self. According to the common view, the self is co-extensive with self-awareness. For Lawrence, however, the mind can only illuminate a fragment of the total self. 'I don't care so much about what a woman *feels*—in the ordinary usage of the word', he writes in his correspondence with Edward Garnett. 'That presumes an ego to feel with. I only care about what a woman *is*—what she IS—inhumanly, physiologically, materially—according to the use of the word.' [10] Allowing for the over-statement of polemic, we may rephrase this: 'What we call feeling is only that portion of instinct illuminated by consciousness, and it is with the greater reality—the darkness, the body—that I am most concerned.' One of the most striking aspects of *The Rainbow*—its emphasis on sexual relationships—is now ex-

61

plained, for all the instincts that attach man to nature, none is more central than the procreative. It is scarcely an exaggeration to suggest that in this novel the test of individual integrity is the capacity to establish a real and lasting relationship with a member of the opposite sex. Lawrence's idea of the self will therefore find further illustration in his treatment of sexuality. Let us briefly consider the contrasting cases of Tom Brangwen and his grand-daughter Ursula.

Tom Brangwen's wooing of Lydia Lensky [11] exhibits a curious mixture of passivity and self-possession. From the very moment he first lays eyes on her, as he is returning with a load of hay from Nottingham, he knows with absolute certainty that she is the woman for him. 'He saw her face so distinctly that he ceased to coil on himself, and was suspended.' "That's her", he said involuntarily.' Lawrence is quite clearly not dealing in the currency of love-at-first-sight. We have seen, up to this point, the gradual building-up in him of a massive self-suppression, which he has occasionally sought to alleviate in drink, but which he has accepted without any attempt at mental interference. What takes place now is an equally massive, and equally involuntary, self-release. To be sure, his mental self remains attentive: he takes in at a glance that 'her face was pale and clear . . . she had dark eyebrows and a wide mouth'. But it takes its directives from his deeper self. The courtship that ensues is conducted under the same conditions of purposeful passivity. In their various casual encounters—in the churchyard after a service, in the kitchen of his ancestral farm-house, in a horse-trap on the Ilkeston road—he submits, we are told, 'to that which was happening to him, letting go his will, suffering the loss of himself, dormant always on the brink of ecstasy, like a creature evolving to a new birth'. And when he comes to a decision at last, it seems more a ritual of obedience than a deliberate choice. The whole event is subtly charged with Lawrence's further significances. One evening in March—the first break in the winter, with a roaring wind outside chasing the clouds across the moon—Tom puts on his best clothes, gathers a bunch of daffodils, and makes his way to the rectory where Lydia lives with her small daughter. For a long while he waits in the darkness, looking into the lighted room at the mother and child. Then he enters, and immediately both he and Lydia are drawn and held together by a 'strangely impersonal' power. Tom's passivity is a condition of his self-assurance : it implies a refusal to allow the mental will to dictate to the deeper demands of his nature.

No such imperatives are felt by the much younger Ursula when she first meets Anton Skrebensky.[12] He rouses her, too, but to the state of heightened self-awareness that leads straight into the game of deliberate coquetry. As the relationship develops we find that both she and Skrebensky are really after the thrill of conscious gratification, for which they devise the usual sort of strategies : provocation in a fast motor-car, stolen kisses in an empty church, and all the tricks of mutual challenge. 'What could either of them get from such a passion', asks Lawrence, 'but a sense of his or her own maximum self, in contradistinction to all the rest of life?' It is scarcely surprising, therefore, that Ursula turns against him, when she discovers that all he has to offer her, apart from love play, is a lame belief in the ethics of good administration. But her betrayal of her deeper self does not leave her unaffected. Before parting, they both attend her uncle Fred's wedding. The excitement of music and dancing in the open air and of the bonfires lighting up the scene provoke her to an almost hysterical exaltation. 'She wanted to reach and be amongst the flashing stars, she wanted to race with her feet and be beyond the confines of the earth.' Forced to respond to Skrebensky, who cannot satisfy this impossible thirst, she suddenly reacts as if possessed. Although what happens is not altogether clear, the scruples of her ordinary life are swept away, and her **buried self viciously asserts itself. She becomes implacable** and destructive and, after a brief struggle, he is emotionally obliterated. We have seen that Tom's wooing had nothing to do with the conventions of romantic courtship. We now see that the treatment of Ursula's triviality bears no relation to the demands of conventional morality. What is at stake in both cases is the new conception of the self. The first shows that true sexuality implies a capacity to surrender to the promptings of the deeper being; the second shows that the sexual life involves one of the dangerous powers of existence.

What Lawrence has called 'the exhaustive method' represents his attempt to express directly the life of the deeper self. We shall see this more clearly if we return to

Will's response to Lincoln Cathedral and locate it in its general context. The episode as a whole, chronologically out of place as it is, provides a further diagnosis of the marital conflict explored in the previous chapter. There we were shown that Will's faith in his essential self was too uncertain for him to achieve real fulfilment either in his relationship with his wife, or in his devotion to church symbolism and architecture. Hence he became excessively dependent on his wife, while she, in reaction, first attacked his commitment to the church, then turned upon herself in the absorption of procreation. The visit to Lincoln brings out what is really involved in Will's passion for architecture. His response to the great nave is subordinate to his essential struggle with his wife. Structurally, it is balanced against the notorious dance she performs in pregnancy, in which she asserts the self-sufficiency of her womanhood, and it represents his masculine challenge to her. This she understands from the start. When she hears him exclaim, as they see the cathedral in the distance, 'There she is!', she inwardly recoils. 'The "she" irritated her. Why "she"? It was "it". What was the cathedral, a big building, a thing of the past, obsolete, to excite him to such a pitch? She began to stir herself in readiness.' And we soon discover that, despite her momentary recognition of the cathedral's power, he cannot withstand the onslaught of her scepticism. This is partly because his attitude to the church is not wholly disinterested. He has tried to make of it a refuge for his uncertainties, and so failed to see what his wife insists on, and what the stone carvings on the building themselves proclaim, that the world of the cathedral is only a part of the greater whole of the created universe. As Lawrence's 'exhaustive' presentation, with its reliance on sexual metaphors, unambiguously suggests, his darker self, foiled and frustrated in his conflict with Anna, illegitimately invades his feelings for the cathedral. The episode at Lincoln marks his partial defeat as a man. Afterwards we learn that 'he was slightly ashamed, like a man who has failed, who lapses back for his fulfilment': and although he eventually regains a measure of sensual assurance, he never wholly recovers.

III

The Rainbow's experimental orientation is the direct product of Lawrence's new concept of the self. We are now in a position to ask how successful this experiment is; in order to consider this question, however, we must raise a further issue. We have seen how the new self affects the style and texture of the book; we have also seen that it is related at every point to the idea of nature elaborated by the novel. **We must now examine it in the further context of society.**

Although *The Rainbow* seems to be informed by a marked experimental impulse, it was not composed in an intellectual and social vacuum. It is an example of the family chronicle, a genre much in favour at the time, and exploited by such of Lawrence's contemporaries as Thomas Mann, Romain Rolland, and John Galsworthy. Moreover, its concern with sexuality and the unconscious is not wholly at variance with an age that produced Sigmund Freud and Havelock Ellis. Nevertheless it remains an astonishingly original performance. Written just before the outbreak of the First World War, it exhibits none of the illusions characteristic of that period; we find in it no echo of Edwardian mellowness, no trace of an innocent faith in the endless summer of English achievement. On the contrary, it represents in its implications a devastating attack on the ethos of the then dominant social class—an attack which is extended and enlarged into nothing less than a radical diagnosis of modern life as a whole.

It has been suggested that the family chronicle is preeminently the genre of the commercial and industrial middle-classes—at least to the extent that, whether their virtues and qualities are celebrated or attacked, they are to be taken seriously. If this is so, then Lawrence's treatment of the family chronicle completely transforms its intentions and purposes. By situating his new concept of the self within the framework of this form, he was able to grasp what has since then been reduced to a commonplace of the politics of protest : the vital inter-connection of sexuality and society. In *The Rainbow* he investigates the challenge and disruptions of modern life, not by engaging his characters in a public conflict with social change as such, but through an exploration of the area in which they most intensely experience the encroachments of modernity —their sexual relationships.

The structure of the novel rests on the indivisibility of private experience and public activity. If, as we have seen, the new self demands a sexual fulfilment deeper than deliberate gratification, then, by the same token, it requires a creative vocation deeper than merely functional bread-winning. The pattern is set in the opening pages of the book where the Brangwen family, confined from time immemorial within the cycle of the agricultural year, can now hear the first sound of foreign activity on the borders of their land. A coal mine is opened in the neighbourhood. 'The sharp clink-clink-clink-clink-clink of the empty trucks shunting on the line vibrated in their hearts with the fact of other activity going on beyond them . . . The shrill whistle of the trains re-echoed through the heart, with fearsome pleasure, announcing the far-off come near and imminent.' From then on the effects of the process are irreversible. The Brangwens can no longer be satisfied with the instinctive physicality so sumptuously evoked in the book's opening movement. Awakened from the drowse of nature, they begin to experience a tension, soon to become a conflict, between the double needs of their being, their craving for a deep sensual relationship, and their desire for self-realization in the world beyond. Tom Brangwen, sent by his mother to grammar-school, and disturbed by a chance encounter with a foreign couple, begins to baulk 'at the mean enclosure of reality', and although he remains rooted in his house and land, he dreams of 'foreign parts' and 'fine-textured, subtle-mannered people'. So he falls in love with and marries a woman who represents this unknown to him. But her foreignness finally proves too challenging: the strength of his native tradition permits him to achieve real fulfilment with her, but he never permanently attains that 'individuality . . . which it depended on his manhood to preserve and develop'. His attachment to his wife's child fills a gap in his life, and the easy-going casualness into which he retreats after her marriage is in part responsible for his death. In his step-daughter Anna, the tension becomes more painful. Married very young to a man too unsure of himself to provide the further meaning she needs —incapable, in the words of the novel, of becoming 'really articulate', of finding 'real expression'—she becomes absorbed in child-bearing, lapsing into 'a vague content', and relinquishing 'the adventure into the unknown'. Left to himself, her husband, like Tom before him, establishes an over-intense relationship with their eldest child, Ursula, and it is on her shoulders that the responsibility finally devolves. Wholly exposed as she is to the demands of modern life, she experiences the conflict in its most racking form. She tries first, with the independence of emancipation, to realize herself in what Lawrence calls 'the man's world'; but it soon becomes clear to her that a career, in itself, cannot satisfy her deep religious needs. So she turns to a former lover. But the man has no profound requirements: he is little more than a conforming puppet of the established order, so the automatic passion he provides proves equally meaningless. Of the protagonists of the novel, Ursula is the least successful, yet in an important respect she remains its heroine. She fails, but she is not defeated, for she continues to cling to the belief that the divergent strains in her nature can be harmonized. She does not relinquish the inherited visionary goal, which the metaphors and symbols of the novel as a whole consistently advance: that the essential self, rooted in the dark of nature, will blossom into the light of further fulfilment; that the horizontal of desire and the vertical of aspiration will blend into the rainbow arch of reconciliation.

The great achievement of *The Rainbow* is its demonstration that man's power over nature, attained at the cost of an immense effort of abstraction and detachment, means a radical alienation from the life of nature, both within and without the self. In conclusion, however, we may ask whether the experimental and exploratory energy which permitted Lawrence this insight has not also betrayed him into moments of unreality. The conceptual scheme of the novel makes it plain that the passionate and the creative sides of man are dependent on each other, and that sexual fulfilment, when wholly divorced from a further search for meaning, is no fulfilment at all. Yet the fact remains that this creative search is not given sufficient imaginative weight or explored with sufficient conviction. We only glimpse Tom Brangwen at work on his farm: the skills, demands, and responsibilities of the agricultural life receive no elaboration. Will Brangwen's talent for wood-carving and his understanding of ecclesiastical architecture are severely subordinated to his erotic problems. Anton Skrebensky's life as an army officer is treated with dismissive contempt. It is not the relative failure or success of the search that is in question here, but the lack of seriousness with which it is realized. Apart from the brilliant pages devoted to Ursula's experience as a teacher, we do not properly participate in the creative struggle of work or vocation. It cannot be argued in defence of this lapse that Lawrence is trying to demonstrate that the conditions of modern life prohibit self-fulfilment in the social realm; I doubt whether any great work can come from such a failure of nerve, and *The Rainbow* is a sufficiently eloquent contribution to the common culture to contradict this sort of rationalization.

One aspect of Lawrence's theme remains strangely unfocused; nor, if I am right, is the other aspect left wholly unaffected. Despite a serious attempt to share the novel's vision of human life, I cannot rid myself of the impression that the sexual element is made to play too strenuous a compensatory role. Some of the implications of this may perhaps be brought out by recalling, for the last time, Lawrence's attempt to express directly the life of the psyche. Bold as the exhaustive method may be, and telling as the insight it permits, it is not wholly free from a certain strain, and even a certain incoherence. I do not reproach him for allowing so large a part to the pre-conscious sources of feeling. Indeed if, as Wordsworth suggested, it is the poet's task to follow in the steps of the man of science, so Lawrence may be said to have tried to humanize some of the discoveries circulated by psycho-analysis. But I am not convinced that the attempt to enact unconscious experience can ever properly succeed. By definition, the unconscious is not directly available to the conscious mind : it cannot therefore be treated mimetically—even when, as I indicated, the authorial voice itself becomes the mimetic medium. If we consider, not the cathedral episode, in which Will's dark self irrupts into his response to the nave, but a parallel and more extreme case, Ursula's 'destruction' of Skrebensky, something of the point of this objection will be illustrated. Ursula's dark self, which turns so savagely against her lover, is translated into a whole complex of material equivalents.[13] For her, Skrebensky becomes 'a loadstone', 'a dark, impure magnetism'; her own hands are 'metal blades', she is 'bright as a piece of moonlight', she seethes 'like some cruel corrosive salt', her soul 'crystallizes with triumph'. I can feel the intensity of this writing, but I do not really understand it: I cannot, even imaginatively, *recognize* this experience. The reason, I suspect, is not that we never lose our heads or our humanity, but that we never experience the unconscious as directly as this. The metaphors are powerful, and Lawrence's narrative voice is compellingly expressive, but these procedures cannot offer enough purchase for the cognitive imagination.

Despite these reservations, however, *The Rainbow* remains a vast and complex innovating work. There is, after all, a kind of imperfection one would far rather have than many kinds of success.

NOTES

1. F. R. Leavis, 'Lawrence and Tradition: *The Rainbow*' in *D. H. Lawrence: Novelist* (Chatto and Windus, 1955); Marvin Mudrick, 'The Originality of *The Rainbow*' in *Spectrum* (Winter, 1959); H. M. Daleski, Chapter II of *The Forked Flame* (Faber, 1965); Mark Kinkead-Weekes, 'The Marble and the Statue: the Exploratory Imagination of D. H. Lawrence' in *Imagined Worlds*, ed. Maynard Mack and Ian Gregor (1968).

2. 5 June 1914: see *Collected Letters*, p. 281.

3. 29 January 1914. *Ibid.*, p. 263.

4. *The Rainbow* (Penguin, 1968), pp. 271–272.

5. Op. cit. p. 202.

6. e.g. George H. Ford, *Double Measure* (New York, 1965), p. 128.

7. Op. cit. pp. 50–55 and 484–496 respectively.

8. See the argument of *Psychoanalyses and the Unconscious*, from which this phrase is taken.

9. *The Rainbow*, op. cit. pp. 344–352.

10. 5 June 1914. *Collected Letters*, p. 282.

11. *The Rainbow*, op. cit. pp. 28–49.

12. Op. cit. pp. 288–332.

13. Op. cit. pp. 318–323.

WOMEN IN LOVE *

Women in Love is the most fascinating and the most disturbing of Lawrence's books. Half a century has passed since it was written, but its compelling strangeness is undiminished. Its originalities of technique and style served a radically original vision; they could not be separated from this and imitated, and have not been much absorbed into subsequent literature. So the book continues to seem essentially new and astonishing, despite the growing number of commentaries which offer to trace its main themes and make it understandable. It is a book we need to understand. Yet if we are not to miss its deeper questioning and its uniqueness, we cannot afford to assume too quickly that we have understood it. For over the years it radiates new meanings.

Written during the first world war, while Western civilization was shooting itself bloodily to pieces, it is a book which probes the human impulse to destruction and disintegration, and finds it not on the battlefield but in the whole fabric of our culture. ' "Di-Di-Di-Di-Oh Di—" ', the cry that rings out with eerie ambiguity over the lake where a girl is drowning,[1] comes like an echo of the age, yet it comes in the midst of a characteristic peacetime event, a social occasion which aims to promote harmony between the classes. In the cry of love itself we hear a murderous exhortation; or perhaps a compulsive death wish. The purpose of the novel is to reveal to us an emotional underlife we had ignored that stirs with just such ambiguities; and to trace within it patterns that serve to anatomize a whole society.

This second task is made difficult by the intensity and at first glance aberrational nature of many of the emotions Lawrence is most concerned with. And most readers will probably admit that the novel has moments of strain. When

* By Richard Drain (University of York).

70

Minette is described as staring 'with an ice-cold look in which there flared an unfathomable hell of knowledge',[2] it is a knowledge for which the reader is not much the wiser. We feel only that Lawrence is striving to make her into the token of a larger hellishness, and has not managed it. But our initial suspicion that lurid and esoteric emotions are being used to further a lurid and esoteric cultural diagnosis, tends to crumble before the unsettling power of many of the most intense scenes, the unexpected coolness of tone in many of the discussions and more analytic passages, and the sharpness of social and human observation that the writing so frequently displays.

These qualities evidence a flexibility in the book that is as important as its urgency, showing that if it is partly about obsessions, it is in no way nailed down by them. But the flexibility serves not simply to resolve tensions but equally to create them: to switch us disturbingly from one viewpoint to another, to reflect discontinuities and arrests, to convey sudden emergings and sudden disintegration, to suggest double significances that point divergent ways. These effects are peculiar to *Women in Love*, and might well make it seem fragmentary, were it not that beneath its surface breaks and starts, the book gathers as it goes a strange inner resonance: the vibrations of one scene evoke echoes of another; and we sense hidden links between disparate impulses. The work seems to grow from a centre. And to understand those dislocations of mood that the book practises, we must first seek this centre. To this end it may be worth trying not to divide the book in our minds into two halves, one about a couple that comes to grief and the other about a couple that comes through; and resisting for a time the consequent impulse to read it as a combined cautionary and exemplary tale. Instead we might consider the degree to which the characters are involved in a common situation and a common plight, and therefore partly subject to common reactions.

Lawrence's primary subject is the emotional life. And the emotions that concern him most vitally in *Women in Love* are the emotions that stem from alienation. One had thought perhaps that the master of this theme in the literature of the period was Conrad; and that Lawrence's gift was to express the opposite states, of living relationship and blood togetherness. A reading of the opening chapters of

Women in Love shows though that Lawrence was quite as concerned with states of estrangement as Conrad, and that he had the sharpest possible awareness of them. He differs from Conrad in that he shows us not the lonely isolation of the human condition, but rather a kind of disjunction at close quarters, a frictional dissonance often turning into grating antipathy, between people and each other, or people and the world they live in. And he does not see it as his task to persuade us, as solid normal readers, that such feelings can exist, by slowly unfolding some extreme situation that explains them. He immerses us in these feelings straight away; he subjects us from the beginning to the emotions and perceptions of the alienated.

So in the opening scene of the book, we are quickly made aware of an acute tension between the two sisters, Gudrun and Ursula, and the world they inhabit. Ursula 'was afraid of the depth of her feeling against the home, the milieu, the whole atmosphere and condition of this obsolete life'.[3] Gudrun, walking through her native colliery town, can wonder only why she submits herself to 'the insufferable torture of these ugly, meaningless people, this defaced countryside'.[4] A predictable jibe from a collier's wife ('"What price the stockings!"') affects Gudrun with a 'violent and murderous' anger: 'she would have liked them all annihilated, cleared away, so that the world was left clear for her'.[5] Hermione would seem to desire the same, entering with 'her long blanched face lifted up, not to see the world'.[6] Gerald has about him a 'strange guarded look';[7] he 'seems always to be at bay against everybody'.[8] Mrs. Crich feels that the people she meets have no identity and finds a blank gulf between them and herself: '"What has Mr. So-and-so to do with his own name?—And what have I to do with either him or his name?"'[9] Birkin agrees with her, and carries her views to their subjective extreme: '"It would be much better if they were just wiped out. Essentially, they don't exist, they aren't there."'[10] In fact, throughout the opening of the book we meet in the different characters a recurring desire to wish other people, or society, or the world, out of existence.

To ask whether such feelings are reasonable is hardly to the point. For Lawrence they are there in the world about him that is his subject. And the vital questions to ask are

72

why, and what now. The book is not out to endorse Birkin's attitude. People *are* there, as Mrs. Crich points out to him, and though he may ask, 'Am I my brother's keeper?' he knows that this is Cain's query, and that if it is anyone's role to be Cain, it is Gerald's and not his.[11] But the first step for both Birkin and us is to acknowledge the existence and reality of such feelings—so Lawrence seems to suggest. Hence the book's starting point is a pervasive alienation, at moments so extreme that it can seem 'like being mad', as it does to Gudrun.[12] Lawrence in *Women in Love* is concerned with areas of feeling that shade at their borders into schizophrenia and paranoia. And he treats the borderline emotions not as symptoms confined to a sick majority, but as reactions that had become alarmingly normal, and that, whether one acknowledged them or not, one might find it difficult to avoid. This affronted his first readers. But now it seems increasingly to show his insight, an insight in advance of his time.

At the beginning of the book, the success of Lawrence's treatment lies not so much in a full explanation of the conditions that cause such reactions; but in the way he makes us see through the eyes of those who are affected by them, and sense how their antipathies and aversions belong to a larger group of responses. The antipathies, whether they reflect an involuntary flinching or a committed judgment, express an acute dislocation between the self and much of the reality outside the self. And this seems in the book to have three effects: it brings about a special way of seeing; a special way of behaving with others; and a special way of feeling about oneself.

The way of seeing we notice most sharply in Gudrun—who as an artist is most conscious of visual perception. 'Gudrun watched them closely, with objective curiosity. She saw each one as a complete figure, like a character in a book, or a subject in a picture, or a marionette in a theatre, a finished creation.'[13] They are cut off from her, and so convey no sense of potentiality. She is a sculptor, but we never see her sculpt; we see her draw. This is the fitting activity for her: she perceives things with a line around them; they are bounded. Her pupil is Winifred, who can draw her dog Looloo in a way that catches him perfectly, and yet does him a 'subtle injury', reducing him to a diagram which is grotesque and comic.[14] Gudrun's art similarly expresses a vision very acute and accurate, but that somehow shrinks reality into something little: Ursula remarks that she likes to 'look through the wrong end of the opera glasses, and see the world that way'. She chooses subjects that are small and controllable, birds and animals 'that one can put between one's hands'.[15]

As her hands can contain the creatures she carves, so her perceptions act as a kind of container, fitting tightly round what she looks at. We recognize here one of Lawrence's recurring themes—the theme of *The Captain's Doll*: and we know that Lawrence had already set himself to find ways of writing which would express those qualities in the living creature that were not to be contained in this way by the analytic understanding, those qualities which made it more than a complex puppet or involved mechanism. But Lawrence in *Women in Love* is not simply setting up for criticism a 'wrong' response to life. The response is not one that the characters choose, but rather one that they suffer. Further, it is a response endorsed by much in the book—where Gudrun is concerned, by the final inadequacies of Gerald; more widely, by the effects everywhere visible of social conditioning, and the general readiness of human nature to limit and repeat itself. 'How well he knew Hermione,' thinks Birkin. 'He knew her statically, so finally, that it was almost like a madness . . . How utterly he knew Joshua Matheson . . . how known it all was, like a game with the figures set out . . .'[16] Such feelings are recurrent in the book, and there is no suggestion that all of them can be refuted. It is consistent with this that a visual impression of things as finishèd or framed is sometimes given by the writing of the book itself. Breadalby is thus framed—'there seemed a magic circle drawn about the place, shutting out the present';[17] and Gudrun's comment, 'It is as final as an old aquatint', is made to seem entirely appropriate. People too are sometimes similarly seen: Winifred's French governess has a 'neat, brittle finality of form. She was like some elegant beetle with thin ankles, perched on her high heels, her glossy black dress perfectly correct . . .'[18] Lawrence describes her as Winifred would draw her. It seems that a perception of things as bounded and finished, reflects an aridity sometimes in the observer, sometimes in the thing observed. This puts the observer in an uncertain position: how can he tell where the fault lies? He may

74

attempt to quench the doubt with a vehement attack on things outside him, but a subtle insecurity remains. It is shared to some degree by the reader. The book is out to make a social critique, in which the primary evidence against modern civilization is the sense of alienation it induces. But the stronger this becomes, the more it creates a subjective distortion of vision and feeling in the observer that prevents his view, and consequently his judgments, from being fully objective. So, for instance, when Gudrun describes her pleasure trip down the Thames, everything is hateful, the boys who plunge after pennies as much as the adults who throw them.[19] Her passionate distaste for the visible sordidness of a society which is alternately money-grubbing and patronizing spills over indiscriminately on to those who are society's most defenceless victims —as, in this case, Ursula suggests.

A further effect of alienation upon the perceptions is suggested in the scene where Gerald forces his horse to stand at the level crossing as a goods train clatters deafeningly by. 'The guard's-van came up, and passed slowly, the guard staring out in his transition on the spectacle in the road. And, through the man in the closed wagon Gudrun could see the whole scene spectacularly, isolated and momentary, like a vision isolated in eternity.'[20] This might remind us of certain passages in Faulkner, where similarly a visible scene is made to create a sense of arrested time, and we become conscious that the image imprinted on our mind's eye brings to focus more than its own passing moment in the narrative. However Lawrence's ethos is not the trancelike timeless ethos of the American south, and the effect he creates differs from Faulkner in that he suggests equally that the scene hangs 'in eternity', and that it is 'momentary'. The two suggestions do not cancel out, for the 'isolated and momentary' shares with the eternal a divorce from the even movement of time and natural change. It is thus difficult for the human being to relate livingly and continuously with either.

With this in mind we may reconsider two apparently opposite effects that we find recurring in the book. On the one hand the writing stresses a sense of fixity, stagnation (Breadalby), or slowness (Hermione), or predictable circular repetitiveness (the activities of the Café Royal set, or Gudrun's sense of the social and industrial machine). On the other hand, such states are frequently interrupted by things happening or people acting rapidly and unpredictably, so that visual effects of sharp suddenness are equally characteristic of the book. 'Suddenly, from the boat-house, a white figure ran out, frightening in its swift sharp transit, across the old landing stage.'[21] In such passages the momentariness of the image is stressed. If it is 'frightening', it is because it seems to threaten the permanence of things—here suggested by 'the old landing stage' with its 'green decayed poles'. But the momentary image shares with the fixedly enduring or identically repetitive image the effect of abolishing our sense of natural process, of things changing and developing coherently within a continuous time flow. This accounts for the marked difference between *Women in Love* and *The Rainbow*, for in the earlier novel it was just this sense that Lawrence was concerned to express.

A subjective impression of suddenness belongs to the alienated vision, because the observer, failing to empathize with what he observes, does not foresee how it is going to move or change, where it is going to appear or disappear. Conversely, actions that are in fact sudden tend to dissociate the observer from what he observes, because its rhythm, its timing, its logic, is not his. The person who performs the sudden act may of course be exemplifying that capacity for spontaneity Lawrence is known to urge. But in fact in *Women in Love* he is more often revealing for us the trickiness of that very concept, for the seemingly spontaneous acts we see are frequently shown to be deeply compulsive, and thus in this way too have something in common with the fixed states they shatter.

That these and so many other of the book's effects are rendered visually, may seem strange when we remember that in 1913, working on what he then called *The Sisters*, the manuscript from which *Women in Love* was eventually to grow, Lawrence wrote in a letter to Garnett that it was 'quite unlike *Sons and Lovers*, not a bit visualized'.[22] And in the novel that emerged first, *The Rainbow*, there are numerous sustained passages in which he attempts to convey the inner life of the psyche without reference to visible outward behaviour. The thinking behind this is probably reflected in *Women in Love* when Halliday says, 'Life is all wrong because it has become much too visual.'[23] Nonetheless the later book, though it makes some play with

76

the concept of darkness, seems less interested in such attempts. Rather Lawrence seems to seek with new energy ways to make the inner life manifest through behaviour and action, and his writing shows a high degree of visual consciousness almost throughout. This does not return him, though, to the mode of *Sons and Lovers*. He brings to the book a new awareness of the relation between different styles of perception and different states of mind, and explores different styles of visual notation as a means of conveying those states. He alerts us to this with a simple example when Birkin suggests changes in the drawings done by Ursula's schoolchildren;[24] their receptive impressionism, which reflects Ursula's own usual mode of seeing, does not satisfy him : he wants post-impressionist areas of flat bold colour, signalling basic inner 'facts'. But this signals too an inner fact about himself : his need to think he has discerned the essentials, and his tendency to restrict his focus to them; the general leaning towards dramatized simplification, that reveals itself in his pungent diagnoses of modern civilization.

If Lawrence withdraws from the attempt to write in a less visual style, it may be at times because he was wishing to express what he thought was a symptom of modern alienation : as the blind man gains increased sensitivity of touch, so we, out of touch, may gain sharper visual consciousness; or it may be because he came to feel that a pure concentration upon the invisible flow of the inward life left unaltered that crucial gap between the inner and outer world that the conditions of modern life tended to create; and was thus in some sense a capitulation to them. A central problem for the alienated person is how to cross that gap, how to manifest his inner feelings outwardly in a way that does not convert them into something divorced from himself. Winifred, a lonely child in an adult world, has a similar problem, and we feel her exhilaration and sense of victory when she finds a way of making visible her feelings for Gudrun by presenting her with a rich bunch of flowers.[25] Throughout there is an interest in such manifestations of the self : hence we may not know the shape of Gudrun's nose, but we do know the style of the clothes she wears. Their vividness is her way of overcoming the basic problem : that for the alienated person, life is a visual surface in which he can make nothing of his inner self visible.

The difficulty is that such a reaction, like Birkin's equivalent attempt to display pictorially the inner facts about the catkins, may seem simply to create yet another surface. 'They saw the two girls appear, small, brilliant figures in the near distance, in the strong light of the late afternoon . . . Ursula had an orange-coloured knitted coat, Gudrun a pale yellow. Ursula wore canary yellow stockings, Gudrun bright rose. The figures of the women seemed to glitter in progress over the wide bay of the railway crossing, white and orange and yellow and rose glittering in motion across a hot world silted with coal-dust.' [26] 'Glitter' suggests a teasing surface, that strikes yet baffles the eye— as we are baffled to know how the sisters could express their individuality in full vividness in a way which would relate them to their background, the world they live in, and not simply turn them into bright shapes against a dullness, more alien, and thus more alienated, than ever.

The effect here, of a surface detached and free-floating, may lead us to our second point: that the alienated person as presented in *Women in Love* is liable to fall into a special way of behaviour in front of other people. His behaviour tends to be likewise a kind of detached surface— he acts a part. So Birkin is introduced as 'clever and separate', yet affecting to be 'quite ordinary'. 'And he did it so well, taking the tone of his surroundings, adjusting himself quickly to his interlocutor and his circumstances . . .' [27] Gerald tends to act a part on principle—the part that social propriety has written for him. He believes that 'you can't live unless you . . . come into line somewhere'.[28] Gudrun affects a cool 'finished' manner very different from her real emotions—she is 'frozen with overwrought feelings'.[29] Hermione's plight is a lack of spontaneity in her outward actions so complete that every gesture seems an artifice. The figures in *Women in Love* display what Nietzsche called 'the most characteristic quality of modern man: the strange contrast between an inner life to which nothing outward corresponds, and an outward existence unrelated to what is within'. Only by some form of acting can they easily mediate between these realms, and give the appearance of fitting into the world from which their true feelings are so dissociated. Moreover, even when their aim is an opposite one, a subtle form

78

of acting may result. The women, for instance, tend to dress in a style which seeks to make a bold assertion of individuality; but it brings them to the point where they hover on the brink of being in costume, like actresses.

Beneath these manifestations Lawrence makes us conscious of a concealed but recurrent feeling about the self: a feeling of radical insecurity, a fear either that the self is in some sense unreal, or else that it is threatened with annihilation. Ursula is perhaps the only major character who is free from such feelings. We encounter them in an extreme form as early as the first chapter in the descriptions of Hermione. Hermione is equipped with a social and cultural superiority of which she is fully aware. And yet in public 'she suffered a torture, under her confidence and pride, feeling herself exposed to wounds and to mockery and to despite. She always felt vulnerable . . . It was a lack of robust self, she had no natural sufficiency, there was a terrible void, a lack, a deficiency of being within her . . . she was established on the sand, build over a chasm'.[30] Gudrun and Gerald are subject to moments when they feel a similar insecurity, and the climax of their disastrous affair is essentially the climax of these feelings. Each experiences with the other a nearly total annihilation of the self. Gerald undergoes a kind of psychic detumescence : he says of his experience with her that 'it withers my consciousness, it burns the pith of my mind . . . your brain might have gone charred as rags . . . you're shrivelled as if struck by electricity'.[31] Gudrun, alone with him in their room in the Alps, becomes paralysed with near psychotic terror as she finds him watching her from behind, and 'getting power over her' to the point where she finds herself unable to turn round to face him.[32] Birkin too has moments when his distaste for others is revealed as fear of others : 'What a dread he had of mankind, of other people! It amounted almost to horror, to a sort of dream terror—his horror of being observed by some other people.'[33] And his relationship with Ursula seems complicated by his suspicion that his nature is threatened with some kind of diminishment at her hands—a diminishment he is determined to withstand. This fear is not always explicit, and when we find him with her insisting on an elusive combination of control and mutual independence, it is not easy to know whether to regard this as token of an independent sufficiency within

79

himself that he knows is best ground for the marriage he wants; or as a defensive strategy unconsciously devised to guard himself from too close and abrasive an interplay of individualities, in which he might come off worst.

The insecurity experienced by the characters in some scenes of *Women in Love* is of so radical a kind that we might well use the phrase adopted by R. D. Laing, and describe it as ontological insecurity.[34] It is a fear for the very being of the person involved. This is an emotion already powerfully expressed in *The Rainbow* (through Tom, Will and Skrebensky), but *Women in Love* significantly extends the exploration of its effects. To protect himself, the person afflicted with this fear needs to be guarded, he needs to preserve warily the barrier between himself and others, himself and society. But that barrier is his alienation, and behind it he lives unnourished, his reality goes unrecognized and unvalidated, he sickens for some dramatic breakthrough to the other person, for some immersion in the larger flow of life. So Lawrence's book offers an alternation of moods. There are scenes in which the characters sense themselves going rigid, tied up with frustrations and social pressures, trapped in the cages of their own ideas, or bypassed by the efficiency of their own organizations. And there are scenes where the inner bonds snap, the repressed energies break out in some sharp assault upon the barrier by which the self is blocked. This assault frequently combines a despairing attempt to break through to another person and thus to life, with a dangerous desire to revenge oneself upon that other person for having failed to restore one to life. There is an impulse to wrest satisfaction from the other and win power over life by subjugating him; and yet maybe equally to extinguish one's fears and despairs by extinguishing oneself, to offer oneself up for destruction by the ruthless forces of life that operate equally through and against the self, but do not sustain the self.

As we see in *Women in Love*, a complex ambivalence results. Characters are tempted to preserve themselves by repudiating the world, society, people; that is, by clinging to their alienation; yet they are also tempted to stake everything on breaking out of this imprisoning isolation, by clutching desperately at another person, or by letting themselves go and giving themselves up to some blind tidal wave of instinctual abandon. They fear intensely to be drowned; and yet they half desire to be drowned. They may long to be invulnerable, their will is a will to power; yet power is a barren mountain peak where their humanness freezes to death. They crave some ultimate physical experience which will wipe out their sense of unreality for ever; yet they sense fatally that this experience may prove to be a kind of Dionysian tearing apart of their own being, a *sparagmos* in which the celebrant is victim. At bottom of all is the tormenting conviction that the surface of life is a façade, a falsity, a constricting artifice—whether it be the social surface of institutions and conditioned public behaviour, or the surface of human personality, the ego that our wills are intent to maintain undamaged. So they long to pierce the surface through. But what lies under it has a dangerous force and a blind destructiveness that they hesitate to release by doing so.

One senses here a deep response to the time in which the book was written—a time when the flimsy surface of pre-war peace had given way to the mass slaughter of war. But however that may be, this cluster of ambivalent responses is at the core of the book, and affects more than the Gerald and Gudrun episodes. It explains why the most intense scenes repeatedly involve the image of a surface either penetrated or assailed—or, to put it another way, why such images trigger a heightened intensity in the writing. Birkin throws stones into the water, demolishing the surface reflection of the moon. Hermione stones Birkin, nearly cracking open his skull with a ball of lapis lazuli. Diana Crich falls into the lake and drowns; Gerald, the 'Diver' of chapter IV, plunges repeatedly after her. Gudrun's sketchbook, with its drawings of water plants breaking through the mud, is dropped into the water, and must be reached after. The boys who follow Gudrun's pleasure boat up the Thames and cause her so much horror, run in the mud ' "going in *up to the waist* . . . they went up to their hips in that indescribable Thames mud." '[35] Birkin and Gerald wrestle as if 'they would break into a oneness'.[36] The flanks of Gerald's horse are pierced by his spurs as he makes it stand at the level crossing. Minette jabs a knife into the hand of a jeering young man. Gerald and Gudrun have their flesh scored and gashed by Bismarck the rabbit, and for Gerald 'The long shallow red rip seemed torn

81

across his own brain, tearing the surface of his ultimate consciousness, letting through the forever unconscious, unthinkable red ether of the beyond . . .'[37] Sexual penetration can evoke hidden associations with these scenes and induce the same psychic tensions—and conversely the various assaults that take place often carry an overtone of sexual gratification.

The kind of ambivalence that Lawrence explores in these scenes may be suggested by a passage like the following, describing Gerald's response to Gudrun : 'like a victim that is torn open and given to the heavens, so he had been torn apart and given to Gudrun . . . This wound, this strange infinitely-sensitive opening of his soul, where he was exposed, like an open flower, to all the universe, and in which he was given to his complement, the other, the unknown, this wound, this disclosure, this unfolding of his own covering, leaving him incomplete, limited, unfinished, like an open flower under the sky, this was his cruellest joy.'[38] The halting movement of the sentence expresses the awkward complication of the feelings described. And the movement of the whole book, though so varied, equally has a relation with the ambivalence Lawrence is treating. We do not find in the narrative the conventional effect of steady linear progress from situation to situation. Ambivalence ties a knot in the emotional life very difficult to undo, and like the knot in a handkerchief recurrently reminds one of its existence. So the book follows the ways of the mind and returns to it or circles it in scenes which carry subtle or concealed echoes of each other, through characters who, because at some point they share a common plight, do likewise.

To appreciate Lawrence's methods and insights, it is worth looking more closely at a couple of these episodes. Let us consider two following chapters, 'Rabbit' and 'Moony'. In the first, chapter xviii, we have one of those remarkable transitions in which the book abounds, from poised commentary, alert to every nuance in conversation and gesture, to writing of startling expressionistic attack and vividness, as the rabbit, dragged out of its hutch to be sketched, thrashes about madly in Gerald's grasp. Yet the two sections are interdependent, there is no sensationalism in the concluding explosion of energy, because its significance has been subtly underpinned by the insights and cool awareness of the opening scene. It is in this opening that we notice a crucial ambivalence in Gerald, revealing itself in his shifting response to the two women, Gudrun and Winifred's French governess. The latter has the quality of finish in her appearance that has been discussed earlier. Here is Gerald's reaction : 'How repulsive her completeness and her finality was! He loathed her. Yet he did admire her. She was perfectly correct. And it did rather annoy him that Gudrun came dressed in startling colours, like a macaw, when the family was in mourning . . . Yet it pleased him . . . He felt the challenge in her very attire—she challenged the whole world. And he smiled as to the note of a trumpet.' [39] Gerald's changing responses to the women result from an ambivalence towards social correctness and 'adherence to society'. In theory, Gerald approves of a measure of social conformity : for one thing, it enables society to run smoothly as a machine for producing goods; for another it restrains people's desire to cut each other's throats. Yet faced with Mademoiselle, the sophisticated image of civilized conformity, he sees her as 'some elegant beetle'—a response in which there lies for the reader a disconcerting association with the primitive African carvings in Halliday's flat—one of which Gerald has seen and hated, and yet recognized as the true totem of the Minette he desires—who in her turn has an obsessive fear of black beetles. Conversely, the 'note of the trumpet' that Gudrun suggests to him, carries an echo of the flowers she has lingered with just before—'she stooped down and touched the trumpets'—and which she has, as it were, absorbed—'her eyes, hot with the beauty of the flowers, looked into his'. So the challenge she offers is the challenge of something disruptive yet natural. 'He smiled'—it pleases him; but what he has not resolved is whether he is pleased because he stands with her in wanting to sound such a challenge—it is Gerald, we remember, who in the midst of the Shortlands wedding party picks up a conch shell and blows a shattering blast on it 'without reference to anybody';[40] or whether he is pleased because he feels the challenge is to himself, an invitation to an encounter in which he will be able to show his superior power.

In fact though his immediate encounter is with the rabbit, and the rabbit, wild one minute, tame the next, functions like the alarming totem of his own ambivalence. In

83

the rabbit we see life caged and domesticated—the powerful Bismarck (for that is his name) lives in a rabbit hutch.
The result reads like an enactment of extreme schizophrenia. The contained or imprisoned energies gather in the
static animal; dragged out to be drawn, as the dog Looloo
has just been drawn—to be, that is, once more contained,
delineated, reduced—the energies explode in a destructive
yet entirely futile outburst. But once they are expended,
the rabbit settles back into harmless domestication : 'And
then quite suddenly it settled down . . . it hobbled calmly
forward and began to nibble the grass with that mean
motion of a rabbit's quick eating.' [41] We discern a sardonic
yet frightening comment on twentieth-century man—we
are 'all that—and more,' says Gudrun, and Gerald, a 'Bismarck of industry' whom she has earlier seen as Dionysus,
is on the one hand stirred to find them equally 'initiate' in
this accidental Dionysian rite, equally aroused and lured
by its total release, its consuming and consummating
aggressivities; but on the other hand, humiliated to find
himself thus exposed, his own energies thus ignominiously
accounted for : he feels 'as if she had torn him across the
breast'.

Every tamed animal has somewhere within it a wild
animal; but the inner wildness is in many ways just a
token of the tameness. We see here that the way past the
ambivalence in which Gerald is locked is to recognize, as
Lawrence makes us do, that the force of the pull towards
one extreme is generated by its opposite. The cage we live
in—the cage of social restrictions, and industrial organization, the cage of the self-controlling will, the cage of
mental alienation—offers a kind of safety; but it creates the
desire for some pseudo-primitive Dionysian outbreak, consummation of a blind and uncreative kind. The fear of this
outbreak, this ripping of the surface, makes us bring to
bear more controls, more pressure to conformity; and this
makes the outbreak still more desired, and still more dangerous. 'Action and reaction, and nothing between' : Birkin's
comment on Halliday [42] fits this situation too.

The chapter takes us way beyond the simplicities of that
often quoted credo from an early letter, 'My great religion
is a belief in the blood . . .' [43] And it implicitly sums up his
final response to one of his preoccupations in that earlier
period, the thinking of Nietzsche. Lawrence's concern with

the will and the ego (for him related concepts) goes back to Nietzsche; and so in some measure does his concern with a dissolving of the boundaries of the self, a flowing into oneness with the vital forces of life, that is symbolized in Nietzsche's revered god, Dionysus. The concepts might seem to be opposed, for will and ego create those walls around the self that Dionysus breaks down. But Nietzsche, via his concept of a superman, or a self which has surpassed the self, of a will charged with life energies and an ego capable of balloon-like expansion, manages to bring them into alliance. Lawrence was positively influenced by Nietzsche's thinking in many ways; Nietzsche's view of prevailing morality as a kind of enforced tameness, motivated by fear and an ignoble obsession with self-preservation, he clearly found persuasive. But in this matter he was not persuaded, and saw Nietzsche principally as a highly significant portent (as certain passages in *Twilight in Italy* make clear). Nietzsche's double emphasis was for him prophetic of a widespread double yearning: for an assertion of egotism and the will to power, and for a dissolution of the caged and limited self. But the will-driven Germanic superman had turned out to be Bismarck; and the Dionysian consummation to be a fling with Minette or, taken further, disintegration with Gudrun—and perhaps ultimately the blood sacrifice of the battlefront. And Lawrence, in reaction, attacks the will as that which jails the natural self and bullies others; and criticises the desire for total abandonment to the submerged drives as a failure of selfhood.

As a result he is left occupying a double position himself. The integral self must be kept whole and distinct, and even to some degree separate, as Birkin's two stars are separate. Yet to be cut off is a kind of death, one must learn to relax one's guards and open oneself freely to the influx of life, the forces of nature, the touch of the other. These two tenets are not as contradictory as they might seem: one cannot risk opening oneself unless one feels that one's self has enough presence and substance not to be endangered by doing so; and without that all things may seem to lack presence and substance. Yet to keep faith with them both can be tricky, as the veering path of Lawrence's later works might suggest, and as he sensitively shows us in *Women in Love* through Birkin. The ability to analyse Gerald's case leaves Lawrence, and us, with no easy resolutions of its shared dilemmas. To see this we may turn to the chapter that follows 'Rabbit': chapter XIX, 'Moony'.

Again the expressive power of the writing comes to a focus in an effect we might call totemic: against the characters is suddenly juxtaposed a being of another order; we are startled into recognizing some strange resemblance between it and them, a resemblance which disturbs our preconceptions of what they were. But here the resemblance is a shifting one, and the totem functions as a bright focus of doubts and uncertainties.

The totem is the moon and we are made to see it first as Ursula's totem. The moon is the female principle, and Birkin, as he looks at the water where it is reflected, is saying to himself, 'Cybele—curse her! The accursed Syria Dea!' He is musing, we suppose, on Ursula as engulfing nature goddess or female ego commanding the tides of life —a role left over from *The Rainbow* and not really much at home nor much apparent amidst the prevailing insecurities of *Women in Love*. It is a very different Ursula, at any rate, who unknown to him is present at that moment; and it is a very different resemblance between Ursula and the moon that the opening of this chapter has subtly created.

Described there is an Ursula who has become an embodiment of separateness and repudiation, who feels that in the present state of the world, 'there was nothing for it . . . but contemptuous, resistant indifference . . . she had no contact and no connection anywhere. She despised and detested the whole show.' Further, 'from the bottom of her soul, she despised and detested people': she hates the way they refer themselves 'to some detestable social principle', and she detests their 'soulfulness and tragedy'. There is a sense in which the vigour of her scorn is a device for stimulating her metabolism and throwing off those sicknesses she stands in danger of catching—the sicknesses commonly bred by the alienation she so defiantly embraces. 'She herself was real, and only herself'—no ontological insecurity haunts Ursula. By stoking the fires of her contempt so energetically she gains a warm sense of her own reality, and so survives the cold climates of isolation, much as Lawrence himself did. She achieves by it a 'brightness': 'the strange brightness of her presence, a marvellous radiance of intrinsic

86

vitality, was a luminousness of supreme repudiation, nothing but repudiation'. It is this that relates her in our minds to the moon.

Ursula expresses emotions here which the book seeks to show are well grounded, and which we can hardly doubt had been intensively shared by Lawrence himself. And yet the moon when it appears is sinister. It has a 'white and deathly smile'. Ursula's search for 'a pure loneliness, with no taint of people', brings her face to face with a moon that mirrors her repudiation and reflects its barrenness. 'Night or day, one could not escape the sinister face, triumphant and radiant like this moon, with a high smile.' If, as the previous chapter suggests, the way of compromise and conformity provokes the dangers it wishes to avert, the opposite way of rejection of all that is dead, may itself immure one in a kind of death.

Birkin, when he stones the reflection of the moon to ' "make it be quite gone off the pond" ', is equally engaged in rejection, repudiation; there is a rightness therefore in the fact that he cannot succeed. But the significance of the scene does not end here. The description of the disturbed surface of the water is unexpectedly extended, the visual treatment becomes futuristic, and the rhythmic expressiveness of the writing takes on a compelling intensity. It is as if the surface disturbance taps a deeper disturbance, in the mind of the writer: or as if Lawrence senses that his scene is providing him with a visual correlative of those tensions within the book that are most difficult to resolve. We have suggested already one of the ways in which this may be so: one longs to rupture the surface; yet the energies which well out if one does may be deadly. In accord with this, Lawrence's description brings the water alive, its agitation seems not the mere mechanical consequence of Birkin's stone throwing, but a vivid reaction of its own, in which the forces of darkness threaten to consume the forces of light in a dream image of universal war: 'There was no moon, only a battlefield of broken lights and shadows . . . Shadows, dark and heavy, struck again and again across the place where the heart of the moon had been . . .' Further one is conscious of the way the scene prints into our mind an image of radiating vibrations very relevant to the sense of human beings and human acts that the book gives us. Lawrence's characters seem to give out, and be highly receptive to, such vibrations; and this being so, the notion they sometimes cherish of effect-ing a separation from others and shutting down contact seems hardly practicable.

But most interesting of all is the way the writing of this passage creates a subtle fluctuation in our sympathies. We begin by seeing the moon as hard, sinister, repellant. It associates in our minds with the ball of lapis lazuli, Hermione's weapon against Birkin in an earlier chapter: it is equally pure and hard and closed in upon itself; and it functions equally well as an image of egoistic invulnerability, and autonomous mental consciousness. Its staring light we too wish to avoid, and when its reflection begins to form again on the water after Birkin's fusillade, we can accept that its fragments would be coming together 'blindly, enviously', as Lawrence describes them; that the moon would be 'regathering itself insidiously'. But as Birkin obstinately renews his attack, 'like a madness', refusing to admit defeat, it is he who is acting like Hermione, and Lawrence's language subtly changes ground; subconsciously we feel that the darkness has turned brutal and sadistic—'Shadows, dark and heavy, struck again and. again'—and that the moon has become an oppressed victim, desperate to escape, 'tormented': 'Flakes of light appeared here and there, glittering tormented among the shadows . . .' The percussive crashing of the stones, the sense of rhythmic chaos and climactic break-up, recall nothing so closely as the effect of the train upon Gerald's horse when he forces it to stand at the level crossing in an earlier chapter. Birkin, who sides with Gerald then, is in Gerald's role here. The chapter title 'Moony' teasingly echoes the earlier 'Mino', where he has put the case for male control; but he has ignored there what Lawrence's choice of name for the cat wryly suggests: that the fitting mate for a would-be human Mino is not an Ursula but a Minette. Here the effect of the writing is increasingly destructive. And as we see the moon finally, 'trying to recover from its convulsion, to get over the disfigurement and the agitation, to be whole and composed, at peace', we are made to feel that such an attempt is entirely natural. The hallucinatory light show that we have witnessed has shaken our minds free of their initial ideas, and our assaulted consciousness craves now a little wholeness and peace itself.

This subtle swing of attitude relates to a central paradox in Lawrence's thinking, and in the book itself. His rejection of conventional notions of character springs first from his awareness of the living psyche as subject to radical change —people pass through 'allotropic states';[44] and second from the realization most fully explored in *Women in Love*, that the mind may harbour contradictory impulses at the same time. This would seem to put Lawrence in accord with that advanced thinking of the time whose tendency was to dissolve away by empiric analysis all concept of the self as a single unified entity, to reveal its apparent character as an effect of conditioning, and to find within a series of radical dichotomies, or, as in Musil's novel, a 'man without qualities'. And yet of course Lawrence is not finally in accord with this, as his critical views of Freud, Dostoievsky, Proust and Joyce clearly show. Essential to his critique of the structure and aims of contemporary mass society is his sense of the 'disquality', the individualness, of human beings. His view that we pass through allotropic states, that a man may be, to use his own metaphors, coal, then diamond, may function as an attack upon the notion of human nature as fixed and stable; but it also affirms a consistency of nature, for diamond and coal are both carbon : beneath the appearance of change lies a single element, true to its individual nature. And so correspondingly the fixed image of the moon must be shattered and destroyed; and yet be allowed to regather itself, to be whole.

One senses too in this scene a further paradox. What Birkin is doing with his stones is to probe the depths : he is plumbing the waters as Gerald has done when he dives again and again in vain search of the drowned Diana. In that earlier scene it is Birkin who makes him stop : Gerald is wasting himself to track down a corpse, his obsession is an obsession with the dead, and he risks being sucked down into that under-element where life rots and disintegrates. But the book itself is out to explore a darkness and disintegration below the surface, and in that sense Lawrence acknowledges that one may need to run Gerald's risk. However through Birkin he is very concerned to draw some kind of line beyond which the process should not go. To this end Birkin posits a sharp abstract dichotomy between 'the river of life' and the 'river of corruption' [45]—locating Gudrun and Gerald firmly in the latter. It is a dichotomy too rigid to cope with the subtlety of what Lawrence does in *Women in Love*, yet for all that one can hardly deny its importance to the book, and to Lawrence. Its effect is to legitimatize withdrawals—Gerald's withdrawal from the search for Diana, Birkin and Ursula's withdrawal from corrupt England; and also those of a less tangible kind, withdrawals of sympathy which we notice occurring in the treatment of Hermione and perhaps also Gerald. Its effect, one might say, is to encourage sitting on a bank and throwing stones from a distance; and though Lawrence, as we have seen, shows himself well enough aware that there are temptations here to avoid, one may feel that the course he chooses has both gains and losses. The sterilities and constrictions of civilization, the blocks and compulsions of the psyche—these are not life: Lawrence gains a freedom to say this, and it is good to hear. And yet they are life, in the sense that they do not slink away at the voicing of such assertions, but remain, demanding still the same considerable share of our life's energy. So what are we to do? In probing a sickness one risks being further infected by it. But whether it is more dangerous to probe it than to ignore it remains a fine point. There is a time for each perhaps, and we can only hope our instinct will tell us when it is; this at least is what the book suggests, finding its moments to relax tension and obsession and remind us that the best of life is somewhere else.

In the Zen story, the nun Chiyono seeks enlightenment tenaciously for ten years without success. Then one day, as she is bringing water from the well, her daily task, the bottom drops out of her old bucket—and she is enlightened. She writes—

In this way and that I tried to save the old pail
Since the bamboo strip was weakening and about to
  break
Until at last the bottom fell out.
No more water in the pail!
No more moon in the water! [46]

Enlightenment may require obstinate mental seeking; yet gripped tight by that obstinacy one cannot be open to it, one cannot find it. The mind seeks to gather the moon in its small bucket: but what it catches is merely a reflection, that it might better abandon. Lawrence comes by his own path to such truths. Birkin who analyses and 'must pull everything to pieces',[47] Birkin who can be relied on to turn sensuality into a verbal idea or intellectual programme: Birkin must learn to be a changer, and come to know when to fall into the slack waggling dance of spontaneous disresponsibility. In accord with this the vision of the book itself is subject to rapid changes: and from the very beginning the tense perceptions of the alienated consciousness are given their edge and held in balance by a kind of subtle cross-cutting to other, warmer perceptions. The free enjoyment of life, life as spontaneity and vital pleasure, is not dead; it is there for us in the scene between bride and groom in the opening chapter—a scene which seems transposed from Keats' Grecian Urn back into warm reality, and which offers us an image to remember through all the conflicts to come: for the bride flees elusively as life itself does—and yet, fleeing 'with laughter and challenge', flees to be pursued and caught. So that this most fatalistic of Lawrence's books seems still to be saying as Blake said—

> He who kisses the joy as it flies
> Lives in eternity's sun rise.

But Lawrence's moon, unlike Chiyono's, remains reflected on the water. And this is fitting. For his genius in this book is given over first to finding ways of expressing the dilations and contractions of the subjective vision, and understanding the conditions of stress that they unconsciously signal—just as the moon's reflection signals the state of the water it rides on. The stresses he treats are those of our time; and of problems that no doctrine can bring to a final resolution. And for that reason *Women in Love* remains a book that cannot be finished with. Concerned as it is with a whole spectrum of twentieth-century impulses and moods—from the rigidities of alienation to the outbursts of released repression; from the drive towards mass organization to the temptations of opting out; from dreams of *Bludbrüderschaft* to realities of sado-masochism; from neo-Nietzschean vitalism to near-Zen insouciance; concerned with such themes, and displaying a daring imaginative vitality above all his other works, *Women in Love* retains all its relevance and richness, and becomes increasingly a book we cannot afford not to read.

NOTES

(*Women in Love* page references are to Heinemann 'Phoenix', London, 1954).

1. *Women in Love*, ch. XIV, p. 171.
2. *Ibid.*, ch. VI, p. 58.
3. *Ibid.*, ch. I, p. 5.
4. *Ibid.*, ch. I, p. 5.
5. *Ibid.*, ch. I, p. 7.
6. *Ibid.*, ch. I, p. 9.
7. *Ibid.*, ch. I, p. 8.
8. *Ibid.*, ch. V, p. 46.
9. *Ibid.*, ch. II, p. 18.
10. *Ibid.*, ch. II, p. 19.
11. *Ibid.*, ch. II, p. 20.
12. *Ibid.*, ch. I, p. 5.
13. *Ibid.*, ch. I, p. 8.
14. *Ibid.*, ch. XVIII, p. 228.
15. *Ibid.*, ch. III, p. 32.
16. *Ibid.*, ch. VIII, p. 92.
17. *Ibid.*, ch. VIII, p. 76.
18. *Ibid.*, ch. XVIII, p. 231.
19. *Ibid.*, ch. XIV, p. 152.
20. *Ibid.*, ch. IX, p. 104.
21. *Ibid.*, ch. IV, p. 39.
22. Letter to Edward Garnett, 11 March 1913. *Collected Letters*, p. 193.
23. *Women in Love*, ch. VII, p. 71.
24. *Ibid.*, ch. III, pp. 29-30.
25. *Ibid.*, ch. XXI.
26. *Ibid.*, ch. IX, p. 107.
27. *Ibid.*, ch. I, p. 14.
28. *Ibid.*, ch. XVI, p. 197.
29. *Ibid.*, ch. XXVIII, p. 377.
30. *Ibid.*, ch. I, p. 11.
31. *Ibid.*, ch. XXIX, p. 431.
32. *Ibid.*, ch. XXIX, pp. 404-5.
33. *Ibid.*, ch. VIII, p.101.
34. R. D. Laing, *The Divided Self* (London, 1960), ch. 3. My article is indebted to Laing's work.
35. *Women in Love*, ch. XIV, p. 157.
36. *Ibid.*, ch. XX, p. 262.
37. *Ibid.*, ch. XVIII, p. 235.

38. *Ibid.*, ch. XXX, p. 437.
39. *Ibid.*, ch. XVIII, p. 231.
40. *Ibid.*, ch. II, p. 20.
41. *Ibid.*, ch. XVIII, p. 235.
42. *Ibid.*, ch. VIII, p. 88.
43. Letter to Ernest Collings, 17 Jan., 1913. *Collected Letters*, p. 180.
44. Letter to Edward Garnett, 5 June, 1914. *Ibid.*, p. 282.
45. *Women in Love*, ch. XIV, p. 164.
46. *Zen Flesh, Zen Bones*, compiled by Paul Reps (Vermont, 1957), p. 49.
47. *Women in Love*, ch. XII, p. 133.

THE WAY OF FREEDOM . . . FURTIVE PRIDE
AND SLINKING SINGLENESS *

Sons and Lovers can be seen as the record of Lawrence's attempt to break free from his over-involved relationship with his mother, to release his imprisoned sense of his own identity, and to achieve loving relationship with other individuals; and it is a record of the failure of that attempt. The women in the novel—Miriam and Clara—are rarely recognized by Paul as separate individuals, but more as instruments, as manifestations of his own fears and desires. In *The Rainbow* Lydia Lensky urges Will Brangwen to remember in his love-making that 'there is somebody there besides yourself'. This is always Lawrence's problem and theme : to see others not as threats to his individual being, nor as manifestations of it, but as independent beings with whom he can be in satisfying relation. This is a major theme of *The Rainbow* and *Women in Love*—but these novels in fact seem to work away from an apprehension of relationship with independent reality towards the creation of a world where all the characters are manifestations of one central fragmented consciousness.

In his later essay on Galsworthy (written while composing *Lady Chatterley's Lover*) he wrote,

> When [the individual] becomes too much aware of objective reality, and of his own isolation in the face of objective reality, the core of his identity splits, his nucleus collapses, his innocence of naiveté perishes, and he becomes only a subjective-objective reality, a divided thing hinged together but not strictly individual.

However true this may be of Galsworthy, Lawrence is

* By R. E. Pritchard, University of Keele.

94

here touching on his own problem, that he struggled with in the years following *Women in Love*—'his own isolation in the face of objective reality'. Leaving England, where any attempt at community or relationship with others seemed hopeless, he set out in search of a new world where this might be possible. He sought this in the new countries and people that he met, and in foreign literature—most notably, American literature. However, isolated as he was in these cultural environments in which he had no real roots, all he read or saw, or whoever he met, lost 'objective reality' and became only manifestations or symbols of his own internal struggles.

This is in effect the concern of this essay—a survey of the writings of the first five or six years after *Women in Love* (substantially complete by 1916), considering the theme of the isolated outsider, and particularly, the concept of 'singleness' and some of its implications.

In *Psychoanalysis and the Unconscious* (written December 1919—January 1920) Lawrence wrote:

Love is a thing to be learned, through centuries of patient effort. It is a difficult, complex maintenance of individual integrity throughout the incalculable processes of inter-human polarity . . . Who can do it? Nobody. Yet we have all got to do it, or else suffer ascetic tortures of starvation and privation or of distortion and over-strain and slow collapse into corruption. The whole of life is one long, blind effort at an established polarity with the outer universe, human and non-human; and the whole of modern life is a shrieking failure.

Here is the problem, the problem of being in relationship and unison (necessary, but possibly smothering) and also of being separate (equally necessary, but possibly sterile and lonely—and even 'corrupting').

One of the best-known appearances of the concept of 'singleness' may usefully be set against this passage, and is in Chapter 16 of *Women in Love*, 'Moony'. Birkin has set before him two alternatives. On the one hand is the white races' 'mystery of ice-destructive knowledge, snow-abstract annihilation' as embodied in Gerald: this is the mode of isolation, frustration and sublimation of the sensual being (particularly of course the homosexual impulse; there is some implication that Gerald's denial of *Blutbrüder-*

95

schaft with Birkin is a major cause of his destruction). On the other hand is the mode of being that is embodied in the West African fetish, 'the principle of knowledge in dissolution and corruption . . . beyond any phallic knowledge, sensual subtle realities . . .' : this is the way of abandoning oneself to fulfilment of the sensual impulses—particularly the homosexual. 'Dissolution' and 'corruption' here imply a breaking-down into the flux of union, as well as moral turpitude. This unitive flow is seen as surpassing normal sexual union, being the flow of 'the river of corruption' which, according to Birkin in 'Water Party', is 'our real reality'. This river of corruption is partly the excremental flow, which is seen as our fundamental reality (if the pun may be excused); that is, Birkin-Lawrence is inclined to identify the necessary acceptance of our natural bodily condition with acceptance of (sexual) impulses rejected by our conventions as 'unnatural'. To accept these so-called 'unnatural' impulses, he suspects may be essential to self-fulfilment; but he fears the consequences of this course (social condemnation and rejection, and moral degeneration) at least as much as frustration and sublimation. Birkin abandons the struggle of choice—

> There was another way, the way of freedom. There was the paradisal entry into pure, single being, the individual soul taking precedence over love and desire for union, stronger than any pangs of emotion, a lovely state of free proud singleness, which accepted the obligation of the permanent connection with others, and with the other, submits to the yoke and leash of love, but never forgets its own proud individual singleness . . . (XVI)

and in this spirit goes off to propose to Ursula.

In this passage 'singleness' appears in its positive aspect; it appears again, more dubiously, in the young man in the market to whom Ursula and Birkin give their chair. The appearance of this new couple suggests that they are 'parodies' of Frieda and Lawrence. Birkin sympathises with 'the aloof furtive youth against the active procreant female' who is Lawrence's detested overbearing Magna Mater. The young man is

> hardly a man at all . . . strangely pure-bred and fine in one sense, furtive, quick, subtle . . . his eyes had no mind in

96

them, only a dreadful kind of subject inward consciousness . . . He would be a dreadful, but a wonderful lover . . . he had some of the fineness and stillness and silkiness of a dark-eyed silent rat . . . He grinned sicklily, turning away his head. She had got his manhood, but Lord, what did he care! He had a strange furtive pride and slinking singleness. (XXVI)

This singleness is the defensive reaction against the smothering woman and the civilization that have caught and unmanned him: he has not submitted, is unnatural, with a subversive and even subhuman intensity. The qualities sketched in here are further developed in the character Loerke, Birkin-Lawrence's worse self, who has 'an uncanny singleness, a quality of being by himself, that marked out an artist'. A focus for much of the novel's animal imagery (mouse, rabbit, bat, seal and of course 'the wizard rat'), he is furtive like the young man, and gay, bisexual, artistic. a leader or explorer—like Birkin and Lawrence—in the river of corruption.

It is under his influence that Birkin acquires a mocking 'licentiousness (that) was repulsively attractive' to Ursula, when he submits her to anal intercourse. Lawrence attempts to present this action as a liberation from bodily shame, but it is clear that Birkin. acting in the spirit of the other two men, is counter-attacking woman in an act normally associated with homosexual practice, achieving his own sexual satisfaction while denying hers. This too is an aspect of male singleness—a perverse and vengeful self-assertion.

One of the many elements of Women In Love is Lawrence's exploration of the problem of the bisexual. Birkin-Lawrence's inability to unite love and desire in his feelings for a woman, and his homosexual tendencies. were made explicit in the original introductory chapter. Birkin resists love with Ursula, but seeks it with Gerald, whose death indicates both the appalling consequences of passion whether sublimated or indulged, and also the impossibility of the male love that Birkin-Lawrence sought: at the end the problem of Birkin-Lawrence's future role is unsolved.

Lawrence needed a woman who was both wife and mother—but sexual relationships then became regressive, a kind of incest; his consequent sense of guilt meant a kind of psychological impotence, so that, while the woman might obtain satisfaction, he could not. Resentment induced the desire to escape, to find either satisfaction among men, or self-sufficiency. With the first alternative, he felt strongly the dangers of slipping into homosexuality (imaged as subhuman and demonic), with the second the danger was of isolation and frustration. The writing of the years immediately after *Women In Love* display Lawrence's struggles to resolve this dilemma—as for example, the essays on American Literature.[1]

In America Lawrence hoped to find a resolution of his own inner conflict between the frustrating and bloodless 'white' world, and the dark 'savage' world of the passional self, that was savage in its frightening power and in its uncivilized quality. To be civilized and human was to be possessed by woman, so free play of the sensual being (especially in its homosexual aspect) was to be savage or even degenerate.

In the first essay Lawrence suggests that the original North American settlers

> lusted spiritually for utter repression in the sensual or passional self . . . cut and destroyed the living bond (an umbilicus) between men (the species or the sex?), the rich passional contact. And for this passional contact was substituted the mechanical bond of purposive utility. (p. 27)

However, to balance this Gerald-spirit Lawrence imagined the influence of the new but ancient world to which they had come :

> They breathed a savage air, and their blood was suffused and burnt . . . their first and rarest life-stuff transmuted . . . (p. 29)

So, in America, there was the hope of 'the mystic transubstantiation', reconciling the two forces. All the essays on American literature are concerned with the outlining, exploration, and attempted solution of Lawrence's problem (which he saw as the problem of his time), so those authors—such as Thoreau and Emerson—who do not fit his scheme are excluded, and the rest ruthlessly pressed into service. Recognizing his need to understand and accept his own nature, he criticizes Benjamin Franklin's effort at

98

rational self-analysis and self-control, but agrees that

> it is not until man has utterly seized power over himself,
> and gained complete knowledge of himself, down to the
> most minute and shameful of his desires and sensations,
> that he can really begin to be free. (p. 43)

Freedom depended on releasing his sensual self from inhibition, the influence of his dead mother living on in him
(as he indicates in his essay on Fenimore Cooper); freedom
depends on the constant struggle and interaction of the opposed principles of frustrating civilized tenderness and
savage sensual desire. So long as the struggle continued intensely, intense, painful life is assured.

The first requirement is to resist absorption by woman's
love, as in the sexless love of two men :

> They are the dual centre of all the whirl of life . . . Two
> mature, silent, expressionless men, they stand on oppo-
> site shores of being, and their love, the inexpressible
> conjunction between them, is the bridge over the chasm.
> (p. 102)

Procreative sexuality is dismissed as only 'a mechanical
marking-time of the creative process', and marriage is
simply a tender trap for those frightened of being alone.

> Most men would rather have a home which is misery
> and torment than suffer from the sense of exposure to
> the winds of fate . . . It is a shrinking from the sheer
> communion in isolation which lies ahead, the mystic
> consummation of the White soul with the Red. (p. 105)

—that is the reconciliation of the civilized with the
savage, the rational with the passional. Lawrence is clearly
speaking for himself : the fear of isolation and 'exposure'
is ever-present, qualifying his search for singleness. In discussing Poe's tales of murderously consuming incest, he
indicates that love—particularly incestuous love—is the
desire for merging and identification, but that to pull away
from unison is also dreadful. His concern is clear :

> La Bruyère says that all our human unhappiness *vient
> de ne pouvoir être seul* . . . the triumph of love . . . lies
> in the communion of beings, who, in the very perfection
> of communion, recognize and allow the mutual other-
> ness . . . each self remains utterly itself . . . (p. 130)

99

But that is only an ideal; the condition of our civilization is expressed in Hawthorne's *The Scarlet Letter* which reveals the futile attempt of woman-dominated, idealistic men to suppress primary sensual being, both in themselves and in women (whose sexuality seems particularly threatening): 'it is the age of fatal, suffocating love'. There is no fulfilment possible in escape, for then one becomes only the perverse outsider. Lawrence sees a parallel between his and Frieda's wandering life, and that of Hawthorne's characters, when

> Hester . . . urges Dimmesdale to go away with her to a new country, to begin a new life . . . When a man responds to the prompting of a woman to a new life, he has not only to face the world itself, but a great reaction in the very woman he takes . . . If Dimmesdale had fled with Hester they would have felt themselves social outcasts. And they would have had to live in secret hatred of mankind, like criminal accomplices; or they would have felt isolated, cut off, two lost creatures, a man meaningless except as the agent, or tool, or creature of the possessive woman; and when a man loses his meaning, the woman one way or another destroys him. (p. 145)

Here, clearly is Lawrence's own condition: the (natural) fear of 'facing the world', the fear of becoming the outsider, excluded from normality, drifting into 'criminality', and unprotected against the woman.

The 'sensual male in complete subordination, as we have him in modern life' appears in Hawthorne's characters Chillingworth and Hollingsworth, the latter described as a 'dark, black-bearded monomaniac' with 'criminal' obsessions; the sensuality asserted by such characters has a savage intensity, destructive of the spirit, and of normal humanity. Hollingsworth's submissive—even masochistic —wife is dehumanized by this absolute sensuality, acquiring—like Adela, in *The Lost Girl*—the

> infernal reality such as is suggested by the old legends of werewolves and metamorphoses . . . the last processes of mystic disintegration out of being. The last lust is for this indescribable sensation—whose light we can see in the eyes of a tiger, or a wolf. (p. 158)

The second part of the Hawthorn essay had provided some introduction to Lawrence's own 'science' derived from 'alchemy and astrology and the Hermetic science', and the next essay, 'The Two Principles', turns aside from literary criticism to explore Lawrence's theories of duality and polarity. He posits the existence of two principles, as fire and water—that is, the male and female principles. The two sexes (whether actual men and women, or as impulses present within an individual) may meet 'in the youth of an era' so as to produce a being 'harmonious and at one with itself'; however they may meet in 'the times of disintegration, the crumbling of an era', in

> the tremendous conjunction of opposition, a vivid struggle, as fire struggles with water . . . it is the birth of a disintegrative soul, wherein the two principles wrestle in their eternal opposition: a soul finite, momentaneous . . . (p. 185)

Lawrence sees an imbalance in his parentage and in himself, and a movement towards abandonment of normal sexuality, and towards isolation. In this plight, he then adopts another scheme promising more hope. Here he contrasts the upper half of the body, associated with the idealistic and social qualities, with the lower, sensual half, where he finds

> a magnificent central positivity . . . a state portrayed in the great dark statues of the seated lords of Egypt . . . Here, in the navel, flowers the water-born lotus, the soul of water begotten by one germ of fire . . . the symbol of our perfected sensual first-being . . . (Here) we have our passionate self-possession, our unshakable and indomitable being (p. 186)

Rooted in the lower, rear portions of the body,

> from the lumbar ganglion and from the sacral ganglion acts the great sensual will to dominion. From these centres the soul goes forth haughty and indomitable, seeking for mastery . . . as also in the tiger and the cat the power-centre is at the base of the spine, in the sacral ganglion. (p. 189)

For Lawrence, the source of strength, the sense of identity, is to be identified with the ultraphallic source at the rear that Ursula had sensed in Birkin; this is ignored by the 'civilized' consciousness and cannot be possessed by woman : this is the core of a man's sensual being.

Returning to literary criticism, Dana's voyages are interpreted as an escape from the repressive forces of idealistic civilization, and as a confrontation with the female element of the sea that would overwhelm the solitary exposed male. The notorious incident of the ship-board flogging is interpreted by Lawrence as a release of tension, 'spontaneous passional morality, not the artificial ethical', that is 'a natural form of coition, interchange', that brings the men on board into harmonious relation again. He likens this violent and passionate outburst to divine male thunder—thunder that, because of its sulphurous smell, is apparently called by some tribes 'the dung of the gods'. Balance between water and fire, frustration and passion, has been restored, and the ship can sail on, in harmony with the elements :

> There is no violation . . . only a winged centrality. It is this perfect adjusting of ourselves to the elements, the perfect equipoise between them and us, which give us a great part of our life-joy. (p. 209)

But this equipoise is very unstable and transient, and in his discussion of Melville, Lawrence returns to the eternal struggle between the civilized and the savage. Melville's wandering in the Pacific islands provide a rebirth into 'the green Eden of the first, or last era, the valley of the timeless savages', a culture that contains the remnants of the lost savage but innocent past. Here Melville finds himself

> at once in a pure, mysterious world, pristine . . . naked simplicity of life, with subtle, non-mental understanding, *rapport* between human beings. (p. 224)

However, this rediscovered savage world is only a corrupted and degenerate remainder of the 'sensual-mystic civilizations now gone'. Primitive art once embodied a religous vision, but now it is only decadent, sensuality gone rotten :

> No man can look at the African grotesque carvings, for example, or the decoration patterns of the Oceanic islanders, without seeing in them the infinitely sophisti-

cated soul which produces distortion from its own distorted psyche, a psyche distorted through generations of degeneration. (p. 223)

Likewise, the savages' devouring of human flesh was once a 'sensual-mystic' communion, but now it is only disgusting cannibalism, just as love between men is now degenerated into perverse homosexuality.

Melville-Lawrence is too much possessed by modern idealist consciousness-ridden civilization to be able to indulge in self-conscious savagery and primitivism.

The true spontaneous existence, though he longed for it achingly, was yet a torture and a *nullification* to him. This is the quandary of the idealist, the man who stakes all his being on his upper consciousness. He cannot be made free. He cannot even enjoy his own being. (p. 226)

There can be no going-back : regression means degeneration; Lawrence must continue his struggle to come to terms with his divided self, and with the real world.

Moby Dick, in Lawrence's brilliant account, seems almost to have been written for—or by—him, including as it does so many Lawrentian *motifs*. There are the lonely wanderer, Ishmael, briefly finding male love, with Queequeg; the idealist Ahab, equally solitary but doomed, blasted and scarred by lightning (this is the scar of sexual conflict and agony, as it appears in 'The Blind Man', the essay 'David', and on the pine-tree in *St. Mawr*), hunting down the embodiment of the phallic being, 'the deep, free sacral [or sexual] consciousness in man,' embodied in other myths as the dragon (see *Apocalypse*); there is the solitary individual white albatross; the vision of 'the heaven beneath the wave' in the sight of the mother whales suckling their young, central in the clear depths; the vision of the phallic being in its terrifying, negative aspect, in the appearance of the squid (cf. the squid on Gudrun's lantern), and, in the vision of the white whale swimming in the surface, the phallic being in beneficent majesty; and finally, the disastrous consequences of attempting to suppress and destroy 'the dragon of the primary self, the sensual psyche' (as Lawrence writes, in the Hawthorne essay).

The last essay is concerned with the solution of the problem. For all his praise of Whitman's 'supreme spiritual

consciousness' Lawrence opposes the celebration of the
spirit of unison,

> the motion of merging [which] becomes at last a vice,
> a nasty degeneration, as when tissue breaks down into
> a mucous slime. There must be the sharp retraction from
> [surely 'to'?] isolation, following the expansion into
> unification, otherwise the integral being is overstrained
> and will break . . . (p. 259)

Whitman's merging involves self-sacrifice,

> the ecstasy of *giving himself*, and of being taken . . .
> He knows nothing of the other sacrament, the sacrament
> in pride, where the communicant envelops the victim and
> host in a flame of ecstatic consuming, sensual gratificat-
> tion, and triumph. (p. 260)

This sounds much like the savage cannibalism that Lawrence excused, as religious, in his first Melville essay; sensual
pride involves some cruelty and sacrifice of others, it would
seem. Lawrence then concludes by taking up the theme of
common male activity : when

> man acts womanless it is no longer a question of race
> continuance. It is a question of sheer, ultimate being, the
> perfection of life, nearest to death . . . And the polarity
> is between man and man (p. 260)

as the plant in Whitman's poem 'Calamus' produces 'without the intervention of woman, the female . . . It is the
cohering principle of final *unison* in creative activity'. That
Lawrence is aware that he means homosexual love is clear
when he declares that he does not wish to '*épater les
bourgeois*' :

> The relation is a relation between fearless, honourable
> self-responsible men, a balance in perfect polarity. (p.
> 261)

The love between men has been purged of its unacceptable
'savage' elements, and made morally respectable; the relation
with woman is not denied, but firmly put in its place.

> True marriage is eternal; in it we have our consumma-
> tion and our being. But the final consummation lies in
> that which is beyond marriage . . . then, at last we shall
> know a starry maturity. (p. 264)

So, in these essays, Lawrence works out his problems and fears. He cannot endure in the civilized world of women and the masses, where he does not feel pre-eminent, but only relative, and therefore inadequate. He needs to assert himself, and his repressed sensual being, without becoming isolated from normality by his 'unnatural' tendencies. The hope is that 'self-knowledge' will bring the power to produce integrated being, that the repressed being will become dominant, and that he will find community in a purged male love and common activity in a new world.

However, this 'ideal' solution was only a fantasy, and the repressed being was soon insurgent again, appearing in demonic criminal or unnatural guises, and taking its revenge on the opposing 'white' forces. In the stories of the time, such as 'The Fox' and 'The Captain's Doll', the 'blocking' women are killed off. In *Movements in European History* (finished by January 1919) and in *Fantasia of the Unconscious* he celebrates the savage phallic-paternal tree of life that demands submission and sacrifice. In the history book he celebrates a demonic outsider, Attila the Hun, the 'scourge of God', who was eventually destroyed by his sexual passion, marrying a fair princess and dying in a blood-soaked bed.

This demonic outsider appears again in an essay from the autumn of 1920, 'America, Listen to Your Own':

> That which was abhorrent to the Pilgrim Fathers and to the Spaniards, that which was called the Devil, the black Demon of savage America, this great aboriginal spirit the Americans must recognize again, recognize and embrace. The devil and anathema of our forefathers hides the Godhead which we seek. (*Phoenix*, p. 90)

For a while, Lawrence sought to overwhelm his sense of being a 'furtive' and 'slinking' outsider, leading only as a 'wizard rat' might lead, by giving the reins, if only in imagination, to the savage and loveless sensual being repressed and ignored by the world of civilization and women. The consequences of this are the concern of *The Lost Girl*, begun before the war under the title *The Insurrection of Miss Houghton* as a counterblast to Arnold Bennett's *Anna of the Five Towns*, discontinued during the war, and rewritten in the period February to May, 1920.

The heroine, Alvina Houghton, was probably first

105

thought of fairly simply as a young woman brought up as a 'nice girl' who gradually discovers in herself a passional being unsatisfied by provincial ethical values; however, this self turns out to be a perverse one, that finds satisfaction in submission. Her instincts are barbaric, opposed to Christian morality: she has a sardonic, derisive attitude, ' a look of old knowledge' that can give her face 'a gargoyle look'.

Her first suitor is an Australian, from 'down under', a dark demonic sensuous figure, with 'cruel, compact teeth'. She does not 'love' him in any sense that her society would appreciate, rather he excites her in a perverse sexuality. 'She felt him an outsider, an inferior', but when with him

> found herself in a night where the little man loomed large, terribly potent, potent and magical, while Miss Frost [her nurse-governess] had dwindled to nothingness. (II)

Miss Frost's sterile respectability is an obstruction to her taste for *fleurs du mal*.

> It was time now for Miss Frost to die. It was time for that perfected flower to be gathered to immortality. A lovely *immortel*. But an obstruction to other, purple and carmine blossoms which were in bud on the stem . . . Black, purple and red anemones were due, real Adonis blood, and strange individual orchids, spotted and fantastic. (III)

Alvina's search for suppressed underworld experience leads her to a visit to a coal-mine: her response is reminiscent of Gudrun's, to Beldover. The coal-miner seems 'not human' and

> there was a thickness in the air, a sense of dark, fluid presence in the thick atmosphere, the dark, fluid viscous voice of the collier making a broad-vowelled, clapping sound in her ear. He seemed to linger near her as if he knew—as if he knew—what? Something forever unknowable and inadmissible . . . knowledge humiliated, subjected, but ponderous and inevitable. (IV)

The surface, civilized world seems insubstantial as a bubble, and she imagines the eruption of this buried underworld force

of darkness which had no master and no control . . .
it would be simply disastrous, because it had no master.
There was no dark master in the world. The puerile
world went on crying out for a new Jesus, another
saviour from the sky, another heavenly superman. When
what was wanted was a Dark Master from the underworld. (IV)

Here in Alvina is Lawrence's fearful desire for demonic
male sexuality. Alvina then works in her father's little
theatre, where she becomes involved with a fantastic group
of 'Red Indian' mime artists, the Natcha-Kee-Tawaras, who
provide a (rather absurd) glimpse of barbaric splendour
and quasi-religious ritual. Here she meets her demon lover,
Cicio, the loutish, sensual Italian who is to be Dis to her
Persephone. Though she fears he may be simply 'stupid
and bestial', yet she sees in his features

a certain *finesse* . . . refined through ages of forgotten
culture . . . the clean modelling of his dark, other-world
face . . . decided her—for it sent the deep spasm across
her. (IX)

Cicio soon establishes a wordless sexual dominance over
her, like death; when she first submits to him, it is an
annihilation :

. . . the spell was on her of his darkness and unfathomed
handsomness. And he killed her. He simply took her and
assassinated her. How she suffered no one can tell. Yet
all the time, his lustrous dark beauty, unbearable. (IX)

With her dark Italian she is 'beyond the pale' of normality,
where

. . . life was not her life. It was as if she had fallen from
her own world on to another, darker star, where meanings were all changed . . . In all the passion of her lover
she had found a loneliness, beautiful, cool, like a
shadow . . . (X)

After a separation, an almost last-ditch attempt by Alvina
to reconcile herself with normality, the 'unintelligent
forces' of nature (as one of Lawrence's characters calls
them) return in Cicio, who takes her again, and marries her.

There was no wonderful intimacy of speech, such as she
had always imagined, and always craved for . . . His love

did not stimulate or excite her. It extinguished her. She had to be the quiescent, obscure woman . . . under all her questionings she felt well; a nonchalance deep as sleep, a passivity and indifference so dark and sweet she felt it must be evil. Evil! She was evil. And yet she had **no power to be otherwise. (XIII)**

As for Cicio, 'now something unfolded in him, he was a potent glamorous presence, people turned to watch him'. In him is seen now what Lawrence felt man (especially himself) could be, if women were completely subordinate. But the central experience is Alvina's : through her Lawrence explores the consequences of self-abandonment to forbidden male sexuality. The Italy Cicio takes her to is no easy, sun-drenched world, but terrifyingly cold : for the civilized person to go back to the primitive is to release inhuman horrors.

She seemed to feel in the air strange Furies, Lemures, things that had haunted her with their tomb-frenzied vindictiveness since she was a child and had pored over the illustrated Classical Dictionary. Black and cruel presences were in the under-air. They were furtive and slinking. They bewitched you with loveliness, and lurked with fangs to hurt you afterwards. There it was : the fangs sheathed in beauty : the beauty first, and then, horribly, inevitably the fangs. (XV)

The title of this much underrated novel is not wholly ironic. In Alvina Lawrence lives-out the consequences of **abandonment to 'furtive pride and slinking singleness'** : unnaturalness and dehumanization. The obliteration of civilized consciousness is too high a price for the release from a divided self.

Certainly Lawrence dared not make the attempt by himself, in the present ordering of society : the results of such a mode of existence were only too apparent in the person of Maurice Magnus, whom he had met in Florence (and who figured in *The Lost Girl* as Mr. May).

In his first days in Italy, in Winter 1919–20, Lawrence not only felt very isolated (he was at first without Frieda) but, in the English colony, in Florence, found himself in an *ambience* of parasitic bohemianism and homosexuality (recreated in *Aaron's Rod*). Here he met Magnus, and in this cosmopolitan *poseur*, bisexual dandy, and parasitic con-man he found a curious affinity, an affinity with that element in himself portrayed in Loerke. While he found much to loathe in Magnus, yet he recognized their common condition as perverse outsiders, and respected in him 'the terrified courage of the isolated spirit' exploring 'the boundaries of human experience'.

Lawrence's 'Introduction to *Memoirs of the Foreign Legion* by M[aurice] M[agnus][2] (written in January 1922, but based on experiences of 1919–20) is a brilliant and too little-known work, that ranges from painful comedy to hysteria and elegy, from fine travel-writing to keen insight.

After the light comedy of the opening, where Lawrence recounts how he met Magnus with Norman Douglas in Florence, and briefly and with uncertain disapproval shared in their bohemian life, Magnus invites Lawrence (but not Frieda—he himself is separated from his wife, and does not care for women) to visit him at the monastery of Monte Casino, where he is staying (and which he claims, preposterously, to intend joining).

Magnus receives him almost wooingly in the ice-cold monastery, set high above 'the gulf where the world's valley was' (the scheme dating back to *Twilight in Italy* reappears : the cold mountain of unnatural isolation, and the hot crowded valley of life); it is so cold that, to make their tour of the monastery, Magnus lends Lawrence his enormous expensive overcoat, which is—and how life accords with Lawrence's private symbology!—'lined with black sealskin, and having a collar of silky black sealskin'. So the extraordinary couple make their tour, returning to Magnus's room; there Magnus shows Lawrence a photograph of 'a lovely lady' (the hostility in the phrase appears in the later story of that title) who, Lawrence tells him, looks 'a bit cheap, trivial'; unfortunately, it is Magnus's mother.

The morning after, looking out, Lawrence is overcome with yearning for the unattainable religious intensity of the past.

I looked down on the farm cluster and the brown fields and the sere oaks of the hill-crown, and the rocks and bushes savagely bordering it round. And the poignant grip of the past, the grandiose violent past of the Middle

Ages, when blood was strong and unquenched and life was flamboyant with splendours and horrible miseries, took hold of me till I could hardly bear it. It was really agony to me to be in the monastery and to see . . . all that lingering nonchalance and wildness of the Middle Ages, and yet to know that I was myself, child of the present. It was so strange from M-'s window to look down on the plain . . . To see the trains stop in the station and tiny people swarming like flies! . . . this was almost a violation to my soul, made almost a wound. (pp. 318–9)

Savage bushes, mountain-top, monastery, and Magnus all reveal this viewpoint as sterile and perverse self-assertion and withdrawal. On their morning walk Lawrence sees the negative aspect of this regressive mode, that involves the brutalization of the peasants outside. Magnus, whose views parody Lawrence's, approves of the isolated 'aristocratic' mode, but Lawrence realizes that, bitter as modern life may be,

here on the mountain-top was worst: the past, the poignancy of the not-quite-dead past . . . 'I think one's got to go through with the life down there—get somehow beyond it. One can't go back,' I said to him. (p.325)

Heartbroken at this self-denial (even though of a mode of being associated with Magnus) he leaves, the steamer that carries him away seeming 'to be making its way away from the old world, that had come to an end in me'.

However, he has not seen the last of Magnus, who turns up again at Lawrence's home, demanding help and money. The next section is filled with the painful comedy of the confrontation of Magnus's outrageous effrontery, parasitism, and pathetic pride with Lawrence's scrupulousness and lower-middle-class carefulness with money. Eventually Magnus's demanding submissiveness seems an encroachment, a threat (like 'the beggar-woman love . . . demanding more of me, yet more of me', of the early poem 'End Of Another Home Holiday'), and Lawrence refuses any more help: Magnus must be responsible for himself. Lawrence outlines Magnus's further brief career of cheeky parasitism and fraud before, eventually cornered by the police on the barren island of Malta, he commits suicide.

His death-note is characteristic: 'I want to be buried first class, my wife will pay'.

Lawrence is filled with guilt at having said, in effect, 'yes, he must die if he cannot find his own way', but also insists on the rightness of this judgment. Magnus was a Judas betraying everyone's trust (but Lilly, in *Aaron's Rod*, says: 'A Jesus makes a Judas inevitable. A man should remain himself, not try to spread himself over humanity. He should pivot himself on his own pride.') Yet Lawrence also commends his perverse integrity as a

> courageous isolated little devil, facing his risks, and like a good rat, *determined* not to be trapped . . . He went through vile experiences: he looked them in the face, braved them through, and kept his manhood in spite of them. For manhood is a strange quality, to be found in human rats [like Loerke] as well as in hot-blooded men. M carried the human consciousness through circumstances which would have been too much for me. (p. 357)

Lawrence implicitly identifies himself with Magnus, and his 'fear of his own self and its consequences' with the recent inhuman mechanical war (in his symbolism, the struggle against suppression, and 'inhuman' homosexual passions) against which he rages hysterically.

The dehumanizing influences in humanity can only be conquered by understanding them.

> This is true of all the great terrors and agonies and anguishes of life: sex, and war, and even crime . . . it is the great command *Know Thyself*. We've got to *know* what sex is, let the sentimentalists wiggle as they like . . . We've got to know the greatest, and most shattering human passions, let the puritans squeal as they like for screens. And we've got to know humanity's criminal tendency, look straight at humanity's deeds of crime against the soul . . . Knowledge, true knowledge, is like vaccination. It prevents the continuing of ghastly moral disease. (p. 358)

So Lawrence confronts himself in Magnus, who like Loerke, Poe, Dana and Alvina Houghton, has ventured on his behalf where he dared not go, and accords Magnus a generous elegiac farewell as a self-destroyed hero of the human spirit. Like Birkin after Gerald's suicide, Lawrence mourns, and goes on (in the words he applied to Magnus) 'a strange, quaking little star'.

Though he, of course, was not alone, with Frieda to support him; yet he felt very solitary and exposed, desperate for new identity and fulfilment. The desperation appears in several works of the time, both fiction and non-fiction (the distinction is not very meaningful: all are 'thought-adventures'—as he described Kangaroo—where conventional forms of feeling and expression are to be exploded by volcanic energy). So the essay 'David'[3] may be set with the novel Aaron's Rod (especially perhaps Chapter 16).

The essay is concerned with Michelangelo's statue of David in Florence (with which David Lawrence identified himself). Here is the opposed duality of the fire of intense male individuality and the water of submergence in the world of woman and the amorphous masses. By day the rain-water seems to drench and extinguish the city, but at night the river howls with threatening cat-like passion. In the midst is the corpse-white sensitive figure of David, not altogether quenched but tensely awaiting renewal in the miraculous annual orgasm on New Year's Eve that popular myth accords him. He is the embodiment of Florence (the city of the flower of manhood), the lily, 'the flower of adolescence, of incipient sexuality'.

> Too naked, too exposed . . . half self-conscious all the time . . . stripped so bare, the very kernel of youth. Stripped even to the adolescent orgasm of New Year's night—at midwinter. Unbearable.

A favourite image, of the nut fallen open and exposed to the fearful possibilities of new life, is implicit in this dream-like vision of self-exposure in the crucifixion of sexuality (an image found in the 'Tortoise' poems of about this time). As a figure of threatened sexuality, David is the 'Dionysus and Christ of Florence' filled with male fire that the maternal waters almost quenched. David, as Dionysus, is the son of Semele, who was destroyed by the divine sexual power of Zeus.

> Semele, scarred with lightning, gave birth prematurely to her child. The Cinquecento. Too fierce a mating, too fiery and potent a sire. The child was sewn again into the loins of the lightning. So the brief fire-brand. It was fire

over-whelming, over-weening, briefly married to the dew,
that begot this child. The South to the North. Married!
The child, the fire-dew, Iacchus, David.

In the lightning-scar, Lawrence sees male sexuality as
frighteningly powerful; his own parentage is seen almost
as a mis-mating between divine and human; his mother has
pushed him too early into conscious being, so that he has
to return into the phallic body of the father, which provides a new cosmic womb, the security and ease of identification with the potent male.

Though adolescence may be the time of sexual crucifixion, it is also a brief period of poise, before the fall—
that is, in Lawrence's historical myth, the Cinquecento.
Three art-works figure the Fall: David, poised on the brink
of sexuality, Botticelli's Venus on her scallop-shell (born
of the white foam of her divine father's castration), and
John the Baptist, head separated from body because of
woman.

> Fire and dew one moment proportionate, immediately
> falling into disproportion . . . [Then comes the modern
> world], morality, chastity . . . equality, democracy, the
> masses, like drops of water in one sea, overwhelming
> all outstanding loveliness of the individual soul.'

This flood has prevented the full growth of the bud (the
immature phallus and being), but David, still unquenched,
will one day complete his development and receive recognition. 'One day he reaps his mates . . .' (not female, but male
companions) to achieve 'the pride of the fulfilled self . . .
Not the frail lily . . . But the full tree of life in blossom' of
which Lilly speaks at the end of Aaron's Rod: the essay
provides an excellent introduction to the novel.

In Aaron's Rod (a novel overrated by Middleton Murry,
and underrated by most other critics) Lawrence is split
into two characters: Lilly, whose name identifies him with
'spontaneous' transcendent male power, and Aaron, who
synthesizes manhood and art in his phallic flute, and who
as ex-working-class artist and husband seeks to avoid psychological and financial parasitism on his wife and society,
to achieve independence and maturity in the world of men.

Aaron is incapable of melting into self-forgetful sensual
bonhomie, held back by his 'strained, unacknowledged

opposition to his surroundings, a hard core of irrational, exhausting withholding of himself'; in argument with the Indian doctor in the pub, the thought of large numbers of independent, self-responsible people (in an independent India) seems a threat to his own shaky self-confidence. A few night later he retreats to the dark night outside his home, whence the human domestic world of wife and children seems threatening and claustrophobic to the solitary outsider, driving him to run away.

In London he is seduced by one of the arty-literary set who have taken him up, which induces extreme psychosomatic illness. From this he is rescued by Lilly, who restores him in a ritual rubbing and anointing (a variation of the 'bath of life' of *The White Peacock*, 'Odour of Chrysanthemums' and *The Plumed Serpent*). On his recovery, Aaron and motherly little Lilly unite in mutually consoling criticism of marriage, and women who possess and disposses their men.

> The man's spirit has gone out of the world . . . marriage wants readjusting—or extending—to get men on their own legs once more . . . (IX)

Men must 'stick together', they agree. An extended interruption by a visiting officer-friend of Lilly's about the horrors of the war allegorizes the obsessive agonizing over sexual conflicts that must be left behind, so that the new mode of being may be achieved.

In the ensuing essentially internal dialogue Aaron, as realist-principle, criticizes Lilly the idealist who expresses a theory of self-possession, imaging it as a Nirvana,

> to be quite alone, and possess your own soul in isolation —and at the same time, to be perfectly *with* someone else. (X)

Aaron acutely derides this as being like sitting 'on a mountain top, back to back with somebody else, like a couple of idols'—Lilly is even, he says, his own 'idol on the mountain top, worshipping yourself'. Such criticism is unacceptable, and Lilly drives him away.

Having refused submission, Aaron returns home to attempt reconciliation, only to find his wife, unhumbled, accusing him of being 'too weak to love a woman and give her what she wants : too weak. Unmanly and cowardly, he runs away.' Impotence, whether physical or emotional, is indicated: he will not remain as an unsatisfied sexual tool, but runs away again to the characteristic Lawrentian communion with nature.

> To be alone, to be oneself, not to be driven or violated into something which is not oneself, surely it is better than anything . . . As for future unions, too soon to think about it. Let there be clean and pure division first, perfected singleness. (XI)

Singleness here is more like regression; having chosen singleness, Aaron moves to a new world, to Italy (tracing Lawrence's steps in the winter of 1919–20). There, at the home of a rich patron, Sir William Franks, he defends his chosen course of spontaneous action and trust in providence, while Sir William indicates the difficulties of independence, and the danger of parasitism. Aaron escapes into the town, which is dominated by 'the tiger-like Alps. Tigers prowling between the north and the south'. This imagery suggests returning self-assertion, but the resurgence of suppressed and feared passions is implicit in Lady Franks's dream (displaced from Aaron) of mob revolution.

Aaron-Lawrence now relives the fight with himself and his wife. She seems to see his fulfilment in service of herself, but he will neither submit nor give himself to her, in spite of their—only apparent—sexual intimacy. Aaron abandons the struggle, again choosing to be alone.

> His intrinsic and central aloneness was the very centre of his being. Break it, and he broke his being. (XIII)

The old conception of self and of reality disappears, and a new 'underworld' is revealed.

> . . . the accepted idea of himself cracked and rolled aside like a broken chestnut-burr, the mask split and shattered, he was at last quiet and free. He had dreaded exposure: and behold, we cannot be exposed, for we are invisible [like Wells's *Invisible Man*, to which Lawrence refers]. We cannot be exposed to the looks of others, for our very being is night-lustrous and invisible. (XIII)

Man must not give away this newly discovered self, in love, but remain in loneliness, which is rapidly redefined as singleness, and so find fulfilment: the lily reappears as an image of such 'life-rooted, life-central' singleness, untroubled by anxiety, even about love. Having determined on this, Aaron can even contemplate sexual relations, of a more passionate kind than Lilly's ideal, where one might be

> happily alone in all the wonders of communion, swept up on the winds, but never swept away from one's very self ... like Whitman's Dalliance of Eagles. (XIII)

So Aaron moves on to Milan, where he actually sees Lady Franks's allegorical rebellious mob. Here is male force, inhuman, demon-looking and vicious; out of this mass springs a youth, who is watched admiringly while he climbs up a building to snatch a flag in 'one unending wiggling movement' like a lizard (a smaller version of Lawrence's dragon of 'the fluid, rapid, invincible, even clairvoyant potency that can surge through the whole body and spirit of a man', in *Apocalypse*); when the police, the forces of conventional order, return, the youth is left exposed, alone and deflated. Likewise in Florence, the statue of adolescent David is contrasted with the statues of the 'big lumpy Bandinelli men'. The desire is to assert and be recognized by the male, the fear is of isolation and inadequacy. Aaron senses in Florence and in himself 'the end of the old world and the beginning of the new' and contemplates the manly Florentine men,

> red lilies ... Flowers with good roots in the mud and muck, as should be: and fearless blossoms in the air, like the cathedral and the tower and the David; (XVI)

and in this male world, even the stripes on the tower are likened to the stripes on the tiger-lily, by Lilly, who now reappears.

Lilly is still arguing for an easy, indifferent isolation, but Aaron still has to make one last attempt at relations with a woman. In his affair with the Marchese's wife, he dominates her, and with the aid of his phallic flute releases her from inhibition. The Marchesa is slightly frightening to him, her full, mature figure evoking the Magna Mater, her cosmetics the Scarlet Woman; though he dominates her at first, so that she becomes like a child, her dependence comes to seem a threat. Her sexual demands make him feel used, the God who is sacrificed, torn apart by sexuality, and once again he withdraws from involvement with women.

He returns to Lilly, who in a rather tiresome café-argument is proposing a fascistic system of slavery, effacing the multitude's independence in subordination to a great leader (the scheme proposed by Lawrence in *Fantasia of the Unconscious*, where he was to be such a leader). The discussion is interrupted by a bomb-explosion that destroys Aaron's flute: self-assertion, whether sexual or artistic, must be abandoned. Lilly's dream of the sticks in the shallows striking his exposed limb allegorizes the harm done to his phallic nature by women; when he returns to the 'deep, unfathomable' waters where the fish swim (embodiments of sensual being, that appear in 'The Captain's Doll' and 'The Flying Fish') he is at ease in the womb of unconscious being.

The parent will be Lilly; together they experience quiet, almost foetal centrality in the Italian countryside, 'not passivity, but alert enjoyment of being central, life-central in one's own little circumambient world', before the concluding dialogue. Lilly insists that Aaron must abandon attempts to affect, or be affected by, other people, but concentrate on developing his unique self, his 'own Tree of Life, roots and limbs and trunk'. This will be achieved by developing his inherent power, 'a vast dark source of life and strength', which will give him true being and liberty, both in releasing it in himself, and in serving and submitting to more 'powerful', more heroic men.

Then Aaron looked up into Lilly's face. It was dark and remote-seeming. It was like a Byzantine eikon at the moment.
'And whom shall I submit to?' he said.
'Your soul will tell you,' replied the other. (XXI)

The novel traces a progress from jealous resentment of, and escape from, woman as life-creator and sexual being, to a state of frail isolation and of being able to 'stand up for oneself'; however, this cannot endure, and there is a regression to perverseness and submergence in stronger male power. Singleness appears as inhibition, as self-responsibility, as loneliness, and as a quasi-foetal security in a greater male, when Semele's child returns to the thigh of his divine father.

This unhealthy attitude is not the whole truth about Lawrence's state at this time. While writing *Aaron's Rod*, he went to Sardinia, and in *Sea and Sardinia* he appears, not as a Byzantine eikon, but as a rather wistful married man in search of spontaneous sensual life and precivilized male community—rather like Aaron.

The move is not only a quest, but also a flight—from what is embodied in Mount Etna : the deadly Magna Mater arousing and frustrating desires, creating intense unnatural and dehumanizing passions.

Ah, what a mistress, this Etna! with her strange winds prowling round her like Circe's panthers . . . her strange, remote **exhalations [the breath of the sensual under-world** which Lawrence had discovered in himself]. She makes men mad. Such terrible vibrations and beautiful electricity she throws about her, like a deadly net! [Wrestling with Gerald, Birkin had seemed to throw a net over him—an erotic imprisonment.] Nay, sometimes, verily, one can feel a new current of her demon magnetism seize one's living tissue and change the peaceful life of one's active cells . . . unless a man is very strong, she takes his soul away from him and leaves him not a beast, but an elemental creature, intelligent and soulless . . . like the Etna Sicilians [or the 'Sea-creature' Melville, or Maurice Magnus]. Intelligent daimons, and humanly, according to us, the most stupid people on earth. Ach, horror! How many men, how many races, has Etna put to flight? (I)

So, with Frieda 'the queen bee' (the nickname implies resentment), Lawrence sets off into the interior of Sardinia, seeking not frightening individual passion, but soothing communal being. What he finds however is a brutal and exhausted existence, and the only life is in his own lively observation and engaging personality. Male vitality is not found till the end of the book, at a puppet-show in Palermo. Here, in the all-male audience, and the medieval legend of the play, he finds the male energy he had sought,

the massive, brilliant, outflinging recklessness in the male soul, summed up in the sudden word: *Andiamo! Andiamo!* Let us go on . . . the splendid recklessness and passion that knows no precept and no schoolteacher, whose very molten spontaneity is its own guide (VIII).

(In *Fantasia*, he wrote '*Allons*, there is no road yet, but

118

we are all Aarons with rods of our own'). Even more significant is the account of the conquest of the play's wicked witch, a Magna Mater akin to the spirit of Etna:

> Hear her horrible female voice with its scraping yells of evil lustfulness. Yes, she fills me with horror. And I am staggered to find how I believe in her as *the* evil principle . . . this white, submerged *idea* of woman which rules from the deep of the unconscious. Behold, the reckless untameable male knights will do for it. As the statue goes up in flames—it is only paper over wires— the audience yells! And yells again. And would God the symbolic act were really achieved. It is only little boys who yell. Men merely smile at the trick. They know well enough the white image endures. (VIII)

In reality, Lawrence admits, the male 'unconscious' being cannot overcome the 'female' spirit of frustration and self-division. Whatever his fantasies of male power and of unconscious 'blood-being' in a cosmic womb, there seemed to be no 'way of freedom' that he dared take. Instead he had to resign himself to the spirit that concludes this book, of stoical acceptance of uncertain solitariness, confronting 'the objective world'.

The hopes expressed in *Women In Love*, of a 'proud singleness' the individual in harmony with himself and with the human community, could never be fulfilled by Lawrence in his life. Civilization was for him too deeply imbued with his mother's idealistic, frustrating values, while he could not bring himself to accept the implications of his own sexual uncertainty. Committed to struggle and doomed to frustration, he remained always 'half in love with easeful death'. Until gathered into communion with his dead parents, as in 'Blue Gentians', he felt he could only attain a lonely, insecure position on the outside of life, a 'quaking little star'.

NOTES

1. *The Symbolic Meaning*, ed. Armin Arnold, Centaur Press, 1962.
2. pp. 303–361, *Phoenix II*, ed. Warren Roberts and Harry T. Moore, Heinemann, 1968.
3. pp. 60–64, *Phoenix*, ed. E. D. McDonald, Heinemann, 1936.

ENNUI AND ENERGY IN 'ENGLAND, MY ENGLAND' *

Lawrence personally collected, and considerably rewrote, the ten 'true short stories', as he called them, that were to be published under the title *England, my England*. Fittingly, they are exclusively about English people in English settings, and were written, between about 1913 and 1921, at a time when Lawrence, like E. M. Forster, was perplexed by conflicting feelings about what being 'English' might mean.

A few weeks after the title-story first appeared in the *English Review* in 1915, its author expressed his foreboding in the phrase that Evelyn Waugh was also to adopt in 1928: 'I think there is no future for England: only a decline and fall'.[1] And in the midst of finally revising the stories at the end of 1921, he dismissed the country he was actually preparing to leave as 'a dead dog that died of a love disease like syphilis'.[2] Yet in 1915 he had proclaimed: 'And I am English, and my Englishness is my very vision':[3] and shortly after despatching the amended stories to his American publisher, he wrote:

> We are, have been for five centuries, the growing tip. Now we're going to fall. But you don't catch me going back on my whiteness and Englishness and myself. English in the teeth of all the world, even in the teeth of England.[4]

His concern, in the year of *The Waste Land* and *Ulysses*, was for 'the impulse to carry through':

> I really think that the most living clue of life is in us Englishmen in England, and the great mistake we make is in not uniting together in the strength of this

* By D. Kenneth M. Mackenzie, Open University.

real living clue—religious in the most vital sense . . . I
know now it is a shirking of the issue to look to Buddha
or the Hindu or to our own working men, for the impulse to carry through.[5]

Naturally, then, the stories explore, in a more or less
implicit and quintessential way, the substance of attitudes
that, expressed in the hastily explicit manner of letters,
may seem questionably bald. Read thus, they constitute
much more of a coherent sequence than a mere miscellany.

However, their corporate quality appears most obviously
in their being, on the face of it at least, a series of studies
in 'the relation between men and women':

After all, it is *the* problem of today, the establishment
of a new relation, or the readjustment of the old one, between men and women.[6]

So the ten stories treat, in turn, ten stock situations:
marital breakdown and virtual separation; the philanderer;
'connubial absorption'; seduction; 'the other woman'; the
'marriage of convenience'; marital reconciliation; desertion
and the adulterer; true 'romantic' love; 'marrying beneath
one'. In effect, however, these stereotypes are transformed,
their transformation depending ultimately upon a fresh
and sharply realistic sense of the actual human qualities
of the people into whom the author, for better or worse,
had been born.

But beyond and through even that, the stories explore, or
so it gradually becomes clear, a more abstract concern. A
clue to its scope is the word '*ennui*', used more than once,
italicized or not. The stories repeatedly reflect, in a sensitively exploratory way, upon forms of that very modern
malaise, diagnosed by Baudelaire and Matthew Arnold in
1857,[7] given renewed currency in 1913 by Sickert's famous
painting on the theme, and obtrusive since as an element
in the work of, say, T. S. Eliot, Graham Greene, Philip Lar-
kin and Samuel Beckett.

Lawrence's stories, of course, do not tie themselves to a
word, but they do tend to relate states of depression or
disillusion to others of purposeful energy or vigour; and a
third possibility—some form of refined or highly civilized
sensitivity—may be introduced, modifying the first two
and being itself modified in turn. Not only that, but the

121

stories as arranged in the final volume, even hint at a certain progression : the first three close on a note of ironical disenchantment, the final tone of the last two is resolute or affirmative, while the enigmatic closes of *You Touched Me* or *Samson and Delilah* occur mid-way.

Such bare assertions of pattern or significance inevitably simplify in a schematic way, yet they may be a salutary counter to the habit critics have had of slighting Lawrence's short stories as somehow 'surplus' to his novels.[8] In fact, the adjective 'short' misleads : where the novels work by expansion and exhaustive development, the short story works by intensity and economy, by concentration upon a highly significant incident or phase—'brevity of presentment and a wealth of undeveloped implication'.[9] It can only, for instance, have been a deafness to 'wealth of implication' that led Anthony Beal to summarize the art of *Samson and Delilah, Fanny and Annie,* or *Tickets, Please!* as simply a matter of : '. . . a sort of rough justice being done in a world where not too much is expected of human nature.'[10]

Indeed, critical snobbery has gone from the start with other forms of disdain. When the English edition of the *England, My England* volume eventually appeared in 1924, the *Annual Register* recorded that 'the prolific Mr. D. H. Lawrence' dealt with 'an obsessed and cruel country not familiar to most Englishmen'; the gentlemanly *Morning Post* thought the work restricted to the action of 'sexual attraction and repulsion' upon 'a compound of stupidity and brutality';[11] and in J. C. Squire's *London Mercury*, the potential author of *The Good Companions* trounced Lawrence's 'type of mind' with all the vigour of his own—'He is the champion of those sensitive, rebellious and irrational spirits that want to have their cake and eat it.'[12]

'Cruelty' was to become a common charge,[13] though its source may well be the eye of the beholder. There is undoubtedly a disturbing quality in the stories, as in the *Book of Job, Hamlet, The Taming of the Shrew* or the *Miller's Tale*. Appropriately, one is called *Samson and Delilah*, another *The Primrose Path*,[14] and several have to do with such robust plebeians as kept alive the songs that Egbert, in *England, my England*, was supposed to collect. If *Monkey Nuts* or *Tickets, Please!* seems 'cruel' in spirit, then so must *The Trees they grow so High* or *The Gentleman Soldier*.

A hollow robustness, such as the blustering Daniel Sutton displays in *The Primrose Path*, might indeed prove brutal, if not 'cruel'. But even within the confined economy of the short story Lawrentian art maintains delicacy—a characteristically quick 'flow and recoil' of sympathy. Thus the stories are elusive experiences, neither obsessive nor partisan, as the *New York Times* was quick to suggest when they first appeared together, in America, in 1922:

> By far the greater number of these stories have a subtlety, an evasive quality underlying yet penetrating the texture of the exterior plot. Even when they seem simple, they are in truth intensely complex, composed of innumerable tiny fibres of thought and feeling and instinct, passing into one another by imperceptible degrees.[15]

Such 'evasive' subtlety certainly distinguishes the title-story, where elegiac and satirical notes rapidly interact:

> The timbered cottage, with its sloping, cloak-like roof was old and forgotten. It belonged to the old England of hamlets and yeomen. Lost all alone on the edge of the common, at the end of a wide, grassy, briar-entangled lane shaded with oak, it had never known the world of today ...

> He had not been brought up to come to grips with anything, and he thought it would do. Nay, he did not think there was anything else except little temporary contrivances possible, he who had such a passion for his old enduring cottage ...

And the nostalgic 'poetry of place' is itself more than simply 'Georgian' in quality. Its Arcadian note gives way to another recognition—one that, perhaps, Forster had intended to suggest by the pig-teeth embedded in the bark of the wych-elm at Howards End:

> One day Winifred heard the strangest scream from the flower-bed under the low window of the living-room; ah, the strangest scream, like the very soul of the dark past crying aloud. She ran out, and saw a long brown snake on the flower-bed, and in its flat mouth the one hind leg of a frog was striving to escape, and screaming its strange, tiny, bellowing scream.

That 'fibre of thought and feeling', stressing the 'fierce' seclusion or 'savage' peace of the 'snake-infested' commons, added when Lawrence completely rewrote the story in 1921, is itself in turn qualified—the 'spear of modern invention' has not 'passed through' Crockham. But its effect is to make Egbert's toying with his flower-garden seem all the more 'amateurish and sketchy', a town-bred romanticism. And the young couple are 'caught' in their cottage. Yet further, Crockham's undercurrents, in a profound irony, echo by anticipation the savagery of the war that eventually engulfs the drifting young gentleman; and Egbert's *malaise* consorts, like that of Leontes, with the lethal in nature:

'The sense of frustration and futility, like some slow, torpid snake, slowly bit right through his heart. Futility, futility, futility: the horrible marsh-poison went through his veins and killed him.'

Even the agony of little Joyce, lamed by the sickle her father left lying in the grass, echoes that of the tiny frog, its leg gripped in the snake's mouth.

Moreover, such poetic suggestions 'penetrating the texture of the exterior plot' gradually inform the ostensible 'story', the marriage, with a deeper meaning: the reader is induced to think about the needful continuity, in human living, between a crude energy and civilized refinement: 'Yes, civilization is a beautiful and fine thing if it only remains alive and does not become ennui.' [16]

The weakening of such continuity is implicit in the faltering marital relationship between the robust Winifred and the well-bred Egbert, the 'deeper' and the 'higher' beings:

She moved with a slow grace of energy like a blossoming, red-flowered bush in motion. She, too, seemed to come out of the old England, ruddy, strong, with a certain crude, passionate quiescence and a hawthorn robustness . . . Her hair was nut-brown and all in energetic curls and tendrils.

And it is in her father, the Northern businessman from whom they draw sustenance, that an elemental energy has evolved into the formidably human:

His blood was strong even to coarseness. But that only

made the home more vigorous, more robust and Christmassy.

Nor is he merely a Santa Claus; his powerful Catholic fatherliness fittingly echoes the Old Testament:

> Here was a man who had kept alive the old red flame of fatherhood, fatherhood that had even the right to sacrifice the child to God, like Isaac.

Such a comment was not, of course, fashionably modern, and the reviewer in the *Nation and Athenaeum* duly rebuked Lawrence,[17] but Marshall's 'primitive dominion' is in fact not a possessive domineering. He constitutes a 'pillar of assurance' which Egbert is perfectly free to rival and supplant. In himself somewhat drably stolid, the businessman represents a responsible use of power that his winsome son-in-law fastidiously evades in favour of a permissive liberty increasingly devoid of content—and ironically dependent.

Egbert's quality is certainly not simply weak. Not only is he an 'erect, supple symbol of life', a resolute Ishmael, opposing Winifred's Christ with his own 'Baal and Ashtaroth', but he is positively well-bred, pure of mob passion:

> The distinction between German and English was not for him the distinction between good and bad. It was the distinction between blue water-flowers and red or white bush-blossoms: just difference. The difference between the wild boar and the wild bear. And a man was good or bad according to his nature, not according to his nationality.

Yet to be thus 'fine' is in itself, alas, no more sufficient than the maternal Winifred's cruder robustness: the authority which Egbert abdicates is essential and inward, not merely a matter of work and money, and certainly not of 'sex':

> It was that he stood for nothing. If he had done something unsuccessfully, and *lost* what money they had! If he had but striven with something. Nay, even if he had been wicked, a waster, she would have been more free. She would have had something to resist, at least.

His consequent 'futility' comes out in his straying, quietistic responses to his wife and child after the 'accident'—due in any case to his amateurish negligence. Though his mild or ironical response is partly a reaction against Winifred's 'heavy, unleavened solicitude' he nevertheless lacks a decisive vitality which, in Godfrey Marshall, is at once an organic and a religious force :

> Just a blind acrid faith as sap is blind and acrid, and yet pushes on in growth and in faith. Perhaps he was unscrupulous, but only as a striving tree is unscrupulous, pressing its single way in a jungle of others.
> In the end, it is only this robust, sap-like faith which keeps man going.

Lawrence's expository commentary is as explicit there as it ever is, yet it is contemplative in spirit, not didactic, and certainly not censorious :

> You can't make the columbine flowers nod in January, nor make the cuckoo sing in England at Christmas. Why? It isn't his season. He doesn't want to. Nay, he *can't* want to.
> And there it was with Egbert . . .

That light tone, however, passes into a deeper resonance at the close. Egbert's death, in the 1921 version, is a profound spiritual abnegation, a wintry process of extinction, like the war itself :

> To break the clue, and mingle and commingle with the one darkness, without afterwards or forwards. Let the black sea of death itself solve the problem of futurity. Let the will of man break and give up.

Such suicidal *ennui* anticipates the post-war lethargy of the ex-soldier Krebs, in the 'devastating Oklahoma sketch' from Hemingway's *In Our Time* that Lawrence was to remark on in 1927 [18]—Egbert and Krebs are both 'through' with things, in the American sense, rejecting 'the living clue of life'.

So it is merely distracting to recall the actual Meynell or Lucas families, reducing the art of the tale to 'ill-natured gossip'.[19] Not only does the marital relationship between Winifred and Egbert parallel that of Will and Anna Brangwen in *The Rainbow*,[20] but the short story, unlike the novel, is also something of a political or historical parable, as its title's ironic allusion to Henley's stridently patriotic *Pro*

Rege Nostro must suggest: 'Bit by bit every establishment collapses, unless it is renewed or restored by living hands, all the while.'

It may well be apt to recall the mild Asquith and energetic Lloyd-George,[21] or, one might add, the then Prince of Wales and future 'uncrowned King'. The aspen-like Edgar epitomizes inclinations, common to his generation, that Edward Thomas had to struggle with in his own nature. Nor is Howards End sufficiently far removed from Crockham in spirit, though Kipling's Pook's Hill, or 'Habitation Enforced', is so much closer. Shortly after his story first appeared, Lawrence displayed his share in the national nostalgia:

> When I drive across this country, with autumn falling and rustling to pieces, I am so sad, for my country, for this great wave of civilization, 2000 years, which is now collapsing, that it is hard to live. So much beauty and pathos of old things passing away and no new things coming: this house of the Ottoline's—it is England—my God, it breaks my soul—their England, these shafted windows, the elm trees, the blue distances—the past, the great past, crumbling down . . . But better leave a quick of hope in the soul, than all the beauty that fills the eyes.[22]

The period ethos, the marital *malaise*, and the problems of a refined, or over-refined, civilization, intimately interconnect: Egbert is the English Prufrock. But Lawrence's tale also suggests, notably in Marshall, 'whose soul was quick with the instinct to power', much that is not merely Prufrockian. That Eliot's zany poetic monologue was to receive so much more attention, at least in academic and literary circles, is no doubt a tribute to Egbert's, or Prufrock's, lingering ghost.

Even so, that title-story has excessively over-shadowed its companions. The disturbingly potent *Blind Man*, for instance, has been given nothing like due attention—although Secker apparently had it in mind as the title-story for his English edition.[23]

Perhaps it disturbs one in some way as Egyptian and Assyrian sculpture disturbed Lawrence himself in 1914:

> Then the vision we're after, I don't know what it is—but it is something that contains awe and dread and sub-

mission. not pride or sensuous egotism and assertion. I
went to the British Museum—and I know, from the Egyptian and Assyrian sculpture—what we are after. We want
to realize the tremendous *non-human* quality of life—it
is wonderful. It is not the emotions, nor the personal feelings and attachments, that matter. These are all only
expressive, and expression has become mechanical. Behind in all are the tremendous unknown forces of life,
coming unseen and unperceived as out of the desert to
the Egyptians, and driving us, forcing us, destroying us
if we do not submit to be swept away.[24]

And four years later:

On Butterley platform—when I got out—everything
was lit up red—there was a man with dark brows, odd,
not a human being. I could write a story about him. He
made me think of Ashurbanipal. It seems to me, if one is
to do fiction now, one must cross the threshold of the
human people. I've not done 'The Fox' yet—but I've done
'The Blind Man'—the end queer and ironical. I realize
how many people are just rotten at the quick.[25]

Significantly, the blind man shares the qualities of Egyptian
or Assyrian carvings; there is his 'monolithic way of sitting
. . . erect and inscrutable, remote seeming':

And she turned to the impassive, silent figure of her
husband. He sat leaning back, with folded arms, and face
a little uptilted. His knees were straight and massive.

The blind man's presence, more than merely physical,
is akin to that of Ashurbanipal in the Nineveh reliefs—a
regal composure beyond 'thought and activity', over 'the
threshold of the human'. Lawrence's artistic vision here consorts with that of the young Henry Moore, reading 'the
whole of Lawrence' at the time,[26] and more generally with
the fertilizing extensions in European consciousness, indebted to 'primitive' art, that such artists were helping to
create.

However, Lawrence's prose is not sculptural, and certainly not 'monumental', but works through a fluent play
of 'evasive' suggestion:

She listened with all her ears, but could hear nothing
save the night, and the stirring of a horse.

'Maurice!' she called, softly and musically, though she was afraid. 'Maurice—are you there?'

Nothing came from the darkness. She knew the rain and wind blew in upon the horses, the hot animal life. Feeling it wrong, she entered the stable, and drew the lower half of the door shut, holding the upper part close. She did not stir, because she was aware of the presence of the dark hind-quarters of the horses, though she could not see them, and she was afraid. Something wild stirred in her heart . . .

The condition of blindness is essential to the story, in a way that no cinematic or televisual production could suggest. Here, as in the tale's opening sentences, it is Isabel who is 'blind' : she *feels* the danger to which she is exposing the animals; the sound of Maurice's voice 'seemed to touch her'. And, paradoxically, her husband's 'affliction' intensifies the 'dark, palpable joy' that the married couple share —he, certainly, can be nothing of a *voyeur*.

So their distinctive condition creates an exceptional intensity and gravity—'other people seemed to them both shallow, prattling, rather impertinent'—going beyond any simpler revelation of the manners of the blinded. The blindness is partly a new form of 'vision'; the *persona* of the blind man enacts what 'blood-prescience' may mean :

He seemed to know the presence of objects before he touched them. It was a pleasure to him to rock thus through a world of things, carried on the flood in a sort of blood-prescience. He did not think much or trouble much.

But the intensely married Pervins, as much as Egbert and Winifred, have their forms of *ennui*. The literary wife's composure is a cultivated 'mask' or 'air' :

Her nerves were hurting her. She looked automatically again at the high, uncurtained windows. In the last dusk she could just perceive outside a huge fir-tree swaying its boughs: it was as if she thought it rather than saw it. The rain came flying on the window panes. Ah, why had she no peace?

Her restiveness, which maternity may resolve, significantly increases as she moves from the house's 'regions of

129

repose and beauty' towards what, to her, is 'the animal grossness of the back'. Yet the shadowy barns and stables also seem areas of tranquillity where, like Tom Brangwen, the blind man is at least as 'at home' as within the civilized Grange itself.

Indeed, the Grange,²⁷ split between the educated Pervins and the farming Wernhams, unobtrusively symbolizes the dissociation of civilized refinement from 'blood-prescience' and essential labour—of, in short, Ursula from Tom Brangwen. That 'development' is a fact of history not confined to Granges: the hypertrophy of what had originally been a positive process of civilization has led to a two-way break in transmission—a gap that Maurice Pervin seeks, blindly, to bridge.

He, too, has bouts of 'arrest' when a sense of 'helpless desolation' dismays him and he craves 'some measure of control or surety'. He is an Egbert as much as an Ashurbanipal:

> He came of a good old country family—the Grange was not a very great distance from Oxford. He was passionate, sensitive, perhaps over-sensitive, wincing—a big fellow with heavy limbs and a forehead that flushed painfully. For his mind was slow, as if drugged by the strong provincial blood that beat in his veins. He was very sensitive to his own mental slowness, his feelings being quick and acute.

The merit of that sensitivity is felt in the tentative style of his conversation. His slow utterance is not vacuous, as is that of the bucolic farmhands bent on feeding, nor is it laconic in any ostentatiously 'tough' style. It suggests a radical composure: the blind man 'feels his way' in speech as in bodily movement, as though he moves from a centre:

> 'Maurice', she said, 'you're not wishing he wouldn't come, are you?'
> 'I couldn't quite say,' he answered. 'I feel myself rather on the *qui vive*.'

It is this degree of human delicacy that the opposed *persona* lacks. Bertie Reid—'a Scotsman of the intellectual type, quick, ironical, sentimental'—is, emotionally at least, 'not so very fine'. He gossips clannishly with Isabel, leaving the blind Maurice out of count; nor is he very resourceful when the isolated man seeks to take him into his confidence.

Moreover, Reid also has his deficiency, beyond manners—his inability 'ever to enter into close contact of any sort'. Significantly, it is his eyes that appeal to Isabel. He, one might say, can *only* see; his bodily presence is insignificant, whereas Maurice is not only sculpturally massive—his *hands* are 'intelligent'.

So the art induces the feeling that the Scots lawyer-and-littérateur's kind of 'thought and activity' suffices even less than that of the Pervins, for a fully satisfactory life. At one point, Isabel almost accepts Bertie's resigned 'I suppose we're all deficient somewhere'. Yet both the Pervins feel, in their sensitively inarticulate way, that there is 'something'—'. . . something strong and immediate. There's something strange in Maurice's presence—indefinable—but I couldn't do without it. I agree that it seems to put one's mind to sleep . . .'

The culminating scene, significantly set in the barn, has therefore a symbolic potency—'ritualistic' or 'baptismal', if one likes.[28] The blind man's sculptor's handling of Bertie may appear to break a conventional taboo, but at the deeper level of the tale's psychic drama it dramatizes contact, beyond 'thought and activity', with that 'something' which Maurice's presence, like that of Ashurbanipal, transmits. And through that contact, in his turn, the 'cancelled' man seeks poignantly to be 'included in the life–circle', reaching beyond the confines of his intense 'blood prescience' and 'connubial absorption'.

If anything is broken, it is the professional man's 'insane reserve'. The tale's final note may seem cruelly ironical—Maurice's elation seems ill-founded; the lawyer is 'like a mollusc whose shell is broken'. But such considered art-speech is not crudely scornful in the way of 'rotten at the quick', and a Lawrentian robustness might even turn such an end into a beginning :

> 'One has oneself a fixed conscious entity, a self which one has to smash. We are all like tortoises who have to smash their shells and creep forth tender and overvulnerable, but alive.' [29]

Maurice Pervin may lead one to Willie Nankervis, the husband in *Samson and Delilah*. Each has the presence of a Samson and the Cornish miner, too, has a 'mindless' quality, an 'alert, inquisitive, mindless curiosity' that goes with his potent physical presence 'veering along in a sense of mastery and of power in conflict'. 'Mindlessness', in Pervin or Nankervis or even in young Maryann, is not simply a matter of their not being intellectuals, but, positively, of their displaying an unassertive openness to experience—the equivalent of Keats's 'negative capability'.

Samson and Delilah concentrates on an energetically physical marital relationship—'the beauty of his head and his level drawn brows', her 'handsome flesh' and almost over-ripe Amazonian energy, 'bursting with life and vigour'. There is no fastidious distaste for such robust human qualities. Without glee or relish, Lawrence simply restores to literature appeals and satisfactions that had gone increasingly underground, and deteriorated there. Indeed, an 'energic' atmosphere is induced from the outset by the exhilarating imagery of movement, ocean, wind and stars, and the 'three-pulse flash of the lighthouse'. Moreover, the English story significantly reverses its Hebraic original: Lawrence's Samson, shorn of his strength by the female, is all the more roused to admire and win her over.

Yet the relationship is fully human : it is Nankervis's 'laconic truthfulness' that has power over his wife, and it is her 'fine pluck' that delights him. Further, as with Maurice Pervin, Nankervis's impressive presence also goes beyond the familiarly 'human'—'There was something impenetrable about him, like his eyes, which were as bright as agate.' Beside his contained manner and laconic speech his wife's indignation—'Be a man, and not worse than a brute of a German'—seems blustering claptrap.

Nevertheless, the violence of the 'police action' that her propaganda provokes appears necessary to her eventual submission. It is as if the prodigal husband's humiliating overthrow expiates his offence, satisfying some logic of life.

However, 'submission' is perhaps not sufficiently apt: Mrs. Nankervis still sits 'glowering', even if only into the fire. But the presence of that fire, repeatedly yet unobtrusively stressed, pervades the concluding scene, and its fascination is symbolic. Its warmth, set against the cold night outside, is more than merely external—'her heart beat fiery hot'. Nor is there, on Nankervis's part, any crudely domineering note. Whereas, in Lawrence's first version,[30] the wife 'shrank as if struck'—'Almost a groan of helpless,

desirous resentment came from her lips as he kissed her'—
in the final story, the husband is determined, yet gentle. He
touches his wife' tentatively', 'quietly'. The close is enigmatic, as of two potent natures suspended in an equipoise
of resistance and desire.

By contrast, the whole atmosphere and setting of *The
Horse Dealer's Daughter* is 'depressive', a metaphor for
ennui, as was Sickert's painting. The town clusters 'like
smouldering ash, a tower, a spire, a heap of low, raw,
extinct houses'; the dark weather and dreary landscape form
'a depression of callous wintry obscurity'. A sense of failure,
of foiled and coarsened living, is pervasive.

But the tale is creative, more like *Silas Marner* than like
A Burnt-out Case. Like Silas, both Mabel Pervin and Jack
Fergusson merely exist from day to day, 'mindless and persistent'. Fergusson, also an alien immigrant, similarly drugs
himself with work, while Mabel cherishes her mother's
gravestone much as the exiled Marner does his broken
water-jug—a nostalgic symbol of continuity with the life
of trust and love. And as with the entry of the infant Eppie,
Lawrence's story, originally entitled 'The Miracle', confers
a sense of the marvellous upon the moment when Fergusson first truly 'sees' Mabel, tending her mother's grave:

> . . . She seemed so intent and remote, it was like look-
> ing into another world. Some mystical element was
> touched in him. He slowed down as he walked, watching
> her as if spell-bound . . . It was portentous, her face. It
> seemed to mesmerise him.

But Jack and Mabel, unlike Silas and Eppie, are both
adults, and their mutual renaissance has a correspondingly
painful intensity. Mabel's suicidal *ennui* lacks even the
energy of despair, yet, 'by imperceptible degrees', Lawrence's prose modulates into a high, even exalted, passional
dignity:

> When she turned her face to him again, a faint delicate
> flush was glowing, and there was again dawning that ter-
> rible shining of joy in her eyes, which really terrified
> him, and yet which he now wanted to see, because he
> feared the look of doubt still more.
> 'You love me?' she said, rather faltering.
> 'Yes.' The word cost him a painful effort. Not because

it wasn't true. But because it was too newly true, the *saying* seemed to tear open again his newly-torn heart. And he hardly wanted it to be true, even now.

And when the tale finally restores the couple to a pitch of everyday concern there is no modernist deflation, but a sense of newly-achieved assurance and shy delicacy. The 'stupidity and brutality' of the opening scene has been transformed, like that of *Wuthering Heights*, by an energy of sympathetic passion which is not simply 'sexual'. The couple have become fully human, essentially civilized, redeemed from the condition of draught-horses.

Their story might well, of course, have been called *You Touched Me*, though the latter tale may seem contrastingly 'cruel' in the 'enforced' marriage of Matilda Rockley. In effect, however, *You Touched Me* revises James's *Washington Square*—Lawrence's sheltered spinsters, 'girt in' by walls and hedges, being also deprived, paradoxically by their very wealth and social status, of growth and development:

> They did not quite realize how they missed the shrieking, shouting lasses, whom they had known all their lives and disliked so much . . . In their quiet, melancholy way, the two girls were happy.

The challenge to such happiness comes from Hadrian, the adopted charity-boy charged with plebeian energy:

> He too had his courage, as a rat has indomitable courage in the end. Hadrian had some of the neatness, the reserve, the underground quality of the rat. But he had perhaps the ultimate courage, the most unquenchable courage of all.

In his lack of pathos or plaintive querulousness, he is neither an Oliver Twist nor a Jimmy Porter. He possesses what Egbert lacks. Nor have Lawrence's precedents obliged him, as Shakespeare's arguably did in *King Lear*, to push his upstart 'Edmund' into sheer villainy. Hadrian may be 'unscrupulous' by the Rockley sisters' standards but his refusal to be 'decent' is also a fidelity to his essential self, his innermost need to grow and develop: 'If you wake a man up, he can't go to sleep again because he's told to'. If, that is, Matilda is a somewhat plain Sleeping Beauty and Hadrian a low-born and charmless Prince Charming, then Hadrian

too is 'asleep' and it is Matilda that accidentally touches
him to life :

> But the soft, straying tenderness of her hand on his
> face startled something out of his soul. He was a charity
> boy, aloof and more or less at bay. The fragile exquisite-
> ness of her caress startled him most, revealed unknown
> things to him.

Nor is this new awareness that of the American stage
version with 'little silver Matilda' looking 'breathtakingly
lovely in a delicate, filmy, blue-green dress and a pair of
feather slippers.' [31]

> She was not beautiful, her nose was too large, her
> chin was too small, her neck was too thin. But her skin
> was clear and fine, she had a high-bred sensitiveness.
> This queer, brave, high-bred quality she shared with her
> father . . . And he wanted to possess himself of it. He
> wanted to make himself master of it.

Once again an elemental or 'primitive' energy seeks its
necessary complement in a 'soft delicacy'. Hadrian may
seem acquisitive but, when Emmie charges him with chasing Matilda for her money, the vulgarity turns out to be all
her own. Lawrence's tale not only asserts vigorous growth
('as a striving tree is unscrupulous') where *Washington
Square* resigns itself to a spinsterish fortitude, but it also
admits a more subtle young male :

> He wanted both the money and Matilda. But he told
> himself the two desires were separate, not one. He could
> not do with Matilda, *without* the money. But he did not
> want her *for* the money.

So Matilda's father. in his best Old Testament manner,
breaks the exclusive filial bond that Dr. Sloper's will bound
fast. Ted Rockley's apparent 'malevolence', below the level
of such 'human' feelings. is creative in effect. After all, he is
too old and painfully ill for niceties, and, if his behaviour
seems 'cruel' there is such a thing as being 'cruel in order
to be kind'.

Not that the story suggests any easy outcome. Matilda
holds aloof; Hadrian is 'nipped with fear'. Yet, unlike
Egbert, Hadrian seems fitted to succeed his formidable

father-in-law, and the ceremonious final scene, presided over by the dying old man, conveys a sense of reconciliation, as of a regal handing on or over. Certainly, kisses are symbolic pledges of harmony and forgiveness; any tone of the 'harshly victorious', of 'ruthless disregard' or 'brute will', is thereby ritually dissolved.[32]

Fanny and Annie, on the other hand, might seem to tilt the opposite way, towards the Victorian pathos of a woman of superior manners having to marry 'beneath her'—another loyal tribute, say, to the artist's mother. In fact, this story also summons up a robust 'sap-like faith' beyond mere manners.

For one thing, 'poor Fanny', with her 'nervous, overwrought laugh', is not simply pitiable, however serious her 'come-down'. She is thirty, and has had her other affairs. She knows her own mind, and does not pretend to be marrying for 'love'. She is even, her Aunt feels, 'a woman to be afraid of. So proud, so inwardly violent'.

Moreover, Harry Goodall, who mainly constitutes Fanny's 'doom', is not unpleasant: 'There was something of a mother's lad about him—something warm and playful and really sensitive.' He is even, in his foundryman's way, another Egbert:

He didn't care. He just didn't care. He had no initiative at all. He had no vices—no obvious ones. But he was just indifferent, spending as he went, and not caring. Yet he did not look happy. She remembered his face in the fireglow: something haunted, abstracted about it . . .

Fanny, in fact, has a conflict to resolve, a tension between her physical energies and her cultivated lady-like sense of Harry's 'commonness':

Because there was about him a physical attraction which she really hated, but which she could not escape from. He was the first man who had ever kissed her. And his kisses, even while she rebelled from them, had lived in her blood and sent roots down into her soul. After all this time she had come back to them. And her soul groaned, for she felt dragged down, dragged down to earth, as a bird which some dog has got down in the dust.

136

The note struck by those sentences, which are not in the original magazine version,[33] is emphasized by Lawrence:

> He had even a kind of assurance on his face as he looked down from the choir gallery at her: the assurance of a common man deliberately entrenched in his commonness . . . A certain winsomeness also about him. A certain physical winsomeness, and as if his flesh were new and lovely to touch. The thorn of desire rankled bitterly in her heart.

But what the story goes on to reveal is that the 'common' working-class *milieu* which the genteel Fanny thus re-enters does not consist solely of 'stupidity and brutality' —neither the harsh emptiness of *This Sporting Life* nor the cosy banality of *Coronation Street*. The comedy is Chaucerian in depth. If Mrs. Nixon is even more outrageously obstreperous—comically inverting Harry's anthem solo 'They that sow in tears shall reap in joy'— and certainly more 'cruel' than the Wife of Bath, the local minister is more than equal to the poor parson: 'He was a little simple, one of God's fools, perhaps, an odd bachelor soul, emotional, ugly, but very gentle.' His plangent chapel charitableness turns out to be quite free from prudish righteousness, and the story's ironical comedy, by avoiding all unction or flattery, makes his human grace (there is no hint of his blaming anyone) seem all the more poignantly fine.

The humane considerateness of which the community is thus capable also comes from the very source Fanny might least expect—the 'clannish' Goodalls. Harry's composure is distinct from complacency, the family gossip is fair-minded in tone, and even the crudely robust Mrs. Goodall—a subtle irony—defends their assailant. More crucially, the family brings no hint of pressure to bear on their prospective daughter-in-law: they are essentially civilized.

So Fanny's spontaneous decision to stay with them has the effect of resolving both the tale's and her own difficulties. The firmly decisive manner of her final announcement displaces her earlier sense of 'doom'. It is as if Mrs. Nixon's brutal revelation, like Ted Rockley's outrageous will, has precipitated a basic human reaction. At that stern level, Fanny not merely survives but seems, like a 'striving tree', to overgrow apparent obstacles. In her

137

feminine way, she draws upon such 'acrid sap' as flowed in Godfrey Marshall and receives 'the impulse to carry through'.

Indeed several of the tales implicitly question 'Victorian', or for that matter modern, sentiments about the truly feminine. They restore a robustly realistic sense of female qualities, such as had been admitted in folk song and anecdote, in Elizabethan Drama, by Chaucer (or Dunbar), and everywhere in Greek Drama and Mythology. Certainly, the mobbing of the womanizing 'Coddy' by the maenad conductresses in *Tickets, Please!* accords with 'How the maidens served Will Sommers for his sawcinesse' in Deloney's *Jack of Newbury*—though the modern tale dispenses with any gross Elizabethan coarseness.

However, Lawrence's story is more than a simple revelation of 'rough justice' or of the truth that women, too, may be violent on occasion. For one thing, its 'energic' prose disperses, as in *You Touched Me* or *Monkey Nuts*, a key modernist *ennui*: work, in this industrial-urban war-time scene, does not simply provoke pangs of 'alienation':

> . . . With a tram packed with howling colliers, roaring hymns downstairs and a sort of antiphony of obscenities upstairs, the lasses are perfectly at their ease. They pounce on the youths who try to evade their ticket-machine. They push off the men at the end of their distance. They are not going to be done in the eye—not they. They fear nobody—and everybody fears them.

Nor is this 'gusto' sentimentally indulgent—the conductresses are 'fearless young hussies'; Annie is 'peremptory, suspicious'; Lawrence's narrative tone is bantering.

The upshot of the story, moreover, is ironically complex. It entails not only the discomfiture of the philanderer, but of the girls themselves. Certainly the original ending in the *Strand* magazine, had simply suggested an unembarrassed satisfaction:

> The girls continued in silence to dress their hair and adjust their clothing, as if he had never existed.[34]

In the final version, however, they are 'anxious to be off' with 'mute stupified faces'. The story thus works 'evasively' in one's mind in a way beyond the elementary art of Deloney. It is as if the 'rough justice' has broken some obscure natural law.

Monkey Nuts might also be read simply as a 'cruel' account of a young woman's frustration. But the true centre of attention is Joe, the shy and callow young soldier at whom Miss Stokes sets her cap. In its undidactic bantering way, the tale is a study in male chastity, or of an initiation into manhood of the kind Conrad did not, perhaps could not, handle. The uncouth 'cruelty' of the 'softhearted' youth's final jeer at his temptress is an accident of his clumsy lack of *savoir-faire*. Neither he, nor Albert, is the callous male deliberately taking an offensive delight in humiliating the female. Nor does the tale suggest any such insane fear of women, deadly in its outcome, as is implicit in Hemingway's comparable tale of male initiation, *The Short Happy Life of Francis Macomber*.

Lawrence's Miss Stokes, then, is not a 'shrike' but she is 'offhand and masterful', more than capable of exchanging tit for tat with the seasoned corporal Albert. Her craving for the shy stripling therefore seems all the more unsuitable, though far from the sensational oddity of a Blanche Dubois. She eyes young Joe as though he were a delicacy whose 'slender succulent tenderness' she relishes.

Yet the young woman is not the object of blame or pity. Her tears dismay the corporal—clearly, if she is a siren, she 'can't help it'. The spirit in which the tale treats her forwardness is that of Albert's village-landlord: 'they be artful, the women'. The affectionately tolerant yet wary shrewdness implicit in that phrase's leisurely rhythm is such as the curt art-speech of Hemingway cannot convey. Beside the latter's English hunter, with his 'flat, blue, machine-gunner's eyes', Lawrence's corporal is richly humane, in the way of the prose that creates him:

. . . steady, decent and grave under all his "mischief"; for his mischief was only his laborious way of skirting his own ennui.

NOTES

1. Letter to Constance Garnett, 17th November, 1915. (*Collected Letters*, p. 383).
2. To S. S. Koteliansky, 10th November, 1921. (*Ibid.*, p. 673).
3. To Lady Cynthia Asquith, 21st October, 1915 (*Ibid.*, p. 371).
4. To Lady Cynthia Asquith, 30th April, 1922. (*Ibid.*, p. 702).
5. To Robert Pratt Barlow, 30th March, 1922. (*Ibid.*, p. 698).
6. To Edward Garnett, ? 18th April, 1913. (*Ibid.*, p. 200).
7. 'The predominance of thought, of reflection, in modern epochs is not without its penalties; in the unsound, in the over-tasked, in the over-sensitive, it has produced a state of feeling unknown to less enlightened but perhaps healthier epochs—the feeling of depression, the feeling of *ennui*. Depression and *ennui*; these are the characteristics stamped on how many of the representative works of modern times!' *On the Modern Element in Literature*, Inaugural Lecture, Oxford, 1857; first published in *Macmillan's Magazine*, February, 1869.
8. e.g. *The Dark Sun*, Graham Hough, (1956), p. 168. *D. H. Lawrence*, Anthony Beal (1961), p. 99. *D. H. Lawrence*, A Collection of Critical Essays, ed. Mark Spilka (1963), p. 11.
9. *D. H. Lawrence, Novelist*, F. R. Leavis (1955), p. 256.
10. Beal, op. cit., p..99.
11. *The Morning Post*, 8th February, 1924, p. 10.
12. *The London Mercury*, March 1924, pp. 546–548.
13. See *England, my England*, (1950), introduction Richard Aldington, pp. v, vi, viii. Hough, op. cit., p. 173. Beal, op. cit., p. 99. *Selected Tales*, D. H. Lawrence, ed. Ian Serraillier, (1963), introduction, p. x.
14. See *Hamlet*, Act I Sc. iii. ll. 49–51.
15. *New York Times Book Review*, November 19th, 1922, p. 14.
16. To Baroness von Richthofen. 28th February, 1922. (*Collected Letters*, pp. 694–5).
17. *The Nation and the Athenaeum*. 23rd February, 1924, p. 738.

18. See: *Phoenix*, ed. Edward McDonald (1936), p. 366.

19. Anthony West, *D. H. Lawrence*, 1966 (1st ed. 1950), p. 94.

20. See: Barbara Lucas, 'A propos of "England, my England" ' (*Twentieth Century*, March 1961).

21. See: 'A. J. P. Taylor and the "Rise of the People",' J. C. F. Littlewood, *Cambridge Quarterly*, Autumn, 1966, pp. 326–327.

22. To Lady Cynthia Asquith, ?9th November, 1915 (from Garsington Manor). (*Collected Letters*, p. 378).

23. To Martin Secker, 19th September, 1922 (*Letters of D. H. Lawrence*, ed. Huxley, p. 551).

24. To Gordon Campbell, 21st September, 1914. (*Collected Letters* p. 291).

25. To Katherine Mansfield, 21st November, 1918 (*Collected Letters*, p. 566). Ashurbanipal, King of Assyria, was represented on extensive reliefs from his palace at Nineveh, displayed in the British Museum, which Lawrence must have seen.

26. See: *Henry Moore on Sculpture*, ed. Philip James, 166 (1968 edition, p. 50).

27. The word originally meant a barn or granary.

28. 'Ritual Form in "The Blind Man",' Mark Spilka: in *D. H. Lawrence, A Collection of Critical Essays*, ed. Mark Spilka, 1963, pp. 112–116. 'D. H. Lawrence and the Short Story', Frank Amon: in *The Achievement of D. H. Lawrence*, ed. F. J. Hoffman and H. T. Moore, 1953.

29. To J. O. Meredith, 2nd November, 1915. (*Collected Letters*, pp. 373–4).

30. *The English Review*, March, 1917.

31. *You Touched Me. A Romantic Comedy in Three Acts*, Tennessee Williams and Donald Windham, New York, September, 1945. Act III, Scene 1.

32. Cf. R. P. Draper, *D. H. Lawrence* (New York, 1964), pp. 124–125; Hough, op. cit., pp. 173–174.

33. Cf. *Hutchinson's Magazine*, November, 1921, p. 465.

34. *Strand Magazine*, April, 1919, p. 293.

APHRODITE OF THE FOAM AND
THE LADYBIRD TALES *

". . . But the mode of our being is such that we can only
live and have our being whilst we are implicit in one of
the great dynamic modes. We *must* either love, or rule.
And once the love-mode changes, as change it must, for
we are worn out and becoming evil in its persistence,
then the other mode will take place in us. And there will
be profound, profound obedience in place of this love-
crying, obedience to the incalculable power-urge. And
men must submit to the greater soul in a man, for their
guidance: and women must submit to the positive
power-soul in man, for their being."

This pronouncement of Rawdon Lilly in *Aaron's Rod*
(1922) may serve as a gloss on the central issue of the three
tales published in 1923 in the volume called *The Ladybird*.
Despite their difference of milieu and mode, all three tales
are primarily concerned with the same theme, with the
necessity for the abandonment of romantic love as a basis
for relationship between the sexes and with its replacement by the woman's submission to the 'power-soul in
man'. *The Ladybird* tales, indeed, are best read in the light
of the novels of this period, particularly *The Plumed Serpent* (1926); for in this novel the conception of the new
relationship that is first adumbrated in *Aaron's Rod* is fully
developed, and Lawrence is explicit about the nature of the
submission demanded of the woman in the sex act,
whereas he is reserved on this matter in the tales. The
sexual submission of the woman in *The Plumed Serpent* is
total, involving, as it does, her voluntary forgoing of

* By H. M. Daleski, Hebrew University, Jerusalem.

orgasm. It is an extreme position, to which Lawrence had been led in reaction against the kind of assault on a man that is figured in Ursula Brangwen's ferocious 'annihilation' of Skrebensky in *The Rainbow*—an assault that the novelist had come to envisage as a concomitant of romantic love. It is a position, moreover, that he abandoned, for in *Lady Chatterley's Lover* (1928) relationship between a man and a woman is based not on power and submission but on a reciprocal tenderness, and Connie Chatterley achieves a less questionable form of sexual fulfilment with Mellors. *The Ladybird* tales, in other words, should be regarded as exploratory ventures in a large undertaking that was to lead, eventually, to *Lady Chatterley's Lover*. But Lawrence's assertion in these tales of a male dominance unwittingly suggests that the concomitants of the doctrine of power are as unfortunate as those of romantic love. *The Ladybird* is a most impressive volume, a testimony to Lawrence's remarkable power and range in the long story; but it seems to me that both 'The Ladybird' and 'The Fox' are seriously marred.

II

Lady Daphne in *The Ladybird* is introduced as having 'her whole will' fixed in 'her adoption of her mother's creed', fixed, that is, in a belief in loving humanity and in a 'determination that life should be gentle and good and benevolent'. But it is at once intimated that her adherence to such a creed is a perverse denial of her essential self, for she has 'a strong, reckless nature'—she is 'Artemis or Atalanta rather than Daphne'—and her eyes tell of 'a wild energy damned up inside her'. Such a fixing of the will in frustration of natural being is inevitably inimical to life, and Daphne moves, as it were, in death : her two brothers have been killed in the war, her baby has been born dead, and her appearance fills 'the heart with ashes'. She is, indeed, Proserpine—though in a sense different from that in which her husband, Major Basil Apsley, uses the name when he refers to her 'wonderful Proserpine fingers' and says that 'the spring comes' if she lifts her hands. Daphne, though given to life, is wedded to death, embodying in herself the deathliness of the creed of Love.

This deathliness is further projected in the marriage

143

of Daphne and Basil. When he comes back from the war, he is 'like death; like risen death', and 'a new icy note' in his voice goes 'through her veins like death'. We are meant to register, I think, that the death Basil carries in himself is not only the mark of his experiences in the war. 'A 'white-faced, spiritually intense' man, Basil maintains that, having been through the ordeal of the war, he has arrived at 'a higher state of consciousness, and therefore of life. And so, of course, at a higher plane of love'. It is the constant burden of Lawrence that, where life is viewed in terms of the achievement of a state of heightened mental consciousness, it is life as well as 'blood-consciousness' that is denied; and it follows that the love which is a correlative of such a state of consciousness is as sterile as the life with which it is equated. This, at all events, is what Basil's love for Daphne is shown to be. After his love-making she has 'to bear herself in torment', she feels 'weak and fretful', she '[aches] with nerves', and cannot eat; he in turn becomes 'ashy and somewhat acrid'. In Basil, we are to understand, the consciousness of loving has usurped the body of love, leaving him ineffectually prostrate before Daphne:

He suddenly knelt at her feet, and kissed the toe of her slipper, and kissed the instep, and kissed the ankle in the thin, black stocking.

'I knew,' he said in a muffled voice. 'I knew you would make good. I knew if I had to kneel, it was before you. I knew you were divine, you were the one——Cybele—Isis. I knew I was your slave. I knew. It has all been just a long initiation. I had to learn how to worship you.'

He kissed her feet again and again, without the slightest self-consciousness, or the slightest misgiving. Then he went back to the sofa, and sat there looking at her, saying:

'It isn't love, it is worship. Love between me and you will be a sacrament, Daphne. That's what I had to learn. You are beyond me. A mystery to me. My God, how great it all is. How marvellous!'

The act of kneeling and the kissing of feet are charged with significance in Lawrence's work of this period. In this instance, we may feel, they are even somewhat overcharged, but their purport is unmistakable. Abnegating his independent manhood, Basil becomes a slavish idolater; and his worship of Daphne turns her into a goddess, turns her, indeed, into Cybele, whose name Birkin invokes when (in the scene at the millpond in *Women in Love*) he attempts to smash the reflection of the moon, thus demonstrating his opposition to the possessive *magna mater* figure that is destructive of a man's virility. When Basil says that his feeling for Daphne 'isn't love' but 'worship', what he means is that he has attained 'a higher plane of love'. It is too ethereal a plane to support life, however, and not unexpectedly his worship of her postulates the kind of sacrifice of self that conceals a desire for death : 'I am no more than a sacrifice to you,' he tells her, 'an offering. I *wish* I could die in giving myself to you, give you all my blood on your altar, for ever.'

Basil is distracted from his worship of Daphne when, returning to the sofa, he slides his hand down between the back and the seat and finds a thimble. The thimble belongs to Daphne, a present given her as a girl by a Bohemian count, Johann Dionys Psanek, with whom, wounded and a prisoner of war in England, she has renewed acquaintance. This interruption of Basil's adoration of his wife is premonitory of the Count's irruption into their relationship. The Count, whose own marriage has failed, regards himself (like the Indians in 'The Woman Who Rode Away') as 'a subject of the sun' rather than of a woman; and a 'dark flame of life' seems to glow through his clothes 'from his body'. 'I belong to the fire-worshippers,' he tells Daphne; and what he slowly, even unwillingly, proceeds to do is to fire her into life, to release the wild energy that is dammed up in her. At the same time, contact with her also helps to heal him—'Let me wrap your hair round my hands, like a bandage,' he says—for he does not at first wish to live.

Daphne's sewing of some shirts for both the Count and her husband is made to reveal the different demands that the two men make of a woman. Basil is enraptured at the thought of having a shirt she has sewn next to his skin : 'I shall feel you all round me, all over me,' he says to her. What he wants in his relationship with her, we see, is to be encompassed, as in a womb. The Count, on the other hand, having told Daphne that the hospital-shirt he is wearing is too long and too big, insists that she herself, and not her maid, should sew a shirt for him : 'Only you,' he maintains, 'might give me what I want, something that buttons round my throat and on my wrists.' What he wants of a shirt is that it be a good fit—just as what he wants of a woman is that she be a 'mate'. 'Everything finds its mate,' he is fond of remarking; and he makes it clear to Daphne that what interests him is not the gentle mating of doves but the fiercer mating of wild creatures. The tale, that is to say, seems to be moving to a Dionysian mating of Artemis and Dionys, for Daphne becomes aware of a 'secret thrilling communion' with the Count, of a dark flow between them; and, though she resists him with her mind and will, she is nevertheless drawn by his account of a 'true love' that is 'a throbbing together in darkness, like the wild-cat in the night, when the green screen [with which her eyes are closed] opens and her eyes are on the darkness'. She comes to recognize too that, in contradistinction to the 'superconscious' finish of Basil and herself, the Count, like her father, has some of 'the unconscious blood-warmth of the lower classes'; and she is prepared to grant that his 'dark flame of life . . . might warm the cold white fire of her own blood'. We are led to expect, in other words, that the union of these two will be the contrary of the deathly 'white love' of Daphne and her husband; in fact the new relationship proves to be merely the obverse of the old.

The new form that Daphne's life appears about to take is symbolized by the thimble the Count has given her, which she puts on when she sews his shirt. The thimble has 'a gold snake at the bottom, and a Mary-beetle of green stone at the top, to push the needle with'. The Mary-beetle or ladybird, placed opposite the snake at the top of the thimble, may be thought of as instinct with flight; and the thimble, I suggest, figures the kind of union that is represented by Quetzalcoatl in *The Plumed Serpent*, a union of bird and serpent, of spirit and flesh. Certainly, as Daphne moves closer and closer to a vital relationship with the Count, it appears to be the hope of a release into unified being that is held out to her. It is the ladybird alone, however, that is the Count's crest, and as such, as 'a descendant of the Egyptian scarabaeus', it is emblematic of a rather different urge on his part. Lord Beveridge declares that the ball-rolling scarab is 'a symbol of the creative principle', but the Count suggests (though he smiles 'as if

146

it were a joke') that, on the contrary, it symbolizes 'the principle of decomposition'. He is not joking, however, for, confronted with a world that 'has gone raving', he has chosen 'the madness of the ladybird' and found his God in 'the blessed god of destruction'. His God is a 'god of anger, who throws down the steeples and the factory chimneys', and he proposes to serve him by helping to beat down 'the world of man'. The Count, it emerges, is bent on disrupting the established order, an order founded on democracy and love, and substituting for it an order based on 'the sacredness of power'. Basil maintains that 'there is really only one supreme contact, the contact of love', but the Count insists that he 'must use another word than love' and suggests several: 'Obedience, submission, faith, belief, responsibility, power'. The Count talks here like Lilly in *Aaron's Rod*, and it is in the novels, particularly in *The Plumed Serpent*, that the political implications of this doctrine of power are pursued to a logical conclusion. In 'The Ladybird' the superiority of the doctrine of power over that of love is asserted domestically, as it were, in the Count's conquest of Basil's wife.

The Count's power as a man is evidenced by the 'spell' he casts on Daphne when, prior to his departure from England, Basil invites him to spend a fortnight at Thoresway, the 'beautiful Elizabethan mansion' of Lord Beveridge. At night, when he is alone in his room, the Count croons to himself 'the old songs of his childhood'. Daphne, who is 'a bad sleeper', and whose nights are 'a torture to her', hears the singing, which, 'like a witchcraft', makes her forget everything. Thereafter it becomes 'almost an obsession to her to listen for him'. She is sure he is calling her, 'out of herself, out of her world', and in the day she is 'bewitched'. One night she cannot resist going into his room, and they sit for some time apart, in the dark:

> Then suddenly, without knowing, he went across in the dark, feeling for the end of the couch. And he sat beside her on the couch. But he did not touch her. Neither did she move. The darkness flowed about them thick like blood, and time seemed dissolved in it. They sat with the small, invisible distance between them, motionless, speechless, thoughtless.
>
> Then suddenly he felt her finger-tips touch his arm,

147

and a flame went over him that left him no more a man. He was something seated in flame, in flame unconscious, seated erect, like an Egyptian King-god in the statues. Her finger-tips slid down him, and she herself slid down in a strange silent rush, and he felt her face against his closed feet and ankles, her hands pressing his ankles. He felt her brow and hair against his ankles, her face against his feet, and there she clung in the dark, as if in space below him. He still sat erect and motionless. Then he bent forward and put his hand on her hair.

'Do you come to me?' he murmured. 'Do you come to me?'

Great stress is laid here on the lack of consciousness of the lovers: they sit 'speechless, thoughtless', and the Count, having moved to Daphne 'without knowing', sits 'in flame unconscious'. In contradistinction to the superconsciousness of Basil and Daphne, they are immersed in a flow that is thick and dark, 'like blood'; and where Basil is prostrate before her, the Count sits 'erect, like an Egyptian King-god in the statues', sits, that is (like Birkin in *Women In Love*) in 'immemorial potency'. The Count's sense of his own potency certainly communicates itself to Daphne, for it brings her sliding down to his feet. But the relationship which Daphne now embraces is not, after all, so different from that which obtains between her husband and herself. There is a significant reversal of roles, it is true, but the relationship is still founded on the worship of one partner by the other, even though it is now 'the sacredness of power' that elicits the devotion. What is disturbing here is that Lawrence, intent on asserting the Count's power and on emphasizing the difference between his attitude to Daphne and that of Basil, seems to be unaware that Daphne, clinging to the Count's feet and with 'her brow and hair against his ankles', is (for all the heightened prose of the description) in no less objectionable a position than Basil at her feet.

It is a position, we cannot help feeling, that figures more than a woman's necessary sexual submission to a man. The 'small' man has brought the 'tall' woman—their difference of stature is repeatedly stressed—to her knees; and her clinging to his feet is the overt sign of a kind of submission to him that has far-reaching implications for their sexual

148

relations. This is how Daphne is described on the following morning:

> She felt she could sleep, sleep, sleep—for ever. Her face, too, was very still, with a delicate look of virginity that she had never had before. She had always been Aphrodite, the self-conscious one. And her eyes, the green-blue, had been like slow, living jewels, resistant. Now they had unfolded from the hard flower-bud, and had the wonder, and the stillness of a quiet night.

The reiterated allusions to Daphne's stillness at first sight seem to betoken no more than her achievement of the **peace of fulfilment after the strain of her sexual relations** with Basil, but taken in conjunction with the references to her 'delicate look of virginity' and to her always having been 'Aphrodite'—we remember that Basil, 'in poetry', has called her 'Aphrodite of the foam'—the emphasis on her stillness has a concealed significance. A passage in *The Plumed Serpent* makes clear, I think, what is only hinted at in the story:

> [Kate] realized, with wonder, the death in her of Aphrodite of the foam: the seething, frictional, ecstatic Aphrodite. By a swift dark instinct, Cipriano drew away from this in her. When, in their love, it came back on her, the seething electric female ecstasy, which knows such spasms of delirium, he recoiled from her. It was what she used to call her 'satisfaction'. She had loved Joachim for this, that again, and again, and again he could give her this orgiastic 'satisfaction', in spasms that made her cry aloud.

With Basil, we are told, Daphne has known 'the fierce power of the woman in excelsis', the power of 'incandescent, transcendent, moon-fierce womanhood', but her inability to 'stay intensified' in her 'female mystery' has left her 'fretful and ill and never to be soothed'. What the Count has done, it seems, presumably by refusing her 'satisfaction', is to bring her not a release of, but from, her own wild energies. Hence the 'quiet, intact quality of virginity in her' and her 'strange new quiescence' which Basil finds so puzzling; and hence her own sense of having 'suddenly collapsed away from her old self into this darkness, this peace, this quiescence that was like a full dark river flowing eternally in her soul'.

Daphne's achievement of a new self should be distinguished, therefore, from that of Connie Chatterley, of whom she is evidently a prefigurement, for it is said that at Thoresway 'there was a gamekeeper she could have loved— an impudent, ruddy-faced, laughing, ingratiating fellow; she could have loved him, if she had not been isolated beyond the breach of his birth, her culture, her consciousness'. Connie, responding to the tenderness of Mellors, also dies to the Aphrodite in her, but she is reborn as a woman who finds a different kind of 'satisfaction', a consummation that I think we are to understand is denied Daphne, as it is denied Kate in *The Plumed Serpent*:

> Oh, and far down inside [Connie] . . ., at the quick of her, the depths parted and rolled asunder, from the centre of soft plunging . . ., and closer and closer plunged the palpable unknown, and further and further rolled the waves of herself away from herself, leaving her, till suddenly, in a soft, shuddering convulsion, the quick of all her plasm was touched, she knew herself touched, the consummation was upon her, and she was gone. She was gone, she was not, and she was born: a woman.

Daphne's accession into new being, moreover, does not resolve the problem of her relations with the two men. She has to be satisfied, though her relationship with Basil has been demolished, with being 'the wife of the ladybird', for the Count, a prisoner of war, has no alternative but to depart. It is significant, however, that he anyway feels he has 'no future in this life' and that he cannot offer her 'life in the world' because he has 'no power in the day, and no place'. The Count, that is to say, having pledged his power to his god of anger and destruction, appears to have his being in death; and what he finally offers Daphne is a life in the underworld. 'In the night, in the dark, and in death, you are mine,' he tells her; and when he parts from her, he says: 'I shall be king in Hades when I am dead. And you will be at my side.' Proserpine, we see, is Proserpine yet, and the spring seems far behind.

III

'The Fox', until the killing of Banford, has a fine and powerful inevitability of development that makes it, up to that point, one of the most translucent of Lawrence's tales. The established relationship, in this further instance of 'the wicked triangle', is of two girls ('usually known by their surnames'), who have set up home and a farm together. March acts 'the man about the place', but despite their feeling for each other, she and Banford are 'apt to become a little irritable' and seem 'to live too much off themselves'. It is evidently a sterile relationship, March, indeed, being generally 'absent in herself', as if she were not really held by Banford; and this sterility is mirrored in the unproductiveness of the farm, particularly in the 'obstinate refusal' of their hens to lay eggs. Matters are made worse by the depredations of a fox, which carries off hens 'under [their] very noses'.

One evening March, out with her gun, is standing with her consciousness 'held back' when she suddenly sees the fox 'looking up at her'. His eyes meet her eyes, and 'he [knows] her'. She is 'spellbound', does not shoot, and the fox makes off. Thereafter she wanders about 'in strange mindlessness', but she is 'possessed' by the fox and feels that he has 'invisibly [mastered] her spirit'. What is enacted here with admirable economy is parallel to what takes place in repeated meetings between Daphne and the Count. Into the vacancy of March's being there suddenly irrupts, with the force of an epiphany, a manifestation of wild life. Immediately prior to the encounter March has been unaware of the vibrant life around her, of the 'limbs of the pine-trees' shining in the air and the stalks of grass 'all agleam', for she '[sees] it all, and [does] not see it'. Now, at a level deeper than consciousness, she comes under the spell of newly apprehended energies and is possessed by them. What is perhaps specially significant is that she submits to the mastery of the fox—this and the strong sexual overtones of the description preparing the way for her response to the young soldier who suddenly arrives at the farm.

From the moment he appears Henry '[is] the fox' to March. She tries 'to keep her will uppermost' as she watches him, but soon ceases 'to reserve herself' from his presence. Instead she gives herself up 'to a warm, relaxed peace', and, 'accepting the spell' that is on her, she allows herself to 'lapse into the odour of the fox', remaining 'still and soft in her corner like a passive creature in its cave'. In the light of Daphne's experience in 'The Ladybird', March's still, relaxed passivity under the spell is worthy of notice. That it is to a sexual potency in Henry that she is responding is indicated by the dream she has on the night of his arrival. Hearing a strange singing—a call (like the Count's crooning) to a new mode of life—she goes outside and suddenly realizes that it is the fox who is singing. She approaches the fox, but when she puts out her hand to touch him, he suddenly bites her wrist. At the same time, in bounding away, his brush (which seems to be fire) '[sears] and [burns] her mouth with a great pain'. If March in her dream experiences the fire of passion that she desires (for when Henry later kisses her it is 'with a quick brushing kiss' that seems 'to burn through her every fibre'), she is also warned, as it were, not to play with fire, for the fox is no doll, as his bite testifies.

What playing with fire means, in the first instance, is resisting Henry's determination to master her. He is 'a huntsman in spirit', and deciding that he wants to marry her (initially with the shrewd idea of gaining the farm for himself but soon with a genuine and disinterested passion), he sets out to hunt his quarry, knowing 'he [is] master of her'. He also hunts the fox and kills it. It is a remarkable stroke. The killing of the marauder functions, first, as a ritual supplanting of the fox by which March is possessed. At the same time Henry is paradoxically aligned with the fox he kills, and his hunting of it is made the occasion of an extension of his significance:

As he stood under the oaks of the wood-edge he heard the dogs from the neighbouring cottage up the hill yelling suddenly and startlingly, and the wakened dogs from the farms around barking answer. And suddenly, it seemed to him England was little and tight, he felt the landscape was constricted even in the dark, and that there were too many dogs in the night, making a noise like a fence of sound, like the network of English hedges netting the view. He felt the fox didn't have a chance.

For it must be the fox that had started all this hulla-baloo.

. . . He knew the fox would be coming. It seemed to him it would be the last of the foxes in this loudly barking thick-voiced England, tight with innumerable little houses.

Henry, we see, should not be regarded merely as a rather nondescript young man who has been fired into the pursuit of a woman. He suddenly emerges here as the represen-tative of a wild, passionate spirit for which there seems to be no room in a tight England. It is a spirit, we are to understand, that has been assailed in England during the war, for the passage should be related to Lord Beveridge's bitter thoughts in 'The Ladybird' of 'the so-called patriots who [have] been howling their mongrel indecency in the public face' and of an 'England fallen under the paws of smelly mongrels'. Henry, like James Joyce's Stephen Deda-lus, is determined to fly by the nets that threaten to drag him down; and he wants a freer, more expansive life than seems possible in a land fenced in by the conventional pieties of such as Banford. It is a measure of Lawrence's despair of England at this time that Henry and March are made to leave for Canada at the end of the tale.

But before they can finally come together, Banford's hold on March has to be broken. The way in which Banford is disposed of arouses our gravest doubts; and it is at this point that the crystal-clear depths of the story become suddenly muddied with obsessive matter. Banford is disposed of when Henry, refusing to accept March's withdrawal from her promise to marry him, comes back to the farm to claim her and chops down a tree which falls on and kills his rival. It is true that this climactic event is carefully prepared for. Prior to it March dreams that Banford is dead and that the coffin in which she has to put her is 'the rough wood-box in which the bits of chopped wood' are kept. Not wanting to lay her 'dead darling' in an unlined box, March wraps her up in a fox-skin, which is all she can find. The dream points clearly enough to March's desire for Banford's death, and, in its association of the dead woman with the fox that Henry has killed, seems to express a wish that he will be the one to bring about her death. It is March's unconscious complicity in Banford's death that in part explains her immediate capitulation to Henry the moment the deed is consummated. It is true, too, that the killing is technically an accident, and that Henry warns Banford to move (though in a manner that ensures her refusal) before he strikes the blows that fell the tree. 'In his heart', however, he has 'decided her death'—and the fact remains that he murders her.

It is furthermore true that the symbolism of the story insidiously suggests that Henry kills Banford as naturally, almost as innocently, as a fox kills chickens, and out of a similar need to live, March being essential to his life. It may also be granted that the killing frees March for life. That does not mean to say, however, that we should celebrate the murder as 'an inspired and creative deed', as Julian Moynahan has suggested. Henry, after all, is not a fox, and calling murder by another name does not make it smell any sweeter. We can only conclude, I think, that when Lawrence, who has such a reverence for life, can be taken to justify murder, it is because the murder is incidental to a compulsive justification of something else.

What strikes us about the murder of Banford is that it is strictly unnecessary. The moment Henry returns to the farm and faces March, her upper lip lifts from her teeth in a 'helpless, fascinated rabbit-look', and as soon as she sees 'his glowing, red face', it is 'all over with her'; she is as 'helpless' as if she were 'bound'. She is as powerless, that is, as a rabbit before a fox; and her helplessness surely implies that Henry has only to insist on her leaving the farm with him for her to yield, irrespective of the opposition they might be expected to encounter from Banford. That Henry is nevertheless made to kill Banford is a means, I suggest, not of freeing March but of ensuring her submission to him as a woman. In *The Plumed Serpent*, when Cipriano executes the men who have tried to kill Don Ramón, he repeatedly intones 'The Lords of Life are Masters of Death'; it seems to be the covert intention behind Henry's murder of Banford that his mastery of death establishes him as a lord of life. For March not only has to be freed from Banford; she has to be released into a new mode of being.

She has to be won, first, to a new conception of relationship between a man and a woman. When she writes to Henry and goes back on her promise to marry him, she says that she has 'been over it all again' in her 'mind', and that she does not see 'on what grounds' she can marry him since he is 'an aboslute stranger' to her, they do not 'seem to have a thing in common', and she does not 'really love' him. What she has to be made to respond to, though not with her mind, is the existence of an affinity between them that goes deeper than conventional ideas of love and compatibility; what she has to be made to accept, in a word, is the compulsion of a life-force—and of a lord of life. It is this acknowledgement that is wrung from her when Banford is killed, it being an indication of the lengths to which Lawrence is driven in asserting the doctrine of power that murder should be made the means of ensuring the acknowledgement. March faces Henry, gazing at him 'with the last look of resistance', and then 'in a last agonized failure' she begins to cry. 'He [has] won,' we are told; and looking at him with 'a senseless look of helplessness and submission', she realizes that she will 'never leave him again'.

Henry's demonstration of his mastery in the killing of Banford is intended to effect a further submission on March's part once they are married:

> If he spoke to her, she would turn to him with a faint new smile, the strange, quivering little smile of a woman who has died in the old way of love, and can't quite rise to the new way. She still felt she ought to *do* something, to strain herself in some direction. . . . And she could not quite accept the submergence which his new love put upon her. If she was in love, she ought to *exert* herself, in some way, loving. She felt the weary need of our day to *exert* herself in love. But she knew that in fact she must no more exert herself in love. He would not have the love which exerted itself towards him. It made his brow go black. No, he wouldn't let her exert her love towards him. No, she had to be passive, to acquiesce, and to be submerged under the surface of love. . . .

Lawrence is not as explicit here as he is in *The Plumed Serpent*, but in view of the previously quoted comments in that novel on Aphrodite of the foam, I think there can be little doubt what a woman's exertion in love should be taken to mean. March, having 'died in the old way of love', is required (like Daphne) to be reborn into a new passive acquiescence and foamless submergence in the sex act. It is a saving grace that March is left not quite accepting her submergence.

IV

F. R. Leavis has discussed 'The Captain's Doll' at length in his chapter on the tale in *D. H. Lawrence: Novelist*, leaving little to be added to his account. I should merely like to draw attention to the presence in the tale of what might be called the Aphrodite motif. It is perhaps only our recognition of the importance of this motive in 'The Ladybird' and 'The Fox' that makes us aware of it in the third tale in the volume, for in 'The Captain's Doll' it is presented symbolically.

Captain Hepburn, like Count Dionys and Henry, possesses the kind of mastery that casts a spell over a woman. He speaks to Countess Hannele with a 'strange, mindless, soft, suggestive tone' that leaves her 'powerless to disobey'; and when he makes love to her, she is 'heavy and spellbound . Hannele, in a word, cannot 'help being in love' with him. Nevertheless, Hannele, who makes dolls and cushions and 'suchlike objects of feminine art', has made a doll of the Captain, a 'mannikin' that is 'a perfect portrait' of him as a Scottish officer; and the making of the doll clearly indicates that his mastery over her is far from absolute. At the same time the doll projects an image of the Captain that is not altogether unfair, for we discover that his wife has made a living doll of him: 'Why, on our wedding night,' Mrs. Hepburn tells Hannele, 'he kneeled down in front of me and promised, with God's help, to make my life happy. . . . It has been his one aim in life, to make my life happy.' The mannikin, that is, suggests the diminishment of self, of true being, that is implicit in such a limitation of a man's purposive activity. Hepburn is thus both a masterful man and a doll, and it is this complexity that makes the conflict between old and new modes of love a more subtle affair in this story than it is in 'The Ladybird', of which we may be reminded by the recurrence of a man on his knees before a woman. In 'The Captain's Doll' the conflict is first internalized, as it were, for Hepburn himself comes to repudiate 'the business of adoration'. When his wife dies, he realizes that he no longer wants to love in that way; and he insists to Hannele that 'any woman . . . could start any minute and make a doll' of the man she loves: 'And the doll would be her hero: and her hero would be no more than her doll.' Hannele, however, is inwardly determined that 'he must go down on his knees if he [wants] her love'. The ostensible drama that is played out between them consists in his attempt to make her abandon this position.

But since a man's being no more than a woman's doll also implies that she may use him as a toy in the sex act—implies, indeed, the kind of relationship that Bertha Coutts is said to have forced on Mellors in *Lady Chatterley's Lover*—the drama here not unexpectedly turns out to have a further dimension. We are adverted to this dimension at the beginning of the long, superb description of the excursion which Hannele and Hepburn make to the glacier. Sitting silently in the car that is taking them to the mountains, they watch the glacier river. The river is 'roaring and raging, a glacier river of pale, seething ice-water'; it is a 'foaming river', a 'stony, furious, lion-like river, tawny-coloured'. When the car can go no further, they begin to climb the mountain; and then there follows this passage:

> This valley was just a mountain cleft, cleft sheer in the hard, living rock, with black trees like hair flourishing in this secret, naked place of the earth. At the bottom of the open wedge forever roared the rampant, insatiable water. The sky from above was like a sharp wedge forcing its way into the earth's cleavage, and that eternal ferocious water was like the steel edge of the wedge, the terrible tip biting into the rocks' intensity. Who could have thought that the soft sky of light, and the soft foam of water could thrust and penetrate into the dark, strong earth? . . .

What we have here, it seems clear, is another rendering of 'the intercourse between heaven and earth' that is described at the beginning of *The Rainbow*; and what the 'rampant, insatiable' water, the 'ferocious' water, symbolizes, I suggest, is 'the seething, frictional, ecstatic' Aphrodite of the foam. Such a reading helps us to understand the reactions of Hepburn and Hannele to the scene. He 'hates' and 'loathes' it, finding it 'almost obscene'; she is

157

'thrilled and excited' by it 'to another sort of savageness'. They proceed on their way to the glacier, and Hepburn suddenly decides he wants to climb on to it: it is 'his one desire—to stand upon it'. The ascent of the glacier is for Hepburn an 'ordeal or mystic battle' and, as he prepares for it, 'the curious vibration of his excitement' makes the scene 'strange, rather horrible to her'; she shudders, but the glacier still seems to her 'to hold the key to all glamour and ecstasy'. He has earlier declared that the mountains 'are less' than he, and been filled with 'a curious, dark, masterful force'. What he demonstrates, I take it, as he climbs 'the naked ice-slope', the ice that looks 'so pure, like flesh', is his determination to pit himself against the source of the seething water and so really to get on top of it.

On the way down Hepburn makes it clear to Hannele that he will not marry her 'on a basis of love'. What he demands of her in marriage, he tells her, is 'honour and obedience: and the proper physical feelings'. The word 'proper', we may feel, is highly ambiguous, but he leaves it at that. Lawrence leaves it at that too, and 'The Captain's Doll' is consequently not marred, as the other two tales are, by an attempt to enforce a total surrender on the woman. After a fierce argument Hannele finally makes her submission, movingly and convincingly, when she tells Hepburn she wants to burn the picture of the doll that he carries with him. The ascent of the glacier has shown beyond question that he is no doll.

THE FIRST *LADY CHATTERLEY'S LOVER* *

Many of those who have read *Lady Chatterley's Lover* and other novels and stories by Lawrence are still perhaps unaware that he wrote the novel three times, that each of the three versions is a different story, different—often astonishingly so—in mood and characterization and that the first two versions have survived in manuscript and are still waiting forty years after they were written to be published in Lawrence's own country and in Lawrence's own native language.[1] The fact that, except for one or two pages, which leave no serious hiatus in the text, the first two drafts of the novel have survived, may of course appear to be of concern only to those whose interest in Lawrence is 'specialized' or fanatical. And the indifference of publishers, who are understandably supposed to know what it is in their own best interests to look out for and put on the market, may have encouraged this view. Yet the few, I find, who have read the three versions agree that the first is by far the best, that it is among the finest things that Lawrence ever wrote and that if he altered a great deal in rewriting the novel, he certainly failed on the whole to improve it. This is what I wish to argue in this essay. I also wish to maintain that it is the novel which provides the most relevant touchstone by which to judge the still notorious third version, to judge it both as a work of art and, since the two considerations are inseparable, as the expression of certain moral beliefs.

The nature of these beliefs, the nature, that is, of what in the final version Lawrence wished to make abundantly clear, is suggested by Frieda Lawrence in her preface to *The First Lady Chatterley* :

* By G. R. Strickland, University of Reading.

He wrote the novel three times and the third version is the published one. My favourite is the first draft. Lawrence said grimly after he had written the 'First *Lady Chatterley*', 'They'll say as they said of Blake: "It's mysticism", but they shan't get away with it, not this time. Blake's wasn't mysticism, neither is this. The tenderness and gentleness hadn't enough punch and fight in it, it was a bit wistful.' Anyhow, another mood came over him and he had to tackle the novel again. He wanted to make the contrast between the cynicism and sophistication of the modern mind and the gamekeeper's attitude sharper. To give a glimpse of living spontaneous tenderness in a man and the other mental, fixed approach to love. 'The First *Lady Chatterley*' he wrote as she came out of him, out of his own immediate self. In the third version he was also aware of his contemporaries' minds.

Frieda is probably referring here to the introduction in the second and third versions of the rather pathetically over-civilized Brigadier Tommy Dukes and in the third version of Michaelis. She might have added, however, that in the third version Lady Chatterley's lover, Oliver Mellors, though not a cynic like Michaelis (Michaelis believes only in the 'bitch goddess', success), is none the less a man of education, a former grammar school boy who can read French and German, a former officer in the war and a perfectly suitable partner for Connie. He is socially at ease with Connie's father, more at ease in fact than Sir Malcolm himself and he is able, with no sense of being overawed by his surroundings, to give what seems like a devastatingly just and far from unsophisticated appraisal of the fashionable Duncan Forbes' would-be 'unsentimental' Cubist-inspired 'tubular' paintings.

Mellors is not only a suitable partner for Connie. He is also, unlike Lady Chatterley's lover in the first version, ideally suited. Lawrence's overwhelming sense of the absolute rightness of the relationship comes out in the beautiful declamatory prose of Mellors' letter to Connie which concludes the novel. And it is this perhaps which, more than anything else, accounts for the discomfort which many readers feel, at least after several readings of the novel, why they find many things difficult to 'swallow' and why as a consequence they are unable altogether to share the beliefs which inspired the novel. For such readers, and I include myself among them, if *Lady Chatterley's Lover* is an immoral novel, it is not because Connie or her lover say or do anything which in itself seems particularly wrong. It is because of the state of mind in which Lawrence seems to have imagined such a man and the life he offers. The novel is immoral, in other words, in the sense in which Lawrence himself defines the term :

> The novel is not, as a rule, immoral because the novelist has any dominant *idea*, or *purpose*. The immorality lies in the novelist's helpless, unconscious predilection. Love is a great emotion. But if you set out to write a novel, and you yourself are in the throes of the great predilection for love, love as the supreme, the only emotion worth living for, then you will write an immoral novel.
>
> Because *no* emotion is supreme, or exclusively worth living for . . . If the novelist puts his thumb in the pan, for love, tenderness, sweetness, peace, then he commits an immoral act : he *prevents* the possibility of a pure relationship, a pure relatedness, the only thing that matters : and he makes inevitable the horrible reaction, when he lets his thumb go, towards hate and brutality, cruelty and destruction.[2]

It will by no means be obvious to every reader that in *Lady Chatterley's Lover* we have an example of what Lawrence is describing here. And I don't regard it as necessarily proof of naïveté or obtuseness on my part that when I first read the novel it was not obvious to me. (Similarly it is not perhaps immediately obvious that if Lawrence has 'put his thumb in the pan', he also betrays 'the horrible reaction . . . towards hate and brutality, cruelty and destruction'. Lawrence's most distinguished critic has recently surprised many of his readers by talking of Lawrence's 'animus' against Sir Clifford Chatterley.[3]) My point is simply that in *The First Lady Chatterley*, these misgivings, that can grow into certainties, are no longer possible, that the 'punch and fight' which, according to Frieda, Lawrence put into the third version, impose a strain on our credulity and our sympathies.

This would matter less if it were not for the obvious importance of what Lawrence has to say in all three versions of the novel, not only about the relationships between men and women, but about fundamental aspects of the England of his day, an England which is recognizably very similar to our own. Perhaps the most striking differences between the first versions and the third lie in Lawrence's presentation of English life, the life of the managers and the working people in the industrial midlands in which he grew up. The difference can be seen for example if one compares one of the most often quoted passages in Lawrence: 'The car ploughed uphill through Tevershall . . .' (chapter 11) with the original version which reads as follows:

The country was looking its most dismal in the rain, the spring not yet burst through. The car ploughed uphill through Tevershall, a long dark-red straggle of small dwellings with glistening black slate roofs like lids and poky shops with stacks of soap, or turnips and pink rhubarb, or huddled drapery; and Wesleyan Chapel, then Methodist Chapel, then Congregational Chapel, then Christadelphians or whatever they were: but all alike dreary and ugly to a degree. And at the top of the hill the old church and old stone cottages of the previous agricultural village, before the mining had started . . . She sighed. It was the hopeless dismal ugliness that depressed her. She was used to Sussex, and a lovely old house in the fold of the downs. She could never get used to this awful colliery region of the North Midlands. And yet she liked it too: it gave her a certain feeling of blind virility, a certain blind, pathetic forcefulness of life. If only it could realize how ugly it was and change a bit. (Page 42)

Lawrence's sense of dismal ugliness does not blind him to the fact that there are human beings for whom a Tevershall is home and to whom it is not wholly intolerable. There is a reason for which, unexpectedly, Connie should 'like it too'. Tevershall is her *lover's* home: 'And yet . . . in one of those dwellings he was brought up, and his old mother lives in one of them with his child!' In the description of the drive through Tevershall in the third version only hopelessness prevails. The condemnation is absolute.

In the third *Lady Chatterley* Connie and her lover reject utterly and with gladness the England of Tevershall and Wragby Hall, the world of the managers and the world for whose ugliness the managers must bear most of the respon-

162

sibility.[4] They do so obviously with Lawrence's approval. Mellors, unlike the gamekeeper in the first version, expresses what we know and could have guessed anyway to be Lawrence's own beliefs about contemporary industrial 'civilization':

> I'd wipe the machines off the face of the earth again, and end the industrial epoch absolutely, like a black mistake. But since I can't, an' nobody can, I'd better hold my peace, an' try an' live my own life: if I've got one to live, which I rather doubt. (Chapter 15)

The third *Lady Chatterly* is impressive. And there is something fiercely salutary in the positive unhelpfulness of Mellors' (and Lawrence's) considered opinion of modern English life, in the 'punch and fight' which are here a refusal to compromise with essential human needs or hold on to false hopes:

> They talk a lot about nationalization, nationalization of royalties, nationalization of the whole industry. But you can't nationalize coal and leave the other industries as they are . . . Even under a Soviet you've still got to sell coal: and that's the difficulty. (Chapter 19)

Forty years after this was written (which was during the period of the Sankey Report and Tawney's *Acquisitive Society*) the unhelpfulness seems, apart from anything else, like a very remarkable political realism.

Yet the unhelpfulness is not only of the positive kind which we find here, of the kind, that is, which can remind us of Arnold's scepticism with regard to all social 'machinery'. If Lawrence over-reaches himself in the third version and stands in his own light, it is because of the unhelpfulness too of what he has to say to the individual trying, in Mellors' words, to 'live his own life'. We know that at the end, having rejected Teneshall and Wragby Hall, Connie and Mellors will settle for farming, that they will realize the town dwelling Englishman's nostalgic dream and become members of what we can now only think of as a privileged and fortunate minority. (If a comparison with Arnold seems relevant here it is with the Arnold of the *Scholar Gipsy*.) We are not shown how the individual might 'live his own life' while living, as most of us have to live, in Teneshall or its suburban equivalent. We are not

163

shown, in other words, what a positive choice can be like, the best conceivable choice that an individual can make for himself, given the *circumstances* of his life, in the far from ideally satisfactory conditions of the world as it is. We *are* shown this in a number of stories which, from this point of view resemble one another and which seem to me for this reason superior to *Lady Chatterley*: *Daughters of the Vicar, Fanny and Annie, You Touched Me* and *Mother and Daughter*. We are shown this also in *The First Lady Chatterley*.

Oliver Parkin, the gamekeeper in the first and second versions of the novel, is a workman who has a rooted objection to being or seeming anything else. He is not like Mellors a man who is capable of speaking 'educated' English.[5] His obstinacy springs from his hatred and mistrust of the ladies and gentlemen who come to shoot the pheasants he rears and who patronize him with loud voices, and from a revolt against the conditions of life he experiences as a lorry driver working for a Sheffield steel foundry. At the end of the novel we are told that he has become an active member of the Communist Party. For Connie, Parkin is 'culturally of another race' and the decision to become his wife is made with immense misgivings and after long contemplation of all that the choice involves. The Clifford of this version is a friend and companion for Connie and their life together leaves her free. The spaciousness of Wragby Hall enables her to have her own rooms and to furnish them elegantly. Isolated in the ugly Midlands, she is nonetheless not too remote from the life of London and the continent. Her companionship with Clifford, furthermore, is a matter of constant deliberate, delicate adjustments. It is in fact against the empty burden of her freedom and against an excess of good feeling and 'understanding' between Clifford and herself that she finally revolts. In the very difference between herself and Parkin we are able to see what draws them together, what it is that makes it possible for each to recognize the uniqueness of the life in the other.

Connie, throughout the novel, is torn between her lover and her paralysed husband. Yet the uncertainty and constant ambivalence of judgment are not registered as confusion on her part or on the part of the novelist, nor even as agony or strain. On the contrary in *The First Lady Chatterley* the effect is at times one of high-spirited comedy, of a kind almost wholly lacking in the third and of a clarity and freshness of registration which we find only in Lawrence's finest writing. One could say in fact that it is the ambivalence of *judgment* and, going with this, the novelist's fidelity to swift changes of real instinctive appraisal which make the freshness and clarity of effect possible:

> Ah if she could be in the cottage with him now, just lighting the lamp! Perhaps they would have—she tried to think of something really common—bloaters, yes bloaters for supper, grilled bloaters. The house simply reeked of grilled bloaters. And he sat with his elbows on the table in his shirt sleeves and picked bits of bloater bones away with his fingers. And drops of tea hung on his fierce moustache. And he said:
> 'These 'ere bloaters is that salty, they're nowt but brine. Pour us another cup o' tea, lass.'
> And he would nudge his cup towards her. And she would rise obediently to get the brown teapot from the hob to pour him his cup-a-tea . . .
> But she laughed to herself at the picture of the bloaters and the cup-a-tea. She would still love him because of the loveliness of his flesh-and-blood being . . . She would love to sleep with him. He wouldn't even wear pyjamas. Probably he slept in his day shirt. But curiously, nothing would make him physically unattractive.
> But if they lived together they would humiliate one another. She, because she was in another world of culture than his. And he, because his state of nature would ignore so much of her; and he had no goal, no onwards in life. He was static . . . (pages 63–4)

The simplification of issues in the final version leads often to a blurring of outline and a blurring of what in the first version are vital distinctions. Reality takes on a nightmare or phantom quality or is merely an irritant to raw nerves:

> The fault lay there, out there, in those evil electric lights and diabolical rattlings of engines. There, in the world of the mechanical greedy, greedy mechanism and mechanized greed . . . lay the vast evil thing, ready to destroy whatever did not conform. (Chapter 10)

It is perhaps significant that the realism in Mellors that can seem all the more remarkable now that forty years have gone by should take the form of *general* truths.

The *First Lady Chatterley*, though less ambitiously prophetic than the third, gives us more of the essence of modern England.[6] And in saying this one may suggest an answer to the inevitable question: why should Lawrence have made Lady Chatterley find a lover so different from herself? One answer I have half suggested already: the difference is itself a condition of the recognition of what is unique in the other; one is reminded here of other novels and stories by Lawrence, perhaps most obviously of the long short story which Lawrence wrote a year before beginning the *First Lady Chatterley*. It is in fact *The Virgin and the Gipsy* which, for Professor Leavis, provides the touchstone by which to judge the final version of *Lady Chatterley*: 'The point of the comparison', he writes, 'is perhaps plain enough . . . its essential aim commits it, for success, to the achievement of *The Virgin and the Gipsy*; that of disengaging unambiguously the fact, and the crucial significance, of desire—of indicating desire in the sense of compelling a clear and clean and reverent recognition'.[7] Yet *The First Lady Chatterley* (while obviously also similar in 'essential aim') carries on, so to speak, from *The Virgin and the Gipsy* and explores the possibilities of the kind of relationship which by comparison seems merely hinted at in the earlier story. Lawrence explores, for example, what it is that makes for profound differences of feeling, outlook and character between the different classes of society, though this is not to say that Connie herself is led progressively deeper into the affair with Parkin by sociological curiosity. She is mortified, when she visits Parkin in his Sheffield lodgings, by her hosts at tea who assume that she is like the socialist Lady Warwick and has merely come to hob-nob with the workers. What leads her, or rather allows her to be led, so much further into intimacy with Parkin than Yvette is ever led with the gipsy is an unusual strength of character of the kind which brings out the best and the worst in those she meets. Connie brings drama into other lives, drama which is essentially revealing. The sociological revelation, if one can call it that, is given by means of dramatic confrontations, such as that which takes place over tea in Parkin's Sheffield lodgings. Bill Tewson, her host, doggedly and good-naturedly fights down his embarrassment and at the same time takes advantage of her presence by seeking confirmation of a cherished belief:

'. . . I know we're not refined nor none of that. We're not *gentry*. But take most of the feelings—they're the same aren't they? Most of your feelings are the same as most of ours, aren't they? I don't mean you personally, because your father was a painter and painters are more free anyhow. That's how I can understand you might like to come here—something new for you, like, to see us in our own homes . . . But take even Sir Clifford! His feelings and my feelings, are they so very different?'

Constance had thought many things during this tirade. So! They took her visit for a sort of bohemian curiosity. And they didn't mind, they put up with it. And they had not the faintest suspicion that she was Oliver Parkin's lover. The sly little devil, he had not let them suspect in the slightest. Even the women didn't suspect. They thought it was bohemian curiosity and boredom. She longed to say to their noses: 'I'm pregnant by this Oliver Parkin here: been pregnant for three months.'

At the same time the queer white flame of earnestness on Bill's face opposite her was pathetic, pathetic. Were his feelings the same as Clifford's? Good God, no!

'Yes!' she said in her soft, composed voice.

'Eh?' he started. 'Yes!'

'Yes!' she repeated.

He stared at her with those bright, grey, intense eyes for some moments as his tension slackened.

'You mean to say there *is* a difference between my feelings and those of a man like Sir Clifford? You mean to say there is?'

'Yes!'

'There *is*? And a big difference? Big enough to matter?'

'Yes.'

He sat slowly back in his chair, his face very pale and as if bewildered. Then he quickly rubbed his forehead and ruffled his hair so that it stood on end. Then he gave a queer, quick, deep little laugh as he looked round, half-rueful, half-roguish at Parkin.

'It's what tha towd me, lad!' he said. (Pages 172-3)

Lawrence of course offers no solution to the problem weighing on Bill Tewson's mind: why there should be

167

these differences. Yet the novel is an immensely honest *airing* of the problem. The clean fresh air of Parkin's, Connie's and Lawrence's honesty blows through every page. I have said that it is less ambitiously prophetic than the third version. One could put it another way and say that it exemplifies Blake's dictum concerning truth. The artist's vision, which is at the same time the social historian's vision can be seen in such minute particulars as Parkin's hands when Connie sees them for the first time after he has moved to Sheffield: 'She was shocked when she saw his hands scarred and swollen, almost shapeless. They had been so quick and light.' 'It's cruel,' Mrs. Tewson explains, 'you know, when you're not used to it. Handlin' that iron all day long, an' those raw edges an' all, oh, it's cruel at the best of times . . .'

'It takes a bit o' gettin' used to,' he admitted slowly.
'But why should you get used to it?' she asked.
He looked up into her face now.
'It's what every man has to,' he said.

(Page 167)

The artist's vision is apparent too in the drops of tea Connie imagines 'hung on his fierce moustache' and in the description of Tevershall quoted above: '. . . it gave her a certain feeling of blind virility, a certain blind, pathetic forcefulness of life.' The forcefulness, which is at the same time 'blindness' and formlessness, is related obviously to the failure of responsibility in those who are responsible for Tevershall's being what it is, the English elite who have let England down, the Sir Clifford Chatterleys with their disastrously conventional and in the worst sense conservative devotion to ideals and to 'forms'. The relation is obvious, though it is characteristic of Lawrence's control over what he has to say in this version that the relation is not insisted upon.

Lawrence's control over what he has to say is evident too in the way in which he introduces the so-called obscene words. So too is his gift for comedy. One is tired of hearing that Lawrence lacked a sense of humour:

'But why?' she said. 'Why should you want to go to Canada? You're all right here.'
'Ay!' he said. 'I'm a gamekeeper at thirty-five **bob** a

168

week. Ay! I'm all right! I'm Sir Clifford's servant, an'
I'm Lady Chatterley's—' he looked at her in the face.
'What do you call me in *your* sort of talk?'

'My lover!' she stammered.

'Lover!' he re-echoed. A queer flash went over his face.
'Fucker!' he said, and his eyes darted a flash at her as
if he had shot her.

The word, she knew from Clifford, was obscene, and
she flushed deeply and then went pale. But since the
word itself had so little association to her, it made very
little impression on her. Only she was amazed at the
diabolic hate—or fury—she did not know what it was
—that flashed out of him all at once, like a cobra
striking.

'But,' she stammered, 'even if you are—are you
ashamed of it?'

He had been looking at her curiously, watchfully,
like a dog that has bitten somebody. His expression
slowly changed to one of perplexed doubt.

'Am I ashamed of it?' he questioned vaguely.

'Yes! Even if you are my "fucker", as you call it, are
you ashamed of it? There's nothing to be ashamed of
in it, is there?'

His eyes slowly widened with a slow wonder, and a
sort of boyishness came on his face again. She was looking at him with wide, candid blue eyes. He pushed his
hat a little off his brow and broke into an amused laugh.
'No!' he said. 'There's nothing to be ashamed of right
enough. If there isn't for you there isn't for me.' He
stood laughing at her oddly, still a little doubtful.

'Why shouldn't you take me if we both want it?' she
said.

'Why shouldn't I fuck thee when we both of us want
it?' he repeated in broad dialect, smiling all over his body
with amusement as a dog does.

'Yes, why not!' she re-echoed.

He looked full into her eyes, and in his eyes a little
flame was dancing with perfect amusement. He pushed
his hat off his brow again, then pulled it back.

'It's a winder!' he said.

She only gazed at him.

'It's a winder!' he repeated, the smile flickering and
moving all over his face.

'What amuses you so?' she asked.
'Yo' do!' he said . . .
He stopped suddenly in his laughter, and his whole
bearing changed.
'Ay!' he said seriously. 'You're right! You're right!
That's what it is to be a proper lady! There's nawt even
to laugh at in it! And you're right, you're right!'
'Then—' she said slowly, 'why were you so cross with
me?'
He took off his hat and looked up at her a little bit
like a schoolboy.
'Was I mad with yer?' he asked.
'Yes!'
He hung his head and ruminated. Then he said:
'Let's go an' sit down. Then 'appen I can tell you.'
(Pages 108–9)

The kind of comedy one finds here and the woodland setting may tempt one to play with the word Shakespearean
when describing the effect of this scene. Yet the broad-
minded comedy of *Much Ado About Nothing* or *As You
Like It* seems, by comparison, merely the comedy of the
unexpected, the repartee merely the expression of settled
attitudes. Parkin, moreover, is neither a 'wit' nor a clown.
His 'pure amusement', his 'wonder' and his sudden
'seriousness' are those of a man who is capable of making
a genuine discovery. It is because of this than he can seem
'like a schoolboy' and yet, with no contradiction, appeal to
Connie as a man.
A comparison between the first and third versions cannot of course conclude without reference to Lawrence's use
of the obscene vocabulary and without reference to the
question of taste. And here again, it seems to me that
Lawrence lost control, in the process of rewriting, over
what he originally had to say. Although in *The First Lady
Chatterly*, the offending words are used, it is clear that the
Lawrence who wrote this version was aware, as he may
have ceased to be later, of the actual impact they can
produce—their impact, that is, not only on the minds of
those who may shrink from any thought of what they stand
for, but on those too who, through long association, inevitably react to the kind of intention that usually dictates
their use. Parkin himself speaks as he does with the inten-

tion of giving offence. He is astounded to realize that such words can be used in a way that is neither shameful nor offensive. But he realizes too that to use them in the way that Connie uses them calls for unusual character and unusual circumstances, circumstances of the kind that give their relationship its value: 'That's what it is to be a proper lady!' The Lawrence who wrote this version was closer to the English language than the Lawrence who wrote the third,[8] more aware, that is, of the intention and circumstances that in fact determine the impact of words. He was also, in every sense of the word, closer to England itself.

The First Lady Chatterley was begun in the autumn of 1926 when the Lawrences were living near Florence, immediately after a visit to England, a visit which was to be Lawrence's last, and to Eastwood and the country of his childhood. The second version was written in the following spring and the third, the authorized version so to speak, authorized by Lawrence and now by the law courts, during the autumn and winter following that. Why Lawrence altered the novel three times is a matter for speculation. But that he altered it disastrously is beyond question.

Los Angeles
August 1969

NOTES

1. The first two versions can be bought only in the Italian translation by Professor Carlo Izzo published by Mondadori for the first time in 1954 (in *Le tre 'Lady Chatterley'*, volume VII of *Tutte le opere di David Herbert Lawrence a cura di Piero Nardi*). The first version was published in 1944 by the Dial Press in New York with a preface by Frieda Lawrence and two years later in Berne in the Phoenix Books series, but both editions have been out of print for many years. The second version, astonishingly enough, has never once been published in English and my own knowledge of it, for what it is worth, is based entirely on Professor Izzo's translation. We owe it to Frieda Lawrence and to Mr. William Houghland, formerly of the

171

Laboratory of Anthropology in Santa Fe that the first two versions have survived. It was Mr. Houghland who typed up the manuscripts and attempted to find publishers for them. My own page references in this essay are to the 1944 Dial Press edition. (Messrs. Heinemann have now announced that they are shortly to publish both earlier versions).

2. *Morality and the Novel* in *Phoenix* (London, 1961), p. 529.

3. See F. R. Leavis, *Anna Karenina and other essays*, London, Chatto & Windus, 1967, p. 240. It might of course be argued in reply to this charge that one of the main themes of the novel is the tragedy of the years following the war to end all wars, a tragedy of which Clifford is one of the most conspicuous victims. Any cruelty in the way he is presented is not then the author's, it might be said, but simply the cruelty of his own fate. Possibly. But it seems to me that Professor Leavis is right and that the 'animus' he talks of is particularly evident in the conversations between husband and wife. It would be difficult to contemplate without wincing the thought of conversation in which a cripple was reminded that there are men who are 'physical failures' and others who are not, difficult, that is, unless one were carried away by feelings of hatred and malevolence towards the cripple. Yet this is how Connie on more than one occasion speaks to her husband and in doing so she is presented with evident sympathy and admiration. Clifford on one occasion, wishing to be 'nice to her', reads from a scientific-religious book, the theme of which is the slow evolution of matter into the realm of spirit:

> 'She listened with a glint of amusement. All sorts of improper things suggested themselves. But she only said:
> "What silly hocus-pocus! . . . It only means *he's* a physical failure on earth, so he wants to make the whole universe a physical failure. Priggish little impertinence!"' (Chapter 16).

The Clifford of the first version is in no way more intelligent or humane than the Clifford of the third. Yet Connie, for all her usual frankness, has always a natural scrupulous delicacy when talking to him. Lawrence doesn't invite us to amuse ourselves at his expense in the way characterized in the above quotation.

4. Not only of course the world of Tevershall and Wragby. In all three versions of the novel Clifford is an energetic and resourceful captain of industry and a Cambridge-educated intellectual. In the third version he is also a successful author of prose fiction. Lawrence has made him as representative as possible of the culture of upper-class England.

5. Some readers are disconcerted by the way in which Mellors can switch so easily from educated English to dialect speech. However, Mr. William McCance, the art critic and painter, who was born and educated in the Scottish coalfields has told me that he finds this perfectly natural and even on occasions unavoidable. It was Mr. McCance, incidentally, who in conversation with Lawrence probably gave him the idea for an episode in the novel. His own father was killed in a mining accident and his widow, like Mrs. Bolton, in all three versions of the novel, deprived of the full compensation by the owners on the grounds that he must have panicked and run.

6. Not only of modern *England*. In rewriting *Lady Chatterley*, Lawrence sacrificed the description of Connie's journey through Fraance at the time of the hay harvest:

> Yet the country they drove through was strange and fascinating, as if the world had forgotten it. How strange and remote France was! And sometimes they stayed in a village inn where the men came at evening and drank wine. She heard the guttural sound of the dialect, and a certain nostalgia came over her for the warm blindness of life like theirs. She saw them sitting with knees apart and loosely clenched fists resting on their live animal thighs. That was how Parkin sat . . . (pages 134–5).

Compare too with the exasperated description of Paris in the third version, 'weary of its now mechanical sensuality, weary of the tension of money, money, money,' etc., these observations:

How beautiful the midsummer flowers were in the Luxembourg Gardens, so brilliant and so purely decorative! Not at all wistful and a little amateurish as the very lovely and abundant flowers were in Hyde Park!

173

Not in the very least like the pathos of the gardens at Wragby. Fine, splendid, showy, jaunty! She liked them very much. And the thin-legged boys playing games with a ball and crying out with such pseudo-sportsman-like alertness—they might have come out of a Fourteenth Century picture, the clothing merely a little different.

For the first time, even, she rather liked the way the men looked at her: looked to see what she would be like to sleep with . . . Then, after about a week the excitement passed, and though Paris did not cease to be sympathetic, it became depressing. These men, these men, like creatures roving restlessly in Hades, in a sort of after-life, seeking for something in a woman that they had really ceased to want, they were depressed and depressing. They were really terribly disheartened. Only they kept up the old woman-hunt, which no longer really interested them or the woman. Only they could think of nothing else. In their souls they could discover no new impulse (pages 117–8).

7. See *D. H. Lawrence: Novelist* (London, 1955), pages 293–4.

8. He was closer also to the English language than when he wrote *A propos of Lady Chatterley's Lover*, or at least when he wrote the following passage: 'The words that shock so much at first don't shock at all after a while. Is this because the mind is depraved by habit? Not a bit. It is that the words merely shocked the eye, they never shocked the mind at all . . . People with minds realize they aren't shocked and never really were.' The disingenuous distinction between 'the mind' and 'the eye' is not characteristic of Lawrence's thinking at its best.

9. This essay was first published in *Encounter* in January 1971. Permission to reprint it is gratefully acknowledged.

D. H. LAWRENCE'S POETRY: ART AND THE
APPREHENSION OF FACT *

When Lawrence left the school in Croydon where he had
been a teacher for four years, the testimonial he received
included this comment:

> He has also particularly directed the art training of the
> upper divisions, [and] has to a great extent influenced
> the science teaching of the whole school.[1]

The combination may strike us as unusual; and the reform
of science teaching is not, perhaps, what one would guess
to have been Lawrence's distinction as a teacher. There is,
however, a passage in *Women in Love* that makes the
statement intelligible. Birkin, the school inspector, is talking to Ursula:

> 'Give them some crayons, won't you?' he said, 'so
> that they can make the gynaecious flowers red, and the
> androgynous yellow. I'd chalk them in plain, chalk in
> nothing else, merely the red and yellow. Outline scarcely
> matters in this case. There is just the one fact to
> emphasize.'

And after Ursula has objected that it would make the books
untidy,

> 'Not very,' he said. 'You must mark in these things
> obviously. It's the fact you want to emphasize, not the
> subjective impression to record. What's the fact?—red
> little spiky stigmas of the female flower, dangling yel-
> low male catkin, yellow pollen flying from one to the
> other. Make a pictorial record of the fact, as a child does

* By R. T. Jones, University of York.

175

when drawing a face—two eyes, one nose, mouth with teeth—so—' And he drew a figure on the blackboard.[2]

Time and again, in the poems, Lawrence offers us (at whatever the risk of 'making the books untidy') what he calls 'a pictorial record of the fact'—the fact (not the subjective impression) made real, made apprehensible as experience, by the creative imagination. It is this quality that I shall attempt to describe and illustrate in the comments that follow.

Fidelity,[3] which begins 'Fidelity and love are two different things, like a flower and a gem', contains this characterization of the reality of a flower :

> O flowers they fade because they are moving swiftly;
> a little torrent of life
> leaps up to the summit of the stem, gleams, turns
> over round the bend
> of the parabola of curved flight,
> sinks, and is gone, like a comet curving into the
> invisible.

The 'fact' of the flower is apprehended through the imagined draughtsman's line, the gesture of the drawing hand; what the rhythm of the last three of those lines enacts is that imagined action, swift as it must be if the curve of the stem is to run true, but always at the same time carefully responsive to the object—the verbs record the quick-glancing watchfulness of the eyes informing and guiding the uninterrupted hand. What is given to us is not the inert fact of the encyclopaedist, but fact apprehended in a man's consciousness, as the artist must apprehend it in order to recreate it. It is 'a repetition in the finite mind' of the conceivable, if not strictly imaginable, act of creating a flower—'the eternal act of creation in the infinite I AM'.[4] The relation of this activity to botany, and of the creative imagination to science generally, is one that deserves to be investigated.

The analogy that the poem sets up can be illuminating only in so far as its terms are fully present to us as experienced facts. The recreation of the flower's blooming and fading is not ornamental but intrinsic to the insight embodied in the poem. In the same way, the gem, analogue of fidelity, must be made apprehensible; and this is more difficult, because the process of formation of a gem is so long, and involves such enormous masses and pressures, such apparently random and chaotic movements, some sudden and some slow, that no mere speeding-up of events, like running a film projector at high speed, can make its reality imaginable. A gesture of the hand served as a starting-point in experience for the imaginative recreation of a flower, but the attempt to apprehend the birth of a gem has to start from the human extremity of orgasm. It makes use, too, in verbal echoes, of the Book of Genesis, to suggest how the human imagination can be stretched to encompass creation. Something of the slowness of the process is communicated in the diffusion of the description, in contrast with the swift conciseness of the description of the flower; but there remains, in the concept of geological time, a residue of the unimaginable, acknowledged in the poem by the repeated explicit insistence on slowness. By such means the poem creates a metaphor of sensible movement for the geological process.—Not visible movement: that would distort the fact. Here it is Lawrence's respect for the fact in its completeness that differentiates him from the popularizer.

> In the old days, when sapphires were breathed upon
>   and brought forth
> during the wild orgasms of chaos
> time was much slower, when the rocks came forth.
> It took æons to make a sapphire, æons for it to pass
>   away . . .
>
> And when, throughout all the wild orgasms of love
> slowly a gem forms, in the ancient, once-more-molten
>   rocks
> of two human hearts, two ancient rocks, a man's heart
>   and a woman's,
> that is the crystal of peace, the slow hard jewel of
>   trust,
> the sapphire of fidelity.
> The gem of mutual peace emerging from the wild
>   chaos of love.

I need not dwell on the value of the human insight that the poem presents. Obviously it offers a fresh way of apprehending the relation between love and fidelity (a way that can incidentally, help us to discuss the process enacted in Shakespeare's *Antony and Cleopatra*). What I want to draw attention to is the way in which the poem relates human experience to the non-human world, so that each helps to make the other intelligible. The flower and the gem are essential to the meaning of the poem; they are vividly apprehended as real things, and it is their reality, the factual sense of what they are, that throws light on love and fidelity—not the mere idea of flower and gem.

There is a no-man's-land in the neighbourhood of the physical sciences: a place of intuitive gropings and apprehensions where neither scientific fact nor sensory experience is sovereign; popularizers and pseudo-scientists raid it; scientists seem to ignore it, although we may suspect that that is where they go to find their new concepts. Lawrence explored and cultivated this region. He was concerned with the possibility of establishing and communicating truths other than, but complementary to, those that may be scientifically verified; and there is a sense in which much of his poetry might be called 'metaphysical'. Of course I do not want to label Lawrence as one kind of poet—that would be a boring exercise. Nor do I want to say that his poetry is like Donne's, though there is in Lawrence's struggle to build intuitive knowledge on the inhospitable foundation of a modern man's rational education something analogous to Donne's exasperated efforts to seize experience with (or in spite of) the intellectual equipment of an intractable scholastic philosophy. 'Belief', said Lawrence, 'is a profound emotion that has the mind's connivance',[5] and for both poets the mind had often to be coerced into connivance; but they had very different ways of doing it.

My earlier quotation from *Women In Love* may have reminded the reader of another classroom scene: the opening of Dickens's *Hard Times*.

'Now, what I want is, Facts. Teach these boys and girls nothing but Facts. Facts alone are wanted in life. Plant nothing else, and root out everything else. You can only form the minds of reasoning animals upon Facts: nothing else will ever be of any service to them. This is the principle on which I bring up my own children, and this is the principle on which I bring up these children. Stick to Facts, Sir!'

When Birkin says, 'It's the fact you want to emphasize, not the subjective impression to record', he evidently means something different from what Mr Gradgrind means by 'fact':

'Bitzer,' said Thomas Gradgrind. 'Your definition of a horse.'

'Quadruped. Graminivorous. Forty teeth, namely twenty-four grinders, four eye-teeth, and twelve incisive. Sheds coat in the spring; in marshy countries, sheds hoofs, too. Hoofs hard, but requiring to be shod with iron. Age known by marks in mouth.' Thus (and much more) Bitzer.

'Now girl number twenty,' said Mr Gradgrind, 'you know what a horse is.'

'Now you know what a horse is'—this to a girl brought up in the circus, now given the benefit of a definition of a horse by a classmate who, as far as one can tell from his account, may never have been within spitting distance of a horse. It is Sissy Jupe who knows what a horse is, although she is 'possessed of no facts, in reference to' it.

Lawrence's poem *Kangaroo*[6] communicates knowledge of a kangaroo; an encyclopaedia gives facts about it.

Kangaroo (*Macropus*), a genus of marsupial quadrupeds, of which there are many species, almost all Australian, although a few are found in New Guinea and neighbouring islands. The genus, as now restricted, contains, according to the most reliable estimate, twenty-three species. The kangaroos are of different sizes; some of the Wallabies, which really belong to the same genus, being comparatively small, while the Great Kangaroo (*M. giganteus*) attains a length of 8 feet, counting the long tail. They are entirely herbivorous—mainly grass feeders—and the two lower incisors, which are elongated, play upon each other like the blades of scissors and crop the grass. The tail is very thick and strong, while the fore-limbs are short. They are very powerful animals, and the hind-limb forms a very effectual weapon for ripping open the bodies of dogs, with the aid of which they are sometimes hunted.[7]

179

We can't (except in one detail) deny the accuracy of this description, or even, in some circumstances which it is fairly entertaining to imagine, its possible usefulness; but its limitations become apparent in contrast with the poem. As Lawrence wrote in a different context, 'If we try to fix the living tissue, as the biologists fix it with formalin, we have only a hardened bit of the past, the bygone life under our observation'.[8] Here are some of the facts that Lawrence gives us.

> Her little loose hands, and drooping Victorian
>   shoulders.
> And then her great weight below the waist, her vast
>   pale belly
> With a thin young yellow little paw hanging out, and
>   straggle of a long thin ear, like ribbon,
> Like a funny trimming to the middle of her belly,
>   thin little dangle of an immature paw, and one thin
>   ear.
> Her belly, her big haunches
> and, in addition, the great muscular python-stretch
>   of her tail.

If one is more interested in kangaroos than in Gradgrind's kind of facts about them, one is likely to gain more knowledge from Lawrence's description. The difference is not, surely, that the poem is subjective and the encyclopaedia objective. Throughout the poem Lawrence is absorbed in what he is describing: the kangaroo 'out there', not his own feelings about it. 'Little loose hands' is just as factual as 'the fore-limbs are short', and 'the great muscular python-stretch of her tail' gives more information about a kangaroo's tail than does 'the tail is very thick and strong'. What is puzzling is that a phrase like 'drooping Victorian shoulders', which is perfectly factual and precise, strikes us at once as unscientific; whereas 'like the blades of scissors' is scientifically acceptable, although it is a very inaccurate description of the supposed movement. It is very unlikely that the zoologist of the encyclopaedia meant to suggest that the lower incisors of the kangaroo work on the principle of crossed blades as scissors do;[9] he must have meant that they part and meet, edge to edge, to nip grass between them. What makes the comparison acceptable in scientific contexts has nothing to do with precision or objectivity; perhaps it was at first not hard to accept because it is a comparison with a mechanism, not a human characteristic; later writers followed precedent.

But it would be perverse to argue that Lawrence is trying to do the same thing as Bitzer and the encyclopaedist, and does it better. I have only tried to establish that the difference can't usefully be described in terms of the 'objective-subjective' antithesis. Leaving aside that phrase about scissors, which is bad science, the scientific writer prefers to restrict himself to statements that can be verified by counting and measuring: scientific fact generally means numerical fact. The coronation of Mathematics in place of Theology as the queen of the sciences has spectacularly justified itself in many ways; it has led to the discovery of facts which could not have been arrived at by intuition or imagination. But today we are in danger of dismissing as non-fact and mere subjective impression any fact that cannot be formulated in such a way as to be numerically verifiable. Yet the numerically verifiable fact that we have been trained to trust, like 'the Great Kangaroo . . . attains a length of 8 feet, counting the tail', needs to be transformed into imagined experience before we can take it in, respond to it, or remember it: let's see, how long is that?—from here to there—allow so much for the tail, then it would stand about this high. Lawrence gives us, in the rhythms of the passage I have quoted, fully experienced facts about the shape of the mother kangaroo and the smallness of its young. Such observations imply, I believe, a metaphysical position that bases knowledge neither on the scientist's hypothesis that facts have an existence independent of and prior to their discovery, nor on the autonomy of the personal impression, but on the living relationship between the responsive and responsible observer, the thing observed, and the observer's fellow-men with whom he communicates.

The relation between experience and theory, or between the particular experience and the general belief, is explored in a different area of knowledge in *The Man of Tyre*:[10]

The man of Tyre went down to the sea
  pondering, for he was a Greek, that God is one and
all alone and ever more shall be so.

181

And a woman who had been washing clothes in the
   pool of rock
where a stream came down to the gravel of the sea and
   sank in,
who had spread white washing on the gravel banked
   above the bay,
who had lain her shift on the shore, on the shingle
   slope,
who had waded to the pale green sea of evening, out to
   a shoal,
pouring sea-water over herself
now turned, and came slowly back, with her back to
   the evening sky.

Oh lovely, lovely with the dark hair piled up, as she
   went deeper, deeper down the channel, then rose
   shallower, shallower,
with the full thighs slowly lifting of the water
   wading shorewards
and the shoulders pallid with light from the silent
   sky behind
both breasts dim and mysterious, with the glamorous
   kindness of twilight between them
and the dim notch of black maidenhair like an
   indicator,
   giving a message to the man—

So in the cane-brake he clasped his hands in delight
that could only be god-given, and murmured:
Lo! God is one god! But here in the twilight
godly and lovely comes Aphrodite out of the sea
towards me!

So the man of Tyre, like a sensible fellow, does not allow
his dogma to blind him to the experience it denies. Nor, like
a still more sensible fellow, does he abandon a good dogma
—which he may need another day—just because one fact
has collided with it. He carries his conflicting truths, as it
were one in each hand, with a fine tender reverence for
each. One feels that if he were to have more such revela-
tions he might have to reconsider his dogma, but for the
time being he can carry both if he walks carefully.

This poem again presents the experience of a 'man
alive' and of the living moment, but here it is explicitly

opposed to the fixed and apparently impersonal formulation, in this instance a theological one. The confrontation is far from being, as some of Lawrence's essays might lead us to suppose, a mortal battle: the dogma, whether theological or scientific, can be useful as long as it does not exclude fresh experience. The poems invite us to recognize what we see, however inconvenient this may be to our orderly notions of the kind of world we live in—however much it may tend to make our book untidy.

Lawrence's task in this poem is especially difficult because he has to establish a godliness and loveliness: the whole point of the poem requires that apprehended beauty be communicated. As he often does, Lawrence uses the resources of the painter. In the description of the setting, a variety of textures and colours bring the reader's inner eye and finger-tips (and feet perhaps) into active participation; then as we focus on the figure, its physical reality and solidity are conveyed as the painter conveys them, in the delicately recorded variation of lights and shadows, and in the apprehension of weight in the hair and the thighs, emphasized by the slowness of the movements ('lifting').

Of all that this brief account of the poem has omitted, the most important, I think, is the dimension that may be called the 'tone' of the poem: the quality that makes us hear, at the beginning and the end most clearly, a voice that is affectionately and even respectfully mocking. It was in response to this 'tone' that I said that the Greek acts like a sensible fellow; the poet does not declare his attitude, but we know that we are not being invited to scorn the Greek for his theological inconsistency. The affection is conveyed partly by the poet's choosing not to make it clear whether the crucial phrase 'that could only be god-given' is his own or the Greek's, so we read it as both—the poet is with him, or only a very little ironically detached. And 'godly and lovely' summarizes so finely what the poem itself has presented with wholly unironical absorption and delight that again we cannot separate the poet from his Greek. The separation, the ironical detachment, appears only, if at all, in 'Lo! God is one god!' and as this assertion does not in the least obstruct the Greek's vision of Aphrodite, the poet does not begrudge him his dogma. The affirmation, in such a tricky situation, makes us admire his obstinacy and wish him well. It is a part of the total effect of the poem, a very important part that ought not to be neglected in analysis, that the poet's tone is one that we recognize as eminently sane and poised: the voice of a man whom we can, with proper circumspection, trust as a guide among strange and possibly dangerous experiences of thought and feeling.

There is an early poem that illustrates concisely Lawrence's receptiveness to knowledge whatever its sources, and his special interest in the mysterious origins of factual knowledge:

Aware [11]
Slowly the moon is rising out of the ruddy haze,
Divesting herself of her golden shift, and so
Emerging white and exquisite; and I in amaze
See in the sky before me, a woman I did not know
I loved, but there she goes, and her beauty hurts my heart;
I follow her down the night, begging her not to depart.

The fact that he loves her takes him by surprise, and the break at the line-ending ('did not know/I loved') suggests a reluctance, or at least a hesitation, in admitting it to himself. But it can't be denied—'but there she goes', whether he likes it or not, 'and her beauty hurts my heart'. We are not told about the process by which this recognition comes to him, though enough is suggested to make it perfectly credible. Partly it is the visual impression produced by the moon and the clouds that suggests this particular woman, and once her image has defined itself, his involuntary reactions make the fact unmistakable. But the image of the woman has been produced by the observer's imagination working on moon and cloud—external phenomena which to other men might have suggested a ship in full sail or a bowl of steaming porridge. Lawrence does not trace a train of associations as Wordsworth does in 'Strange fits of passion have I known', where again it is the contemplation of the moon that releases a repressed awareness—of Lucy's mortality. Wordsworth relates how, while going to visit Lucy, he fixes his eyes on the moon, and as he approaches her cottage the moon suddenly drops behind it; by this time Lucy and the moon have become so intertwined in his mind that the disappearance of the moon suggests Lucy's death. Lawrence doesn't explain, but presents the delicately recorded experience; he implies no theory to which the reader could with any meaning say 'I don't agree'. There it is, there it goes; it's an accomplished fact, a created experience (whether it ever 'happened', biographically, or not).

Evidently there are dangers in being as open as Lawrence's poem suggests one should be, dangers in a readiness to recognize what one really feels, whether one wants to or not. The mind has its apparatus for suppressing such knowledge, and we may well hesitate to take off the lid; we might discover that we desire our mothers or wish to kill our fathers, or that we are strongly inclined to cruelty, suicide, homosexuality or necrophilia. The counsel of perfection, of course, would be to know oneself anyway, and, knowing the worst, learn to live with it; thus one will at worst know one's enemy, and be free to make moral choices instead of being a mechanism of unacknowledged impulses.

But even choice can be dangerous, even if one chooses well. A poem often studied in schools, not only in England, is *Snake*,[12] which leads one through an experience of liking a snake (a poisonous one) and feeling honoured by its visit, despite the demand of both social duty and self-preservation that it should be killed. After sharing this experience one might still decide to kill a poisonous snake at the next encounter, but the conflict of conscious impulses, however brief, might well delay the blow just long enough for the snake to strike first. I hope this handy example will not seem frivolous to the reader in snakeless England; it is meant to stand for other more subtle dangers. This openness, this readiness to recognize what one really feels, can make life richer and fuller, but also more hazardous and difficult.

But it would be a distortion of *Aware*, and a radical misrepresentation of *Snake*, to suggest that they are about Lawrence's feelings. *Aware* is largely about the moon and the clouds, and *Snake* is about a snake. Of course he does not try, as the scientist does, to exclude himself as observer from the record of his observation. Even *I Wish I Knew A Woman*[13] is really *about* such a woman, and the other kind of woman; it does not for a moment suggest that morbid preoccupation with one's own sensibility that the title might lead us to expect.

I wish I knew a woman
who was like a red fire on the hearth
glowing after the day's restless draughts.

So that one could draw near her
in the red stillness of the dusk
and really take delight in her
without having to make the polite effort of loving her
or the mental effort of making her acquaintance.
Without having to take a chill, talking to her.

This is not a passive yearning, a sentimental daydream wish
that life were nicer than it is. The poem actively creates
the relationship it asks for, rather as a medieval Welsh
poem asking for the gift of a horse recreates the horse
with an intensity of apprehension that convincingly takes
possession of it (the owner must have felt that he might as
well make over the legal ownership too).

Although this poem, like many in *Pansies*, takes the form
of a personal statement, its achieved lucidity implies a
relationship with the reader; it does not rest in the assertion that this is what the poet feels (and if the world doesn't
understand, so much the worse for the world)—but implies
an invitation to the reader to confirm what it observes and
desiderates. In this respect this poem is not unlike *Good
Husbands Make Unhappy Wives*,[14] which is a plain and
apparently verifiable statement :

Good husbands make unhappy wives
so do bad husbands, just as often;
but the unhappiness of a wife with a good husband
is much more devastating
than the unhappiness of a wife with a bad husband.

Lawrence offers no evidence in support of this statement;
he tosses it to us with a certain gaiety, something of 'Take
it or leave it'. We are invited, I think, to try it out and see
if it works—in that sense it is verifiable; and it turns out
to have an alarmingly wide range of applicability. Alarming because it contradicts what we have been accustomed
to assume, our assumption being based on the imprecision
with which we commonly use the word 'good', associating
it with certain stereotyped personal attributes and habits.
A similar perception might have been published in prose,
but then it couldn't decently stand alone, without a more
respectable formulation and a set of case-histories to support it. Or else a single fictitious case-history, recognizably
representative, could imply, without explicitly stating,

some such moral as this poem expresses—in other words, approximately, that the incidence of marked suicidal and murderous impulses among wives appears to be highest where the husbands are most conscientious, considerate and generally impeccable. The poem, though, makes its point less cautiously and less solemnly than my paraphrase can, and more challengingly.

One way in which it challenges our preconceptions is by making us reconsider what we mean by 'good', and the possibility that we are too easily taken in by external appearances in supposing somebody to be a good husband. The goodness may be only for export, and the good man in public may be a terror in the home. What aggravates the misery of the wife in that case is the knowledge that nobody would believe her. But perhaps a more radical questioning is required; it may be that conjugal happiness is quite unrelated to goodness, in any generally received meaning of the word (or the reader's own meaning of it); and, if that is so, it must be a heavy trial to any wife to have a good husband—so that she must feel that whatever may go wrong with the marriage, for any reason, must be her fault. A moderate degree of blameworthiness must be a comforting attribute in a spouse.

This, like many of Lawrence's, is a limited poem. If pressed for a definition of greatness in literature, I should probably offer something like 'inexhaustibility of meaning'. The meaning of this poem is soon exhausted; but in five lines it contributes to our emancipation from the pseudo-logical process by which we are inclined to suppose that good husbands are sure to make their wives happy (it would make the books so untidy if they didn't), and, indirectly, from that sense of a morally tidy universe that leads us to think about human misery in terms of problems —our school arithmetic books having conditioned us to assume that all problems have solutions.

I do not want to claim that Lawrence's best poetry is of this kind—perhaps *Good Husbands Make Unhappy Wives* is not poetry in any strict sense at all, and there is nothing in it that could not turn up in good conversation. But I have chosen it as my last example for several reasons; partly because it is in such poems that it is easiest to illustrate one of the least recognized qualities of his poetry: that attentive curiosity about the world that is not different, in its motive and its concern, from the scientist's; partly because we tend to undervalue such plain and apparently direct statements and find difficulty in discussing them. It is to longer poems, like *Fidelity* and *Kangaroo*, that we must look for Lawrence's best poetry, where the scientist's concern with fact is enlarged and vivified by the range and scope of the creative artist—often that of the painter as well as that of the writer. But the shorter, plainer poems are not negligible, and many of them exemplify finely the triangular relationship I mentioned earlier. We could represent it emblematically in a drawing: the poet stands with one hand on the reader's shoulder, the other pointing at a blossoming tree.

Good conversation, after all, is not to be had every day.

NOTES

1. E. Nehls, *D. H. Lawrence: a composite biography* (University of Wisconsin Press, Madison, 1957), Vol. I, p. 150.
2. *Women in Love*, chapter 3.
3. *The Complete Poems of D. H. Lawrence*, ed. V. de S. Pinto & W. Roberts (London, 1964), p. 476.
4. S. T. Coleridge, *Biographia Literaria*, chapter XII, 'On the Imagination, or Esemplastic Power'.
5. *A Propos of Lady Chatterley's Lover*.
6. *Complete Poems*, p. 392.
7. *Chambers' Encyclopaedia* (1901).
8. 'Poetry of the Present', reprinted in *Collected Poems*, p. 182. This and other printed texts give 'formation', but I believe Lawrence meant 'formalin', which makes better sense.
9. Probably none of the writers who used the comparison really believed that the incisors crossed. Its initiator seems to have been an observant lady who visited Regent's Park Zoo in 1866, and her description stuck. 'Cineradiographic examination of the living animal has established, beyond doubt, that the incisors of the wallaby are separable during biting . . . Our results give no indication that Murie and Bartlett's "scissor action" occurs.'—W. D. L. Ride, 'Mastication and taxonomy in the macropodine skull', in *Function and Taxonomic Importance* (Systematics Association Publication No. 3, 1959), p. 38.

10. *Complete Poems*, p. 692.
11. *Complete Poems*, p. 67.
12. *Complete Poems*, p. 349.
13. *Complete Poems*, p. 506.
14. *Complete Poems*, p. 456.

LAWRENCE AND ART *

There are many reasons why we should be grateful that Lawrence returned, towards the end of his life, to his boyhood hobby of painting. We have the paintings themselves, which are now available for consultation at the lending-libraries in the form of the recent edition of reproductions.[1] Although we are rather put on the spot explaining, to the art-student who regards them with a beady eye, the special character of their value, coming from the hand of a man whose whole *oeuvre* has such an interesting knack of being all-of-a-piece. There is also the art-criticism left by Lawrence, which is of considerable value. Then the sharpening-effect of this painterly enthusiasm on the philosophical and discursive side of Lawrence's thinking should not be underestimated.

The volume of paintings by Lawrence is a rather preposterous book. A charming piece of embroidery and some tasteful early water-colours give place to an acreage of green-tinted white flesh in *Rape of the Sabine Women* (XIII), and then from every page the bodies come burgeoning out, like genii from Aladdin's lamp: in every picture they writhe, or squirm, or flop themselves untidily across the landscape. There is an impression of bulbous big men who cannot find a place to sit down, and wherever you look, so many bottoms!

All of which may appear a little unkind. But it would be wrong to disregard the element of stiltedness, or sense of some complicated emotion's having been set between the painter and his scene in these pictures. It's obvious that by sticking to his limitations Lawrence could have acquired a certain *réclame* as an artist, over and above his fame as a

* By John and Ann Remsbury, University of Lisbon.

writer, if this had been what he wanted. But the embroidery and the water-colours didn't satisfy him. He wanted to paint the human body. This was what mattered to him in painting. It was a compulsion which arose in the most natural way from everything which had gone before, in the novels, poetry and criticism.

Perhaps Lawrence saw the body quite differently from most of us, and perhaps every man who is religious in the way in which Lawrence was religious has known a similar impulse to paint the body. Supposing you really believed that Man was made in the image of God, and you felt the force of this conviction anew each day: how then could it be otherwise? How could you *not* wish to paint the body? How could you *not* wish to express your sense of the loveliness and perfection of the human being? And what better medium is there for doing this than in painting?

For Man, the body is the strangest thing in all the world, and feelings of religious reverence, no less than of fear and shame, are indissolubly bound up with the contemplation of it. What were all those old Venetians, and the fifteenth-century Flemish painters really doing, when they handled their central symbol? Did they not make a free choice of the body, as the most evocative image of the soul? There is the *Adam and Eve* of Hugo Van Der Goes, for instance, with all its ochres and earth-colours, with the delicate luminosity of the figures in the garden, and with the careful toning-in of the figures into the whole composition, so that the warm flesh-tones are reflected by the apples on the trees. His figures have been given real bodies, complete with fine body-hair and delicate little bones set in just the right place at the ankle, wrist and knee. The skill that went into their making was of the rarest kind, as if all the care and attention to detail was informed with affection for the human creature: so his Adam and Eve seem alive and almost a-stir today.

But one returns to Lawrence with a bump, for however praiseworthy his intentions were, his talents were obviously too slender for their execution. The flesh-quality of his nudes is reminiscent—what can one say?—of feet which have been in the water for a long time. The flesh is *idealized*, to use his own word; there is a lack of fine hair, of skin-texture and of bone and sinew in the modelling.

Of course this is not to deny that there are places here

191

and there in this volume where Lawrence truly seems to have enjoyed the things that are to do with painting. *The Feast of Radishes* (V) is a painter's picture. It pleases with its static verticals, simple colours, sustained roughness of texture and with its fine swirl of big, black hats. (It has a familiar, red-bearded, slightly foxy-looking face set just at its point of focus.) *Dance-Sketch* (XII) offers some figures lost in a swirl of movement, and the Spencer-ish *Flight back into Paradise* (IX) has some nice, clear lines and some lively colours. *Red Willow Trees* (VII), with its ver-milions and earth-colours, and formalized recession of rather beautiful, heavy, red, powder-puff trees up the curv-ing hillside is an agreeable picture. Yet it needs something to focus on: some hot, sparky little figures in the centre to replace the pink flopsy-dropsies in the foreground. *Boccaccio Story* (14) is one of the best-known pictures. It has some pictorial sense about it. There is the carved land-scape, the carved, foreshortened legs, the carved dresses and hands, and the fields continuing the ribs of the dresses: and all in delicate pastel-colourings, with nothing amorphous or bloated to spoil the effect. But the face drawn in thick, black lines is a 'strange element', and jars somewhat.

*　　　*　　　*

It is only in the prose-medium that Lawrence was able to render his conception of 'the real existence of the body', and to offer something which was uniquely satisfactory. *Introduction To These Paintings*, especially, is a valuable piece of writing for many reasons. The account of Cézanne's struggle with the cliché it puts forward is as good as any-thing you will find: as perceptive about the man, and as accurate in its grasp of the pictures, as anything which has been written. The philosophical excursions in the essay into the problems of knowledge and imagination perfectly sum-marize the conclusions that Lawrence had been forming on these questions throughout his life. Nor should the comments on science, essential history, and art-history be ignored.

As to the art-history, Lawrence may not say a great deal, but the comments on Watteau and Ingres, on Reynolds and Gainsborough, on the water-colourists, on Impressionism, and on painting after Cézanne, are so much to the point that it may be wished he had said considerably more.

There is always a need intelligently to review the *kinds* of pleasure art is giving people, and it takes a central habit of mind, a relating and organizing habit, to do this. When Lawrence says,

> Van Gogh took up landscape in heavy spadefuls. And Cézanne had to admit it. Landscape, too, after being, since Claude Lorraine, a thing of pure luminosity and floating shadow, suddenly exploded, and came tumbling back on to the canvases of artists in lumps,[2]

he reveals this habit in operation. There is a whole mosaic of local judgements like this in the essay. Together, they arrange themselves in a pattern under the heading of 'the death of the body', with such variants as the case of the Impressionists, who 'escaped from the dark procreative body which so haunts a man'. This simplified way of looking at cultural history is effective in delineating the growth of 'camera-vision' in painting: seen from a distance, the movement of the tradition becomes clearer, so that we *feel* the extraordinary difficulty of making a success of figurative painting today. But 'the novelist's touch' gives rise to a slip of the pen here and there. The portraiture of Hogarth is assimilated, rather clumsily, to that of Reynolds, while Wordsworth is casually grouped with the other 'post-mortem poets' of the Romantic period.

But Lawrence's further opinions on the direction our modern art has taken since his death would certainly be welcome: on all the 'concrete pictorial sensations', as they call themselves, on the scumblings and the impasto, on the pleasures of mental massage from the piled-up heaps of cubes, and on the in-and-out games the eye is invited to play with the perforated sculpture. (His bantering tone is not hard to imagine: 'Isn't it just old hat to you, my dears, the body, as Van Der Goes painted it? Aren't you *intensely* bored? No wonder you have to make holes through it, or flatten it, or stretch it out and make it gangling and spindly, or enlarge its hollows and carve out its stomach, or fashion it into walk-around wire profiles,' etc.)

*   *   *

The account of Cézanne's aim in painting is characterized by its bold simplicity:

I am convinced that what Cézanne himself wanted *was* representation. He *wanted* true-to-life representation. Only he wanted it *more* true to life. And once you have got photography, it is a very, very difficult thing to get representation *more* true-to-life : which it has to be.

The full meaning of these phrases is brought home to us by all the little paragraphs in which Lawrence invites us to look narrowly at the canvases and to make an intelligent effort to see what it was that Cézanne himself saw. What did Cézanne really see, when he took a long, careful look at an apple, or at the head of one of his sitters?

It is the appleyness of the portrait of Cézanne's wife that makes it so permanently interesting : the appleyness, which carries with it also the feeling of knowing the other side as well, the side you don't see, the hidden side of the moon. For the intuitive apperception of the apple is so *tangibly* aware of the apple that it is aware of it *all* round, not only just of the front. The eye sees only fronts, and the mind, on the whole, is satisfied with fronts. But intuition needs all-aroundness, and instinct needs inside-ness. The true imagination is for ever curving round to the other side, to the back of presented appearance.

When this summary is compared with the kind of account Cézanne himself offered, for example,

. . . in an orange, an apple, a bowl, a head, there is a culminating point; and this point is always—in spite of the tremendous effect of light and shade and colourful sensations—the closest to our eye; the edges of the objects recede to a centre on our horizon,[3]

it is of interest to note the course Lawrence has avoided. One way of giving an account of the creative process would consist in turning 'the theory of the culminating point' into a design-principle, and then in laying down a further set of principles of design from this beginning. But what Lawrence has done has been to suggest a necessary link between what is represented on the canvases and the behaviour of the artist himself : the centre of interest in Lawrence's account makes this natural movement towards what is going on in the mind of the painter. We are invited to consider the artist himself, who, it will be recalled, watched this 'all-aroundness' forming before his eyes as he minutely shifted his head from side to side, and *observed* the rotation of the light and colour on an apple, a bowl, or a head, in relation to the culminating point.

Lawrence placed great emphasis on the difficulty of this investigation of the visual world. On the one hand it is only possible to find out what it is that one really sees by fixing an image of the thing seen before oneself; on the other hand ready-made formula for expression springs to the fore every time the effort at true representation is made. Cézanne, more than anyone, thought himself to be in a cleft stick, and he especially wished to escape from his own baroque cliché :

> So he flew at it and knocked all the shape and stuffing out of it, and when it was so mauled that it was all wrong, and he was exhausted with it, he let it go; bitterly, because it still was not what he wanted.

Cézanne never finally discarded this early frustration. It went with him throughout his development as a painter :

> The way he worked over and over his forms was his nervous manner of laying the ghost of his cliché, burying it. Then when it disappeared perhaps from his forms themselves, it lingered in his composition, and he had to fight with the *edges* of his forms and contours, to bury the ghost there. Only his colour he knew was not cliché. He left it to his disciples to make it so.

But Lawrence also affirmed that despite all his difficulties Cézanne remained, for him, by far the most interesting figure in modern painting. He saw something heroic behind Cézanne's struggle with the cliché. He thought that the struggle had a moral weight to it for the very reason that the problem with which Cézanne was dealing was a human and universal one : when a society's vision of the world, and conception of itself, is no longer recruited from the 'quick' of experience, a total cultural failure sets in. Cézanne was to be praised for really coming to grips with his own experience :

> To me these good still-life scenes are purely representative and quite true to life. Here Cézanne did what he wanted to do : he made the things quite real, he didn't deliberately leave anything out, and yet he gave us a

triumphant and rich intuitive vision of a few apples and kitchen pots. For once his intuitive consciousness triumphed, and broke into utterance. And here he is inimitable. His imitators imitate his accessories of tablecloths folded like tin, etc.—the unreal parts of his pictures—but they don't imitate the pots and apples, because they can't. It's the real appleyness, and you can't imitate it. Every man must create it new and different out of himself : new and different.

This is a picture of the great artist as the central kind of man, and a conception of 'the imagination' as a faculty which is developed, after an initial emptying of the mind of all conceptual presupposition, on the basis of the organism's spontaneous and instinctive process of perception. Lawrence says, for example,

He wanted to *express* what he suddenly, convulsedly knew!

'Suddenly' is an interesting word here, for in everday life it is indeed true that insights, such as noticing something for the first time, when they come to us, break in upon the intelligence sharply and quickly. ('I can see it in various aspects according to the fiction I surround it with', says Wittgenstein :[4] and he finds it necessary to speak of 'the clicks' in order to describe the way in which the dawning or the flashing of an aspect heralds the replacement of one field of fictions by another.)

Lawrence's essay is remarkable, and almost unique, for the confident way in which it takes Cézanne's aim—in the artist's own words—of 'realization', or of going 'to the heart of what is before you',[5] at its face-value. The idea that Cézanne, when he studied nature, actually, literally must have seen before his eyes the images he painted, is not easy to accept.

After all, wasn't every canvas simplified from life?
And when I glance around the room, I don't see a world built up from planes in salience and recession!
Cézanne surely meant that there is an *inner* process of seeing the world, no less than an *outer* one, and that his aim was to paint from this *inner* one!

These are the kinds of doubts which have perturbed

196

most of Cézanne's commentators. Of the question of sim-plification, it may be observed that to simplify a composi-tion by omitting from it, for instance, the wall running across the field in front of you, would be to put what is *not* seen in parentheses, and so to draw the attention onto what *is* seen : a critic might comment, 'You have left out just enough detail to enable me to see the slope of the hill clearly'. Of the salient planes, the fact is that we look *through* them, as if through a sort of transparency, rather as we see *through* the lines of a picture puzzle, which is now a duck, and now a rabbit. As to 'inner' and 'outer', the point here is that this naïve (but immensely popular) *schema* of creativity disregards the leading-question of how it comes about that the artist's imaginative concep-tion of the world is shaped and modified by his experience of life.[6]

Lawrence's criticism wasn't to be deflected from its course by such red herrings. For him, even when the artist appeared to be fusing together his images of interior scenes or of landscapes from discrete spatial viewpoints, he wasn't so much 'composing' a scene as making a real discovery about the world he had observed more intently than any-one else. Thus there could be nothing whimsical or merely fanciful about the distortions in Cézanne's pictures. He painted, essentially, what it was forced upon him to paint. It was as if Lawrence admired, not the artist's personal vision, peculiar to *himself*, but the genius of the organism *itself*. The artist can borrow from the tradition, but what the organism sees has always the character of a *donnée*. *This* it is, that has the effect of conjoining the lives of many beholders of the pictures :

> And at the same time he set the unmoving material world into motion. Walls twitch and slide, chairs bend or rear up a little, cloths curl like burning paper . . . he watched the lemons shrivel or go mildewed, in his still-life group. which he left lying there so long so that he *could* see that gradual flux of change . . .
> In the best landscapes we are fascinated by the mysterious *shiftiness* of the scene under our eyes; it shifts about as we watch it. And we realize, with a sort of transport, how intuitively *true* this is of landscape. It is *not* still. It has its own weird anima, and to our wide-

197

eyed perception it changes like a living animal under our gaze.

The force and originality of these little paragraphs can be brought home by comparing them with the kinds of comments on Cézanne's aim and method made by a critic as distinguished as Roger Fry, writing just two years before Lawrence. Fry summarized the creative process behind Cézanne's paintings like this:

> ... the actual objects presented to the artist's vision are first deprived of all those specific characters by which we ordinarily apprehend their concrete existence—they are reduced to pure elements of space and volume. In this abstract world these elements are perfectly co-ordinated and organized by the artist's sensual intelligence.[7]

The difference here is very striking. Fry saw *two* processes, analytic and synthetic, at work. He also portrayed the artist's conflict in terms of a struggle between *the painter and his medium*. (The formulation would appear to reduce the problem down to a matter of technical expertise.)

But it is clear that Lawrence's dictum, 'he wanted it *more* true to life', offers a much simpler way of looking at the creative process, as if only *one* major activity was involved, which was continuous with perception. The reference to Cézanne fighting with the edges of his forms and contours comes to mind here. It is known that Cézanne *did* study the outlines of things with great patience. He noticed that in strong light objects tend to fuse into the surrounding atmosphere. That is why the outlines—of apples, houses, hills—are missing in many of his paintings. This confused him at first because most painters took the outlines for granted and put them in; this was the kind of cliché he had to learn to slough off. Equally relevant is his treatment of shadows, which he noticed were more often blue in reality than the conventional black; and his handling of the culminating points of objects, with all its felt correspondence with the natural field of vision (think of *Man Smoking A Pipe*' in which the face draws the attention, and the body and the arms of the figure appear to surge massively into the darkness at the edge of the picture). All this, like Cézanne's fervour for filling a single carrot with revolution, seems alien in spirit from the organization of 'pure elements of space and volume', by the artist's 'sensual intelligence', in a world contained by the frame of the picture.

Probably, 'Treat nature by the cylinder, the sphere, the cone' has lent more support than any other single statement by Cézanne to the notion that he was the forerunner of a non-representational school of painting, and the founder of such a movement. What must be said here is that 'more true to life' cannot be improved upon. In its very simplicity the phrase suggests a *total* correspondence between what we do when we notice things, and what Cézanne was doing in painting. When he took from the left and the right, and sketched in lines which acquired volume and became objects such as rocks and trees—all without his having to think about it, as he often affirmed—he was re-enacting with a full purposefulness the way in which we quite unconsciously fix an image before our eyes whenever we make an effort to see the world.[8] 'I advance all my canvas at one time together', he used to say. It was like noticing an aspect; and a single brush-stroke would change the whole aspect of the image on the canvas.

Thus what is offered, in Lawrence's criticism of Cézanne, is a revival of the classical definition of art as *Man added to Nature*. The artist, in forming whole symbols from human consciousness,[9] re-enacts the organism's spontaneous perceiving process. He begins by forming his conceptions from conventional types—Cézanne's abstract forms having their indispensable part to play in the total process—and by applying these to his experience of life he works towards a vision which is more concentrated-in upon the 'quick' of what is perceived. It can be said that it is his triumph that he develops his vision on the basis of that state of fusion of 'the two radically different modes of knowing'[10] which exists prior to the consciousness. In great art, according to Lawrence, we have the only form of 'objectivity' in human knowledge which is durable as Man himself:

Cézanne's great effort was, as it were, to shove the apple away from him, and let it live of itself. It seems a small thing to do: yet it is the first real sign that man has made for several thousands of years that he is willing to admit that matter *actually* exists.

Not surprisingly, Lawrence was quite uncompromising in his insistence that Cézanne had inaugurated a tradition which nobody had been able to carry on. His imitators had failed even to understand his surprise, yet alone to apply any of Cézanne's methods to their own experience :

> For who of Cézanne's followers does anything but follow at the triumphant funeral of Cézanne's achievement? They follow him in order to bury him, and they succeed. Cézanne is deeply buried under all the Matisses and Vlamincks of his following, while the critics read the funeral homily.

The thing that Lawrence's essay makes so plain is that, because Cézanne's accomplishment in 'seeing' took immense labour, the artists following him were faced, in assimilating his vision, with all the difficulties this entailed. But what they actually produced was not what Lawrence would have welcomed, a truly imaginative tradition of painting stemming from a more rigorous attempt at seeing the world, *a criticism of life*, but something akin to *a criticism of Cézanne* (and in some cases a pastiche of Cezanne).

A testimony to the fact that Lawrence was not merely raising *a priori* objections to a non-representational style of painting makes an interesting footnote here. It is provided by Knud Merrild, a painter who stayed with Lawrence in New Mexico. After quoting a finely-detailed description of some sea-shells from one of Lawrence's books, in which the writer seems to have held the jeweller's glass up to his eye as he noted down what he saw, he added :

> He talks about lines, colour, pattern, different material, different qualities, transparency, substance and structure —all values the modern painter has accepted and incorporated in his work. And still he denies abstractions.[11]

Looking at the uses to which even such distinguished painters as Braque and Picasso have put Cézanne's telescoped or synthesized perspectives, his culminating points, his segmented colourings and the technique of *plusieurs contours*, we are bound to conclude, following Lawrence, that the assimilation was fragmentary, that the aim was modified, and that representation '*more* true to life' was replaced by the decoration of the picture-space itself; and now that many modern art-critics are working their way round to the view that Cézanne's conception of 'realization' was abandoned quite early in the development of Cubism, and that Cézanne became the 'father of the Tradition' only in the most indirect and unintentional way, there is every chance that *Introduction To These Paintings* will receive more widespread recognition for its impressive contribution at an early date, to the understanding of the art of Cézanne.[12]

*   *   *

It is worth taking note of the similarity between the kind of importance Lawrence attached to Cézanne's achievement, and the significance attributed to it by a philosopher as distinguished as the late Maurice Merleau-Ponty, who was a Professor of the Collège de France. There is virtually a point-by-point resemblance between their commentaries on Cézanne. Of the artist's debt to Impressionism, Merleau-Ponty says:

It is thanks to the Impressionists, and particularly to Pisarro, that Cézanne later conceived painting not as the incarnation of imagined scenes, the projection of dreams outward, but as the exact study of appearances: less a work of the studio than a working from nature.

He quickly parted ways with the Impressionists, however . . . Doing away with exact contours in certain cases, giving colour priority over the outline—these obviously mean different things for Cézanne and for the Impressionists. The object is no longer covered by reflections and lost in its relationships to the atmosphere and to other objects: it seems subtly illuminated from within, light emanates from it, and the result is an impression of solidity and material substance.[13]

When he elaborates on the artist's philosophical conception of the aim of painting, he say that Cézanne,

makes a basic distinction not between 'the senses' and 'the understanding' but rather between the spontaneous organization of things we perceive and the human organization of ideas and sciences. We see things; we agree about them; we are anchored in them; and it is with 'nature' as our base that we construct our sciences. Cézanne wanted to paint this primordial world.[14]

Of the treatment of space in Cézanne's pictures he says:

Cups and saucers on a table seen from the side should be elliptical, but Cézanne paints the two ends of the ellipse swollen and expanded. The work table in his portrait of Gustave Geoffrey stretches, contrary to the laws of perspective, into the lower part of the picture.

By remaining faithful to the phenomena in his investigations of perspective, Cézanne discovered what recent psychologists have come to formulate: the lived perspective, that which we actually perceive, is not a geometric or a photographic one. The objects we see close at hand appear smaller, those far away seem larger than they do in a photograph ... Similarly it is Cézanne's genius that when the overall composition of the picture is seen globally, perspectival distortions are no longer visible in their own right but rather contribute, as they do in natural vision, to the impression of an emerging order, of an object in the act of appearing, organizing itself before our eyes. In the same way, the contour of an object conceived as a line encircling the object belongs not to the visible world but to geometry.

And Merleau-Ponty shows the relationship between the artist's accomplishment in 'primordial perception' and our discovery of the world at first hand:

Cézanne does not try to use colour to *suggest* the tactile sensations which would give shape and depth. These distinctions between touch and sight are unknown in primordial perception. It is only as a result of the science of the human body that we finally learn to distinguish between our senses. The lived object is not rediscovered or constructed on the basis of the contributions of the senses; rather, it presents itself to us from the start as the centre from which these contributions radiate. We *see* the depth, the smoothness, the softness, the hardness of objects; Cézanne even claimed that we see their odour. Cézanne's painting suspends these habits of thought and reveals the base of inhuman nature upon which man has installed himself.

*   *   *

The theoretical side of *Introduction To These Paintings* is concerned with the questions of imagination, instinct, and knowledge. This is a key-statement:

> The reality of substantial bodies can only be perceived by the imagination, and the imagination is a kindled state of consciousness in which intuitive awareness predominates. The plastic arts are all imagery, and imagery is the body of our imaginative life, and our imaginative life is a great joy and fulfilment to us, for the imagination is a more powerful and more comprehensive flow of consciousness than our ordinary flow. In the flow of true imagination we know in full, mentally and physically at once, in a greater, enkindled awareness. At the maximum of imagination we are religious.

On this question of 'imagination', it may be agreed, first of all, that if two men are looking at the clouds, and one of them sees only an amorphous whiteness, while the other sees a galleon in full sail, an ice-floe, a bay full of fishes, etc., we would say that the second is the more imaginative man. He is the one who *selects* from what is offered, in the light of various *contexts of possibilities* for what he sees.

Here Lawrence is saying that these kinds of activity contribute to our perception of the *reality* of things. He thought that 'imagination' in painting had much to do with the capacity for drawing on acquired knowledge. He felt that the painter, in order to convey 'the appleyness of the apple', or 'the horsiness of the horse', must work from the creative side of observation, selecting the essential qualities of things, in the light of their natural evocativeness for the human being. It would follow from what he says that a good painting of a cat would have to summon-up all the changeableness and enigma of a cat. It would have to suggest the whimsicalness of the cat which sleeps in its basket with curled-up little paws, looking like a fluffy toy. It would have to give a hint of the prowling-cat which appears on the window-sill like an inky, undulating shadow, setting its soft pads noiselessly down, one before the other. It would have to suggest the Egyptian-cat, with its lovely, stylized, Cleopatra's-eyes, which sits quite still, as though carved out of stone. It would have to draw out these fields of fictions which exist behind the curtain of the eye and make them more immediately visible.

Lawrence thought that the idea of an 'aesthetic unity' was rather misleading. The new unity shaped by the creative imagination—'the whole consciousness of man working together in unison and one-ness'—would sometimes be put forward in the form of a novel or a painting, and sometimes in the form of a great advance in science.[15]

This insistence that imagination is continuous with perception (and here Lawrence anticipates the thought of Wittgenstein and Merleau-Ponty), must clearly—if we are to be persuaded by Lawrence at all—invite us to ponder the idea of the great artist as a *seer*; and naturally what Lawrence said of painting was a part and parcel of his whole apology for art and literature, with its many comments on the artist's unique accomplishment in giving us a picture of 'man alive'.

'What is the criterion of visual experience?' Wittgenstein asks. And he answers (adopting Lawrence's point of view), 'The representation of "what is seen"'.[16]

How should this affect our attitude to the novel: say, to Lawrence's own novels? There is a scene in *The White Peacock* (III.V) in which Cyril, the Lawrence-figure, presses a florin into the hand of a poor woman sleeping on a bench by the Embankment on a cold night in the drizzling rain. He notices that her hand is soft and warm and curled in sleep, and because he is filled with a variety of conflicting emotions, with grief, and shame, and embarrassment, he recoils from the moment of contact. The touch is on 'the quick', as Lawrence says.[17]

The question here is, what sort of an author would you go to to find out what is *really* happening to the human being in an episode of this kind? Supposing you want to know what 'touching' involves (how it is connected with the entry into the world of another person), or what 'seeing' involves (whether Cyril sees a threatening-hand which may clasp his sleeve, a begging-hand, a sensitive touching-hand): if the criterion of what is seen lies in the representation, wouldn't you go to the work of Lawrence himself, in which scores of similar 'quick' moments are described with perfect clarity and fullness of detail, as the criterion most worth having?

Yet there is a widespread notion that what is *really* experienced requires an *ideal* description to convey it: as if a description couched in rather ordinary language were necessarily an *approximation* to a reality behind the veil of appearances.

Lawrence turned this sort of problem round when he looked at it by discarding the conception of an ideal reality to which the description approximately corresponds, and by starting with the descriptions themselves, inviting us to select the most effective.

He particularly mistrusted descriptions lying over in the 'ideal' direction, concerned with the functioning of anonymous psychic apparatus, etc. He thought that these were the approximations, when compared with what the novel has to offer. The scientist and the philosopher, he said, 'never get the whole hog.'[18]

It is true that *Women In Love*, as a description of human behaviour enjoys a position of relative permanence, compared with the interpretations made of it from the viewpoint of the changing perspectives in psychology. To men of Lawrence's day, who were intensely interested in Freudian psycho-analysis, it seemed that the history of Gerald Crich was the focus of interest in the book. The fate of the doomed Arctic demon of a doomed civilization touched the 'quick' of the reader. The causes of Gerald's collapse and death, in the failed parental relationship, were all there, fully documented. The scale seemed breathtaking. There was a glimpse of a deranged will, and of a whole future in ruins.

A more modern view of the book would see it as a novel which accurately depicts the dehumanizing effects of increasingly rapid social changes. The points of concern, for an age of social and anthropological psychology, include the novel's demonstration of the calling-into-question of the institution of marriage, and the way in which it shows the loss of traditional loyalties to class, country, position and family, with the difficulty of establishing new ties.

The point is that while the psychological blueprint of the human being has been re-drawn many times, and while the neuroses which Freud met and catalogued seem to have disappeared (symptoms of mental illness nowadays being called by new names and given different causes), *Women In Love* has retained its relevance to our needs. It has remained as one of the criteria by which what is really felt and known by an age may be determined.

'But even in literature, how do you know which is the

best description of what is happening to the human being?'

Well, that is the point of the critical discipline. There are no criteria *outside* the works of art. The thing is to keep the whole field under review, and then to move the pieces about, as in a jig-saw puzzle. The local judgements eventually give rise to a constant preference.[19]

*   *   *

It is impossible to read very far in Lawrence's discursive writings without coming across the word 'instinct'. He thought that for Man the desired goal was always a 'natural flowering of life',[20] based on certain human forms of 'instinct'. But how may this 'natural flowering' be recognized, supposing it may be brought into being?

Think of a sculptor carving a figure in stone. He is milling away the material flake by flake, working for the accuracy of his curves, and feeling his way towards the forms he wants on the basis of the resistance of the material. A figure caught in terms of stone (a *stone-person*), has the effect of making the hard thing look soft and pleasing to the touch. In every medium it is possible to catch the figure in this way in terms of the material in which it is executed. The figure might be seen as a lacy statuette in wire, *or* fashioned as a clay figurine from compact pot-forms, made with little pieces of clay rolled between the hands and joined onto the thrown body, or caught, in a limewood carving, in terms of flat chisel-cuts. But to try to execute a spiky, angular design in stone would be to attempt the impossible. Here one would say that the sculptor was *idealizing*. When the artist makes a *stone-person* one says, 'he carves from instinct', seeing how thoroughly at home he is with all the physical processes involved, the weight and swing of the mallet, the resistance of the stone, the chisel-edge, and so forth.

For Lawrence, the capacity to live from 'instinct' was always the great, positive standard for behaviour. He saw a link between the way in which birds, bees, larks, foxes and other creatures developed a physical *rapport* with their environment, out of their need to be wide-awake to it,[21] and the artist's all-round vigilance, born of maintaining a set of relationships in some medium. To the artist he attributed the carrying-forward of the evolution of specifically human forms of 'instinct'.

He also admired those of his fellow-men who seemed to him to be living in harmony with the world around them. *The Rainbow* deals with the life of the farming community, and the travel-essays reflect his interest in peasant-societies. The little sketch *Flowery Tuscany*, with its description of the terraces on the Italian hillsides, turns over the ecological problem in the light of the idea that to shape the environment by 'instinct' is to begin to make art out of it:

> Talk of hanging gardens of Babylon, all Italy, apart from the plains, is a hanging garden. For centuries upon centuries man has been patiently modelling the surface of the Mediterranean countries, gently rounding the hills, and graduating the big slopes and the little slopes into the almost invisible levels of terraces. Thousands of square miles of Italy have been lifted with human hands, piled and laid back in tiny little flats, held up by the drystone walls, whose stones come from the lifted earth. It is a work of many, many centuries. It is the gentle sensitive sculpture of all the landscape. And it is the achieving of the peculiar Italian beauty which is so exquisitely natural, because man, feeling his way sensitively to the fruitfulness of the earth, has moulded the earth to his necessity without violating it.[22]

In this passage one *sees* all the hard work which has gone into the making of the drystone walls. As with allotments and pieces of landscape-gardening, there is this sense of the fascination of something which has been carefully worked-over. One *sees* the resistance of the medium.

One also *sees* the curving contours of the hillsides, once these terraces have been threaded around them. It is as if nature has been softened, and made more seeable and acceptable, by the presence of things made out of natural materials.[23]

Finally one *sees* the man-made things themselves, the walls and little flats of earth, by virtue of the harmony which exists between them and their natural setting. Like the *stone*-person, these walls—the cottages and churches could be included—are caught in terms of the natural materials.

In admiring 'physical consciousness' in the 'peculiar Italian beauty', Lawrence had in mind certain qualities very similar to those he admired so much in Cézanne's pictures.

It comes down to the artist's knack of *making* you see things: to this, and to the links with the body. In the paintings the sense of seeing is similarly enhanced. There is an interesting and fresh untidiness and crookedness everywhere. There are corners with little depths, steps to run up, holes to look through, curves to slide round. You can walk in between the trees, sit on the stones, roll the apples off the table, or wander through the passageways. It is all piled up block on block to give a feeling of plenty, or of accumulation.

One can see what fascinated Lawrence about what he variously calls the 'physical', 'intuitional' or 'instinctive' consciousness by looking at our old English two- and three-hundred-year-old cottages, which he praises in the stories. Built to person-height with corners next to the fire to sit in, windows at a convenient height for looking out of, staircases which lead straight up into the rooms, and with deep window-sills wide enough to put things on or to sit in, these handy cottages give you a feeling of being safely and gently enfolded. The natural materials are comforting, and there is a reachableness about everything. Even the upper storey is so low that you can lean out and talk to somebody in the street. These small, curvy, Medieval-ish dwellings were built to fit round the body by people who worked largely from instinct, rather in the way children satisfy an old instinct in building tree-houses. They picked up stones and packed them together, or hewed them from the rock. There was no grand conception, or attempt at making an impression. How could there be? How could their makers idealize when there was no paper-work, and the houses were not paper-planned? (Here it is to the point that rich architects, being aware of the feelings of irritation produced by high windows, unreachable corners, and walls and ceilings like lift-shafts, when they build houses for themselves often return to the low ceilings with plenty of arches, and to the natural materials, and to the thick, strong walls which give a feeling of protection.)

Ordinarily we like to say, apropos of all that is implied by Lawrence's rueful comment, 'you can't drive a steam plough on terraces four yards wide', something rather like, 'When we have solved the material problem by means of technology we will give the whole of our attention to the higher, spiritual problem.' But according to Lawrence, there is a fallacy in this step-by-step notion of 'progress'. It is an illusion to imagine that Man has a set of needs and problems lying beyond the material ones. The thing to do is to bring all our different ways of being aware of the material world into the right kind of alignment. The test lies in the seeableness of the world we build.

In the past this was done without anyone's having to think about it. In windmills made of wood and canvas, in the sailing-ships, and in lines of men scything their way across the fields at harvest-time, certain natural forms of behaviour for Man fell into place, giving satisfaction to body and soul at once: it was by organizing the converging lines of force of the natural elements among which he lived that Man connected himself up with his fellow-men, and with the universe.

Lawrence's attitude to the future and to technology was that it would not be impossible to discover new, 'natural' forms of behaviour, but that our great machine-tools would make necessary an increasingly high degree of sophistication on the part of the society using them. Here one thinks of the earthy shapes of tube-train tunnels, of the roads cut out of solid rock and swinging round the contour of a hill, and of great bridges spanning the valleys.

Lawrence *hated* the nostalgic attitude to the past.[24] At the same time he saw that a certain amount of difficulty was essential to the business of life, particularly to the problem of making a seeable world. (Think of the way in which one *sees* the effort which has gone into the drystone walls, or of the way in which one *sees* the dexterity which has gone into the making of a woven basket, a bamboo stool, or an egg-carrier fashioned in straw. The sense of *someone doing something* contributes to the sense of there being a *design* to look at.) He would have thought it a very odd notion, that the era of spiritual progress will be inaugurated with the completion of the device of devices, which will maintain and repair itself, and provide us with everything from bread-rolls to buttons. Finally to 'solve' the material problem in this way would preclude the possibility of making further headway with the spiritual one.

* * *

'Imagery is the body of our imaginative life', Lawrence says. The 'philosophy of the body' evolved in his writings, as a solution to the problem of knowledge, with its traditional dualisms of spirit and matter, object and subject, and the primary and secondary qualities of things, looks forward to the main themes of Merleau-Ponty. Here the central idea is that 'the body' is the primary medium in terms of which our consciousness of the world shapes itself, as one form of sense-experience modulates into another.

Possibly there was an analogy at the back of his mind here : as the artist develops his vision of the world by the use of a medium of some kind, like oil-paints and canvas (depicting actual *paint-persons*), so the organism, as it begins to shape its picture of the world, takes its own, immediate, felt life as its primary medium.

Lawrence's ideas about space and time followed consistently from this epistemological standpoint. Of space he said :

> It may seem an absurdity to talk of *live* space. But is it? While we are warm and well and 'unconscious' of our bodies, are we not all the time ultimately conscious of our bodies in the same way, as live or living space? And is this not the reason why void space so terrifies us? [25]

The thought here is that we make the discovery of the existence of space simultaneously with the discovery of the existence of the body. It is initially a matter of feeling warm and well; and then of moving, reaching, and touching. This theme is extensively developed by Merleau-Ponty in this chapter, 'The Spatiality of One's Own Body and Motility',[26] and also in his comments, in his art-criticism, on the displacement of the old *perspective naturalis* of the early Rennaissance paintings by the newly-invented *perspective artificialis*.[27] Lawrence and Merleau-Ponty shared the view that the pure, ideal, mathematical space, corresponding with the laws of perspective, was an abstraction devised by the intelligence, having no experience-content. And further, that a re-discovery of the lived experience of space is to be found in Cézanne's paintings.

(Think of the distended ellipse made by one of Cézanne's saucers. To contemplate it is to want to reach out and run a finger round the hollow interior of the dish; and the sense of 'live or living space' is taken a step further by all the little crookedness in his pictures. This experience is captured in a similar manner by the hugely up-tilted townships of Fra Angelico.)

Of the question of time, Lawrence commented:

> Instead of bewailing a lost youth, a man nowadays begins to wonder, when he reaches my ripe age of forty-two, if ever his past will subside and be comfortably by-gone. Doing over these poems makes me realize that my teens and my twenties are just as much me, here and now and present, as ever they were, and the pastness is only an abstraction. The actuality, the body of feeling, is essentially alive and here.[28]

This should be compared with Wittgenstein's dictum,

> Man learns the concept of the past by remembering.[29]

There is a common concern here to isolate the immediate experience-content in the awareness of the past. The bodily doing-process is seen as the inescapable shaping-influence behind all abstract discussion of the nature of time, or of the past.

It is particularly in Merleau-Ponty's examination, in *The Phenomenology of Perception*, of the theme of the body as our means of belonging to the world, that one is reminded of Lawrence's concept of the living body-medium. One feels Lawrence would have been intrigued with the case-history of Schneider, the patient for whom, owing to a brain-injury, the expression of the simplest concepts involved the use of the whole body. To the military salute Schneider added all the external marks of respect. To the right hand pantomime of combing the hair he added, with the left, that of holding the mirror. When the right hand pretended to knock in a nail, the left pretended to hold the nail. He was unable, or, as it were, too simple, to cut his actions down to a minimum, as a normal subject would. And what is this modern view of *thinking* as 'the modification of a comprehensive bodily purpose' but old wine in new bottles: a variant of the poet's theme of 'the thinking of the body'?

* * *

There is a view of the nature of literature which tells us that, in the words of a modern critic, it is the precise formulation of moral issues in concrete terms that makes a really good novel.[30]

The curious thing about such famous novels as *Women In Love* and *Anna Karenina* is that they tend to go soft in their treatment of 'good' and 'bad' characters. A lack of clarity surrounds Ursula and Levin in their dealings with others. Ursula's scenes are full of unjustified accusations of bullying; Levin abruptly dismisses a guest from his house. Gerald and Anna, on the other hand, appear reluctant to lay down and die when the time comes. So Gerald dances irrepressibly with the Professor's daughters, and Anna cheers herself up by writing a book for children. It is only in the presentation of ambiguous figures that there is no sense of strain. Think of Gudrun playing a rôle, humouring Thomas Crich on his death-bed, or of Oblonsky, soothing the ruffled feelings of Levin or Karenin, and persuading his acquaintances to get on with one another. Here the characters are really in touch with one another. Gudrun and Oblonsky, with their qualities of tact and delicacy, seem to be aware of the other person, or persons, in an all-round way, even while practising deceptions upon them. The effect is of a perfect correspondence with life itself. Here one has the sense that the author, instead of being concerned to bend the shape of the story to fit his moral ideas (saying, as it were, 'This spontaneous person can do no wrong', or 'This dishonest person will come to no good') has taken the simpler course of remaining morally neutral. Sometimes the writer is *actually* most serious when he is unaware of taking himself seriously.

'What is accomplished in the novel must teach its own lesson'. That is the meaning of Lawrence's advice to trust the tale, never the artist. The novel puts forward a set of scenes which arrange themselves in a pattern of relative value, and it is on reflection that various moral qualities are seen to attach themselves to *them*. In the first place one values the scenes and the characters, not the qualities. So it is that eventually such favourite human characteristics for Lawrence and Tolstoy as warmth, spontaneity and generosity come to seem rather glamorized in their work. It is the everyday qualities, like tact, good-humour and commonsense that come to the fore, making the life in which we are immersed seem more interesting to us. This is the 'finer morality' mentioned by Lawrence, which the true artist substitutes for the grosser morality. The criticism of life accomplished in the novel will come to include a criticism even of the artist's own moral conception of life.

The parallel, in literature, with what Cézanne was doing in painting, really consists in a literature of bare facts: in facts without authorial comment and, particularly, without the sense of straining after an effect: in clusters of facts, the more fresh, and interestingly-arranged, the better. When John Synge, at the opening of *The Aran Islands*, says:

> I met few people; but here and there a band of tall girls passed me on their way to Kilronan, and called out to me with humorous wonder, speaking English with a slight foreign intonation that differed a good deal from the brogue of Galway. The rain and cold seemed to have no influence on their vitality, and as they hurried past me with eager laughter and great talking in Gaelic, they left the wet masses of rock more desolate than before,

he brings together a couple of fact—the liveliness of the band of girls and the desolateness of the bare rocks—which convey, with a rare acuteness of sensation, the atmosphere of the locale of Aranmor. It is momentarily as if our emotional lives were illuminated with something of the brightness of the out-of-doors, while the alien indifference of brute things ('the wet masses of rock'), were softened by the presence of an invisible observer who feels things acutely. Lawrence admired this impersonality of feeling in art whenever he found it. He praised Melville for the 'non-human centres' from which he drew his inspiration. He thought highly of Synge, Hardy, and Dana, no less than of Cézanne. He was always drawn to an artist who was capable of accepting life exactly as it was observed to be. Lawrence thought that the great value of art and literature was that they instilled a new criterion of propriety into our way of being aware of the world: you cannot allow yourself to be sentimental, confronted with a work of any quality; at the same time, looking out through the eyes of the artist, you are obliged to shed the habit of observing the world in a literal, photographic way. Of course many literary qualities, like timing, and the selection of detail, go into the making of a description from which the emotions appear to spring unsolicited.)

Lawrence was inclined to be rather impatient with precise formulations of moral issues in art, particularly in the novel. He thought that the deepest *effects* of art did not spring from moral *intentions*. He said that Cézanne's paintings—which can hardly be said to have a 'moral content' in any ordinary sense of the idea—foreshadowed the fall of the whole 'ideal' way of consciousness. It was the long, laborious business of developing a whole new vision of the world which really mattered. (And here we might ask, 'What moral issues are formulated by *The General Prologue To The Canterbury Tales?'*)

*　　*　　*

The history of the appreciation of Lawrence's critical and discursive prose since his death makes depressing reading. Nowadays almost every detail of Lawrence's life is known, while we have no conception of his place in the development of modern thought. This curious neglect of a much-studied man is partly the fault of the critics. There has been a tendency, even among the most distinguished of them, to draw attention to all the wrong things; like Aldous Huxley, in his influential foreword to the *Letters*, writing about Lawrence's interest in Mexico and the solar plexus. But Professor Leavis, with his unfailing insistence that Lawrence's genius was for intelligence, and with his emphasis on Lawrence's greatness as a critic, as well as a novelist, has always been the marked exception here.

The neglect is also Lawrence's own fault. As a discursive writer he was sometimes inclined to force his thought on in a direction against its natural bent, which was always concrete. There are places, particularly in his early essays, in which his self-conscious desire to be a philosopher gave rise to a metaphorical effusion, of hyenas, vultures, insects, poppies, roses, phoenixes, crowns, lions, unicorns, mingled tides, and so on, in which nothing is firmly grasped or clearly presented. One is irritated out of all proportion by the spuriousness of the style, in the work of a man who could write so well: by the portentousness of adjectives erected into nouns, by the privacy of the habit of mind, and by such re-iterated antitheses as 'light and dark' and

214

'systole and dyastole', with which only the play-side of the writer's intelligence was involved.

Lawrence was most illuminating as a *thinker* when he was at his best as a *writer*. He recorded his 'quick' moments most vividly in concrete situations : after meeting a character who had roused his attention and puzzled him, after an encounter with a snake or a bat, or when he had been stirred by a book or a painting; and his most valuable generalities about human existence arose spontaneously, as comments on these situations. It would advance the understanding of his thought better than anything else to publish a slim selection of the scattered 'polyanalytics', edited to show them at their best (which would also bring out their overall coherence at their best).

Here a couple of difficulties indicate further reasons for the neglect. The variety of literary forms is daunting. It is only to be expected that most people, who like to keep one habit of mind for poetry, another for the novel, and a third for philosophy, suffer an initial uneasiness when confronted with Lawrence's thought, which shows itself now as a poem, now as a digression or an episode in a novel, and now as an essay. Again, supposing such a volume were put together, where would it belong on the library shelves? At first glance the discursive writing seems to wander like a maze through every topic under the sun.

Yet it is reasonably plain that a book like Hegel's *The Philosophy Of Fine Art* is close in spirit to much that Lawrence has to say. Hegel was the first great modern philosopher to lift up the whole subject of the principles of art, and to invest aesthetics with the prestige of a 'science of life'. Common to Lawrence and Hegel is a fascination with the theoretical grounding of art and literature, coupled with an insistence that there cannot *be* a 'theory of art', art being the record of life itself. There can only be a 'theory of life', or a metaphysic. What they put forward is a *metaphysical* apology for art and literature, rather than a *moral* one.

Lawrence's work also touches that of a number of modern thinkers at many points. In his theory of knowledge, and in his comments on Cézanne, he has much in common with Merleau-Ponty. Temperamentally and (in the later essays), stylistically, he seems to have been more akin to Wittgenstein. One recalls the moral fervour of their insistence on not cheating yourself, and on not being lead astray by the 'charm' or 'thrill' of a misleading idea, and also their gifts of vigorous and accurate expression, based on the use of the simplest words and phrases from the spoken language. They convey to a remarkable degree the impressions of clairvoyant intelligence, and of a sanity which grew the more deep-rooted as their thought matured. It is finally with Hegel, and with the essays on art, aesthetics and religious belief by Wittgenstein and Merleau-Ponty that Lawrence's discursive writings belong.

NOTES

1. *Paintings of D. H. Lawrence*, edited by Mervyn Levy, 1964.
2. This, and other quotations from *Introduction to These Paintings*, are taken from *Phoenix* by D. H. Lawrence, 1936 and 1961.
3. From the letter to Emile Bernard, 25th July, 1904.
4. Cf. *Philosophical Investigations*, II. xi.
5. From the letter to Emile Bernard, 26th May, 1904.
6. Patrick Heron, for example, in *The Changing Forms of Art*, 1955, says that the art of Cézanne 'was an equation of two great streams of experience—one from inside himself; the other from outside.'
7. Roger Fry, *Cézanne: A Study of His Development*, 1927, p. 58.
8. Cf. *Etruscan Places* by D. H. Lawrence, section 4: 'The ancients saw, consciously, as children now see unconsciously, the everlasting *wonder* in things.'
9. Lawrence makes some illuminating comments on the nature of symbolism in his description of the Sicilian marionettes in *Sea and Sardinia*.
10. The phrase is Martin Buber's. But see *Phoenix*, p. 578, for Lawrence's own account of the two modes of knowing.
11. Knud Merrild, *With D. H. Lawrence in New Mexico*, 1964, p. 226.
12. Sir Herbert Read, in his *Concise History of Modern Paintings*, 1959, p. 96, traces the way in which Cézanne's conception of 'realization' was abandoned; and John Ingamells, in the October, 1965 number of *The British Journal of Aesthetics*, has some sympathetic comments on Lawrence's art-criticism.

13. The quotations from Merleau-Ponty are taken from his essay, 'Cézanne's Doubt', in his collection, *Sense and Non-Sense*, translated by H. L. and P. A. Dreyfus, Northwestern U.P., 1964.

14. 'The spontaneous organization of things we perceive' : cf. Wittgenstein, loc. cit., 'A *concept* forces itself on one. (This is what you must not forget)', and, 'What has to be accepted, the given, is—so one could say—*forms of life*'.

15. It is hard to imagine a modern history-of-ideas thesis which would cut through to essential issues more quickly than an examination of the topic, 'Lawrence and Science'. What conclusion is to be drawn from the resemblance between Lawrence's 'H_2O' passage in *Introduction To These Paintings* (*Phoenix*, p. 574), and what K. Koffka has to say about 'acquired knowledge' in *Principles of Gestalt Psychology* (1936, p. 57), or what W. Koehler says in *Gestalt Psychology* (1947, p. 86)? How do we reconcile Aldous Huxley's well-known comments on Lawrence's apparent obtuseness or perversity before the discoveries of the physical sciences, with his undoubted ability to scent what was in the wind in these territories (when we compare, for example, Lawrence's comments on determinism and 'the mental melting-pot' in Chapter Eight of *Fantasia Of The Unconscious*, of 1921, with Heisenberg's principle of Uncertainty, of 1927)? Lawrence, Wittgenstein, and Merleau-Ponty concur (i) in their insistence that there is all the difference in the world between *knowledge* and *belief*, (ii) in their sympathy for the principles of Gestalt psychology, and (iii) in their antipathy towards investing the discoveries of the physical sciences with any sort of onotologically descriptive status.

16. Loc. cit.

17. 'The quick' : Cf. Lawrence's poem, 'Embankment At Night, Before The War : Charity', which handles the same episode.

18. *Phoenix*, p. 535.

19. Cf. F. R. Leavis, 'Criticism and Philosophy', *The Common Pursuit*. 'The literary critic . . . doesn't ask, "How does this accord with these specifications of goodness in poetry?"; he aims to make fully conscious and articulate the immediate sense of value that "places" the poem.

'Of course, the process of "making fully conscious and articulate" is a process of relating and organizing, and the

"immediate sense of value" should, as the critic matures
with experience, represent a growing stability of organization (the problem is to combine stability with growth).
What, on testing and re-testing and wider experience, turn
out to be my more constant preferences, what the relative
permanencies in my response, and what structure begins
to assert itself in the field of poetry with which I am
familiar? What map or chart of English poetry as a whole
represents my utmost consistency and most inclusive
coherence of response?'

20. *Etruscan Places*, section 3.
21. *The Symbolic Meaning* by D. H. Lawrence, Ch. 7,
'Nathaniel Hawthorne I'.
22. *Phoenix*, p. 46.
23. The quotation might be compared with this:
'Every article on these islands has an almost personal
character, which gives this simple life, where all art is
unknown, something of the artistic beauty of medieval
life. The curaghs and spinning-wheels, the tiny wooden
barrels that are still much used in the place of earthen-
ware, the home-made cradles, churns, and baskets, are all
full of individuality, and being made from materials that
are common here, yet to some extent peculiar to the
island, they seem to exist as a natural link between the
people and the world that is about them.' John Synge *The
Aran Islands, I*. It might also be compared with what Hegel
has to say, in *The Philosophy of Fine Art*, about the ways
in which Man contrives to 'strip nature of its stubborn
foreignness, and to enjoy in the shape and fashion of things
a reality derivative from his own reality.' Lawrence develops this theme in such poems as *Things Men Have Made*.
24. Cf. his poem Piano; also the passage on p. 426 of
Phoenix which concludes, 'I do honour to the machine
and to its inventor'; and his introduction to *Memoirs Of
The Foreign Legion*, by Maurice Magnus, 1924, p. 42.
25. *Phoenix*, p. 298.
26. *The Phenomenology of Perception*, Part I, Chapter 3.
27. *The Primacy Of Perception*, Part 2, 'Eye and Mind'.
28. *The Complete Poems of D. H. Lawrence*, 1964, p.
849.
29. *Philosophical Investigations*, II, xiii.
30. Gilbert Phelps, 'The Novel To-day', *The Pelican
Guide to English Literature*, Vol. 7, 1964.

BIBLIOGRAPHY

I—BOOKS BY LAWRENCE

A. Novels

The White Peacock (London & New York, 1910).
The Trespasser (London, 1912).
Sons and Lovers (London, 1913).
The Rainbow (London, 1915).
Women in Love (New York, 1920).
The Lost Girl (London, 1920).
Aaron's Rod (New York, 1922).
Kangaroo (London, 1923).
The Boy in the Bush (with M. L. Skinner) (London, 1924).
St. Mawr (London, 1925) (including 'The Princess').
The Plumed Serpent (London, 1926).
Lady Chatterley's Lover (Florence, 1928) [*The First Lady Chatterley* (New York, 1944); second version (Verona, 1954)].
The Virgin and the Gipsy (Florence, 1930).

B. Short Stories

The Prussian Officer and Other Stories (London, 1914): 'The Prussian Officer', 'The Thorn in the Flesh', 'Daughters of the Vicar', 'A Fragment of Stained Glass', 'The Shades of Spring', 'Second Best', 'The Shadow in the Rose Garden', 'Goose Fair', 'The White Stocking', 'A Sick Collier', 'The Christening', 'Odour of Chrysanthemums'.

England, My England and Other Stories (New York, 1922): 'England, my England', 'Tickets, Please', 'The Blind Man', 'Monkey Nuts', 'Wintry Peacock', 'You Touched Me', 'Samson and Delilah', 'The Primrose Path', 'The Horse Dealer's Daughter', 'Fanny and Annie'.

The Ladybird (London, 1923): 'The Ladybird, 'The Fox', 'The Captain's Doll'.

The Woman Who Rode Away and Other Stories (London & New York, 1928): 'Two Blue Birds', 'Sun', 'The Woman Who Rode Away', 'Smile', 'The Border Line', 'Jimmy and the Desperate Woman', 'The Last Laugh', 'In Love', 'Glad Ghosts', 'None of That', 'The Man Who Loved Islands' (American edition only).

The Escaped Cock (Paris, 1929).

The Lovely Lady (London, 1933): 'The Lovely Lady', 'Rawdon's Roof', 'The Rocking Horse Winner', 'Mother and Daughter', 'The Blue Moccasins', 'Things', 'The Overtone', 'The Man Who Loved Islands'.

The Tales of D. H. Lawrence (London, 1934).

A Modern Lover (London, 1934): 'A Modern Lover', 'The Old Adam', 'Her Turn', 'Strike Pay', 'The Witch à la Mode', 'New Eve and Old Adam', 'Mr. Noon'.

C. *Poems*

Love Poems and Others (London, 1913).
Amores (London, 1916).
Look! We Have Come Through (London, 1917).
New Poems (London, 1918).
Bay (London, 1919).
Tortoises (New York, 1921).
Birds, Beasts and Flowers (New York, 1923).
Collected Poems (London, 1928).
Pansies (London, 1929).
Nettles (London, 1930).
Last Poems (Florence, 1932).
The Complete Poems of D. H. Lawrence (ed. Pinto & Roberts, London, 1964).

D. *Essays, etc.*

Psychoanalysis and the Unconscious (New York, 1921).
Fantasia of the Unconcious (New York, 1922).
Studies in Classic American Literature (New York, 1923) [The early versions of these essays were published in an edition by Armin Arnold, *The Symbolic Meaning* (London, 1962)].
Reflections on the Death of a Porcupine (Philadelphia, 1925).
Apropos of Lady Chatterley's Lover (London, 1930).
Assorted Articles (London, 1930).
Apocalypse (Florence, 1931).
Phoenix (ed. McDonald, New York, 1936).
Phoenix II (ed. Roberts and Moore, London, 1968).
Note: The two *Phoenix* volumes contain almost all of Lawrence's shorter essays, together with some miscellaneous pieces of fiction, but excluding the first three items above and *Apocalypse*.

E. *Plays*

The Widowing of Mrs. Holroyd (New York, 1914).
Touch and Go (London, 1920).
David (London, 1926).
A Collier's Friday Night (London, 1934).
The Complete Plays of D. H. Lawrence (London, 1965): This volume includes all the above, together with: *The Married Man, The Daughter-in-Law, The Fight for Barbara, The Merry-Go-Round, Altitude* and *Noah's Flood*.

F. Travel Books

Twilight in Italy (London, 1916).
Sea and Sardinia (New York, 1921).
Mornings in Mexico (London, 1927).
Etruscan Places (London, 1932).

G. Translations

All Things are Possible (translated from the Russian of Leo Shestov, by S. S. Koteliansky and D. H. Lawrence; London, 1920).
Mastro-Don Gesualdo (from the Italian of Giovanni Verga; New York, 1923).
Little Novels of Sicily (from the Italian of Giovanni Verga; New York, 1925).
Cavalleria Rusticana and Other Stories (from the Italian of Giovanni Verga; London, 1928).
The Story of Doctor Manente (from the Italian of A. F. Grazzini, il Lasca; Florence, 1929).

H. Miscellaneous

Movements in European History by Lawrence H. Davison (pseudonym of D.H.L.) (London, 1921).
The Paintings of D. H. Lawrence (London, 1929).
Paintings of D. H. Lawrence (ed. Levy, 1964).
Memoirs of the Foreign Legion by Maurice Magnus, with long introduction by D.H.L. (London, 1924).

I. Letters

The Letters of D. H. Lawrence (ed. Huxley; London, 1932).
D. H. Lawrence's Letters to Bertrand Russell (ed. Moore; New York, 1948).
The Collected Letters of D. H. Lawrence (ed. Moore; London and New York, 1962).
Lawrence in Love: D.H.L.'s letters to Louie Burrows (ed. Boulton; Nottingham, 1968).
The Quest for Rananim: D.H.L.'s letters to S. S. Koteliansky (ed. Zytaruk; Montreal and London, 1970).
Letters from D. H. Lawrence to Martin Secker (ed. Secker; London, 1970).
Note: Though Harry T. Moore's edition of 1962 is the largest collection of Lawrence's letters yet published, it omits many included in Huxley's collection of 1932 and most of those in the collections published since 1962. A good many other letters have been published in periodicals and in books by Lawrence's correspondents, and are not yet all collected together; many are still unpublished. A list of books and periodicals containing

Lawrence letters so far uncollected is included in the bibliography of Sagar's *Art of D. H. Lawrence* (see IIc below).

The most reliable English edition is that published by Penguin: it contains all the novels, most of the short stories, the four travel books, and selections of essays, poems and letters. The Heinemann Phoenix edition, which is rather more comprehensive, has many inaccuracies, and the texts of two of the novels —*The Rainbow* and *The Lost Girl*—are incomplete. We are still far from a satisfactory edition of Lawrence's works.

II—BOOKS ABOUT LAWRENCE

A. Bibliographies

The standard bibliography is *A Bibliography of D. H. Lawrence* by Warren Roberts (London : Hart-Davis, 1963, and extremely full and thorough up to that date). Other useful books are :

Edwards, L.: *D. H. Lawrence, A Finding List* (Nottingham: Nottingham County Library, 1968).

McDonald, Edward D.: *A Bibliography of the Works of D. H. Lawrence* (Philadelphia : Centaur Press, 1925); and *The Writings of D. H. Lawrence, 1925–1930: A Bibliographical Supplement* (ditto, 1931).

White, William: *D. H. Lawrence, A Checklist*: Writings about D. H. Lawrence, 1931–1950 (Detroit: Wayne State University Press, 1950).

See also Beebe, Maurice and Tommasi, Anthony: 'Criticism of D. H. Lawrence: A Selected Checklist' (*Modern Fiction Studies*, V : Spring 1959, pp. 83–98).

B. Biographies

Easily the most important biographical work about Lawrence is *D. H. Lawrence: A Composite Biography*, by Edward Nehls (three volumes : Madison, Wisconsin University Press, 1957–59): this gathers together memoirs by very many people who knew Lawrence, including some written specially for the book, together with autobiographical materials and letters. Of more orthodox biographies, the most comprehensive is Harry T. Moore, *The Intelligent Heart* (London : Heinemann, 1955, revised 1960), though some readers will find some of its judgments tendentious. Most interesting are the memoirs written by Lawrence's friends and acquaintances, including :

Lawrence, Ada and Gelder, Stuart : *The Early Life of D. H. Lawrence* (London : Secker, 1932).

Lawrence, Frieda : *Not I But The Wind* (London : Heinemann, 1935; New York : Viking, 1934).

Chambers, Jessie: *D. H. Lawrence, A Personal Record*, by 'E.T.' (London: Cape, 1935; reissued with additional material by J. D. Chambers and others, London: Cass, 1965).

Corke, Helen: *D. H. Lawrence: The Croydon Years* (Austin: University of Texas Press, 1965), containing reissues of several earlier pieces.

Carswell, Catherine: *The Savage Pilgrimage* (London: Chatto & Windus, 1932; revised edition, London: Secker & Warburg, 1932).

Brett, Dorothy: *Lawrence and Brett, a Friendship* (Philadelphia: Lippincott, 1933).

Merrild, Knud: *A Poet and Two Painters* (London: Routledge, 1938; reissued as *With D. H. Lawrence in New Mexico* (London: Routledge, 1964).

Aldington, Richard: *Portrait of a Genius, But . . .* (London: Heinemann, 1950); like all of Aldington's memoirs, this must be approached with caution.

C. *Critical Works*

The list of critical studies of Lawrence is extremely long: the following is highly selective, and larger lists should be sought either in the bibliographies listed under A above, or in those appended to some of the books listed below.

Cowan, James C.: *D. H. Lawrence's American Journey* (Cleveland: The Press of Case Western Reserve University, 1970).

Daleski, H. M.: *The Forked Flame* (London: Faber, 1965); a study of Lawrence's principal novels and one of the very best books yet written on him.

Delavenay, Emile: *D. H. Lawrence: L'Homme et la Genèse de son Oeuvre* (Paris: Klingsieck, 1969—English translation to follow); an extremely elaborate study of Lawrence's early life and work; the resulting picture of Lawrence is highly eccentric.

Draper, R. P.: *D. H. Lawrence, The Critical Heritage* (London: Routledge, 1969): an extensive collection of early reviews and comments, though with some regrettable omissions.

———— *D. H. Lawrence* (London: Routledge, 1969); a very brief but quite useful introduction.

Ford, George H.: *Double Measure* (New York: Rhinehart, 1965); mainly dealing with Lawrence's earlier work, in relation to his own life.

Leavis, F. R.: *D. H. Lawrence* (Cambridge: Minority Press, 1930; reprinted in *For Continuity*: Cambridge, Minority

Press, 1933); although perhaps now superseded by Dr. Leavis's later book, this early judgment remains of great importance.

——*D. H. Lawrence, Novelist* (London : Chatto & Windus, 1955); the most challenging and distinguished book yet written on Lawrence.

Marshall, Tom : *The Psychic Mariner* (London : Heinemann, 1970) : a reading of the poems.

Moore, Harry T. and Hoffman, F. (eds.) : *The Achievement of D. H. Lawrence* (Norman : University of Oklahoma Press, 1953) : a collection of essays.

Moore, Harry T. (ed.) : *A D. H. Lawrence Miscellany* (Carbondale : S. Illinois University Press, 1959); another collection.

Moynahan, Julian : *The Deed of Life* (Princeton : University Press, 1963); an uneven study of the novels, with some illuminating insights.

Sagar, Keith : *The Art of D. H. Lawrence* (Cambridge : University Press, 1966) : a disappointing attempt to identify Lawrence's 'vision', but bibliographically useful.

Spilka, Mark (ed.) *D. H. Lawrence* (Englewood Cliffs : Prentice Hall, 1963) : essays by various hands.

Vivas, Eliseo : *D. H. Lawrence: the Failure and Triumph of Art* (Evanston : Northwestern University Press, 1960) : a helpful study of Lawrence's symbolism.